T. E. LAWRENCE.

(Topical Press)

LAWRENCE
THE
REBEL

BY

EDWARD ROBINSON

LINCOLNS-PRAGER (PUBLISHERS) LTD.
LONDON

A

FIRST EDITION SPRING, 1946

PRINTED IN GREAT BRITAIN
BY LOVE & MALCOMSON, LTD., REDHILL.

INTRODUCTION

THIS story of the impact of one man's life on our history is written, not by a professional historian, but by a soldier who was caught up in the first world war and flung into an exciting campaign which most historians have regarded as a side-show.

I found myself an active participant in most of the campaign and " keeper of the records." Records widen the horizon of a soldier ; the experience of active service puts meaning into the record. So this biography is a history by a man in the street for the man in the street.

I have written it in the hope that it will help him not only to understand Lawrence, but to understand the reasons for the present tangle of trouble in the Middle East. The book is an attempt to bring the mistakes of secret diplomacy out into the open, where the man in the street congregates, because it is, in the end, he who must correct them, and, by so doing, clear the way to peace.

1946.   E. R.

TO

MY WIFE, DOROTHY,

WHOSE FAITH AND LOVE

HAVE REMOVED MOUNTAINS.

" WHERE THE MIND INCLINES, THE FEET LEAD "

THOMAS EDWARD LAWRENCE was born in Wales in 1888, and was one of five brothers (two of whom were killed in action in the 1914-1918 war). His father was descended from an English family which had long been resident in Ireland, and his mother was Scottish.

" T.E." was only eight years old when the family went to Oxford, but even at that age he was a great student. He and his father—a student of church architecture, an enthusiastic photographer, and a cyclist—spent half-holidays at the museums, and looking over the colleges and churches. Before he was nine he had " rubbed " his first brass at Witney Church, and during the next few years he travelled most of England and Wales in search of interesting specimens.

There was another side to Lawrence's character. He was for many years a constant worshipper at St. Aldate's, and he walked six miles, twice every Sunday, to teach in the Sunday School there. He was rarely without his Bible, and when up at the University made a practice of attending the Greek testament readings.

Already a student of ancient crafts, Lawrence added the study of pottery to his many pursuits. This took him constantly to the Ashmolean Museum, where C. L. Woolley[1] was then Assistant Keeper. He helped in the arrangement of the medieval cases, and this brought him into contact for the first time with D. G. Hogarth, the Keeper—a beginning to a life-long friendship which was to have a considerable influence on Lawrence's later activities.

In the midst of all this, he continued his cycling, duly encouraged by his father. It had its novel side, for the latter was practical, and discussed various machine designs with " T.E." In turn the son formulated his own ideas, put some of them to paper, and even had one or two mounts built to his own design.

Oxford then, as now, was the city of cyclists, but if

[1] Now Sir Leonard Woolley.

5

Lawrence's mount attracted attention, he immediately exaggerated it by some eccentricity or other—such as riding his machine up-hill and walking it down.

During these years there had been an intensive pursuit of knowledge among the old castles of England, Wales, and France. In 1909, when he was a candidate for the History Finals, he selected as his thesis the Crusaders and their influence on castle-building in Palestine and Syria. To prime himself on the subject, he decided to make a personal tour of the crusader ruins. Hogarth gave him the benefit of his own experiences, and some introductions. One of these was to H. Pirie Gordon,[1] another experienced traveller in the Near East. One day in May, Lawrence sought him out, tracked him from his home to a restaurant, talked to him for two hours about castles, roads and routes, and borrowed a map. On the last day of the summer term he started for Syria.

He had had some tuition in Arabic before beginning his pilgrimage. Professor Margoliouth, the noted Orientalist, introduced him to the Reverend N. Odeh, who had just retired from the headship of the St. Mary's Mission in Cairo, and they not only gave him advice about the East, but, intrigued by his enthusiasm, drilled into him a slight though useful knowledge of Arabic.

In turn, Hogarth brought Lawrence into touch with Charles Doughty, the Arabian explorer, who talked to him about the Bedouin and their ways. He advised him to go among them, to study their tribal customs. They would give him hospitality for days at a time, he said, and in this way he would be able to pass from tribe to tribe and complete his travels at little cost and in comparative safety.[2]

Lord Curzon was approached, and he obtained an " Irade " (permit) from the Turkish Government to facilitate Lawrence's sight-seeing, and to enable him to map out and plan the castles on which he intended to write his thesis.

After landing at Beirut, in the summer of 1909, Lawrence immediately made for the interior. For three months he tramped the country, searching for the crusaders' castles, carrying a camera and a few articles of underwear. He ran

[1] Later Assistant District Commissioner in Palestine.

[2] Arabs are traditionally bound to extend hospitality to anyone eating their food, but such protection is supposed to expire on the third day, when all that was eaten on the first has presumably passed out of the body.

many risks, inevitable in a land where an "infidel" was always suspect. One robber's revolver shot fortunately missed him. Replying in kind, Lawrence nicked the man in the little finger, walked up to him, bound up the wound with his own handkerchief, gave him some money, and then the two went down the mountain-path together.

Turkomen attacked him during his trek from Aleppo to Latakia. They beat him and left him for dead, indignant because his treasure was no more than his clothes, some Hittite seals, and a few coins.

Lawrence had lived simply, on the food of the countryside. He had plodded from one castle ruin to another, and climbed the walls bare-foot. He saw for himself what he intended to write about, drew his own plans and took his own photographs.

He submitted his Thesis—" The Influence of the Crusades on Medieval Military Architecture "[1]—early in 1910, and obtained a " First " in History.

After his Finals, Lawrence was asked by Hogarth (on behalf of the British Museum) to work under Campbell Thompson, in excavating the Hittite remains at Carchemish, near Jerablus. He left England in December and arrived in Jebail, near Beirut, on Christmas Eve. Here, for two months, he continued his studies in Arabic, learning to read and write it simply and speak it quite reasonably.[2] When he did leave to report at Carchemish, it was at the height of the severest winter Syria had experienced for forty years, but he finished the journey, despite the fact that the roads were blocked, the railroad useless, and the passes through the hills piled high with snow-drifts.

Most of Lawrence's time, from 1911 to the outbreak of the war in 1914, was spent at the excavations at Carchemish, the first season under Campbell Thompson and afterwards with C. L. Woolley, generally under Hogarth's supervision. When the diggings were closed, he wandered on foot in the vicinity, within a radius of about one hundred miles.[3]

He was in constant communication with Hogarth (then in

---

[1] Printed in " Crusader Castles " (Cockerel Press).

[2] Though able later on to speak Arabic fluently in certain dialects, Lawrence never became an Arabic scholar, nor did he read and write the language easily.

[3] Miss Gertrude Bell, already famous in this part of the world, noted in her diary on May 18, 1911, that she had found " Mr. Thompson and a young man called Lawrence (he is going to make a traveller)."

England), giving him long and often breezy reports on matters archæological.

The only records of his first journey to the East took the form of letters to his mother, but he kept a scrap diary of a later walk east of the Euphrates.[1] During this he was plagued with toothache, and with blistered feet, which resulted in temperatures and fevers, making progress a hazy affair of torture and doubt. But to balance his suffering, he found his Bedouin hosts a little overwhelming in their solicitude for him.

At the end of 1912 Lawrence was again at the Carchemish excavations, and remained there practically all the next year. Sir Hubert Young, in his book " The Independent Arab," helped to fill in the picture of Lawrence's activities. He wrote of a journey to the Carchemish diggings in 1913, when he and a friend were " shewn over them by a quiet little man by the name of Lawrence, who was for some reason living there alone."

M. O. Williams, writing in the *National Geographical Magazine* in 1913 of a visit to Carchemish, said : " Both Woolley and Lawrence are disappointing as archæologists. I expected to find grey-haired men with a scholarly stoop. . . . Lawrence is apparently in his early twenties, a clean-cut blonde with peaches-and-cream complexion, which the dry heat of the Euphrates seems powerless to spoil . . . wearing a wide-brimmed panama, a soft white shirt open at the throat, an Oxford blazer bearing the Magdalen emblem on the pocket, short white flannel knickers partly obscured by a decoration hanging from the belt, which did not, however, obscure his bare knees, below which he wore heavy grey hose, and red Arab slippers.

" But I fancy these two young men are competent to hold down the Carchemish digs . . . for better than their years of excavating and their skill in using French, German, ancient and modern Greek, Turkish and Arabic, is their remarkable knowledge of men. I cannot give a correct estimate of their worth as archæologists, but I do say that they know more about handling Orientals than any men I have met during my two years in Syria."

This was amplified by another well-known American writer, L. R. Fowle. Commenting on a visit to Carchemish during the Eastern vacation in 1913, he wrote :

" Lawrence, also fresh from the works, was stepping lightly

[1] Published by the Golden Cockerel Press.

8

across the mounds of earth, clad in what we Americans would call a running suit, and wearing at his belt an ornate Arab girdle with its bunch of tassels in front to denote an un-married man.

" He was out of sight in a moment, and when we gathered for supper a freshly-tubbed young man in his Oxford tennis suit of white flannel, but still wearing his Arab girdle, launched into a fascinating study of the excavations : of relations with the Kurds and Arabs about them : of his trips among their villages in search of rare rugs and antiquities."

Another stay at Carchemish was marked by a riot, caused primarily by the stupidity of a German paymaster on the new bridge-head being built at Jerablus, where the Baghdad Railway was to cross the Euphrates. A Kurd refused payment of five piastres (approximately a shilling) for a month's work. The German ordered his Circassian foreman to hit him : the Kurd retaliated with a stone, and the Circassian with a re-volver shot : then came a fusilade of stones from the labourers, and the riot was on.

A display of diplomacy by Woolley and Lawrence, coupled with an impudent disregard of danger, steered the incident into an atmosphere of ridicule, and it ended with a message of thanks from the Turkish Government for their help in subduing the rioters.

Earlier in 1914, Woolley and Lawrence had explored the desert of the Exodus. The Turkish Government gave per-mission for the area to be surveyed, and Woolley and Lawrence were loaned to Captain S. F. Newcombe, R.E., who was in charge of the five survey parties covering the district. They spent six weeks in January and February, visiting all the remains known between Gaza and Akaba, and then returned to Carchemish.[1]

Lawrence was back in Oxford in the summer of 1914, busy with his part of " The Wilderness of Zin," but when war broke out, Newcombe left the War Office for service in France, his Sinai maps not yet being printed, and his reports incomplete.

[1] A joint report on their part of the survey is to be found in " The Wilderness of Zin," published in 1915 by the Palestine Exploration Fund, and reprinted in 1935 by Jonathan Cape. It is of interest to archæologists mainly, but there are many touches to attract non-specialists, though Lawrence's style is rather different from that which he developed later.

The book was dedicated to Captain Newcombe, " who showed them the way wherein they must walk and the work that they must do."

Lawrence's offer to complete them was accepted, and he finished the essential editing, working in Colonel Headley's department.

Apart from the fact that he was in civilian clothes, he was too much of an individualist to pass unnoticed, and the patriotic mutterings of the uniformed majority reached the ears of the colonel. He immediately suggested to Lawrence that he should " get into uniform."

This was interpreted literally. He ordered a uniform, and had it fitted with leather buttons. Beyond this he took no other step into military service, he was not gazetted, and had no right to wear badges of rank. He was merely godfather to the Sinai map, and just drifted into the British Army.

It was, however, a drift of some significance.

It left its mark on the map of the world, shook an empire to its foundations, and its effects are still evident to-day.

"ONE LIE IN THE SULTAN'S HEAD WILL KEEP OUT MANY TRUTHS."

On the outbreak of war it was evident that Turkey would join the central powers, and her alliance with the enemy which began on November 1, 1914, created a danger to Britain's power hardly less grave than that created by the German attacks on France and Belgium.

Britain was involved inextricably in Egypt and India and all the way between. The Arab territories in the south-west of Asia became, immediately, a vital part of her defences.

The Arabs, who constituted a very substantial proportion of the population of the Ottoman Empire, had been giving trouble to their Turkish masters long before the outbreak of war. The caliphate of the Sultan of Turkey, in Arab eyes, was a self-assumed authority, based mainly on the fact that the Holy places of Arabia were on Turkish territory.

The Sherifs of Mecca had long been rulers of Mecca and its provinces. Sherif Hussein was the senior descendant of Mahomet, and, as such, was the head of the Prophet's family. Mecca was the point to which all Moslems turned their faces in prayer. Mecca, and Mecca alone, could make its voice heard in the world of Islam against a Caliph calling to Holy War.

For some years Syria also had been a ferment of discontent. Some Syrians plotted for out-and-out independence ; some for local autonomy ; some for French guidance ; others for British rule. There were many who wanted to serve a King, but far more who envisaged a great republic. There were too many movements, wasting and frittering, for the Turkish Government to be really troubled about their existence, with the Arabs themselves an agglomeration under emirs and chieftains, each and every one opposed in some way to the other. As a Bedouin would say : " I fight with my cousin against the enemy, but I fight with my brother against my cousin."

It was a very unpromising field which lay before Britain. Even if the " Jehad "[1] had no real effect, Turkey in control of the Red Sea littoral, with its threat to the sea route to the

[1] Holy War.

East, was a distinct peril to the general cause of the Allies, and allied possessions in the middle and farther East would remain accessible to attack from the enemy so long as this dangerous situation existed.

There were complications also for the Central powers. Turkey itself was mainly Mohammedan, she was allied with Christians and had Christian officers and instructors in charge of her Moslem troops. On the other hand, Britain and her allies had Moslem troops perfectly willing to oppose the Turks, if only because of what they believed to be the latter's sacrilegious indifference to the proper control of the Holy cities.

Britain also took a hand in placating Mohammedan opinion. The Government of India issued a statement dealing with the Government's policy in connection with the Holy places :

> " In view of the outbreak of war between Great Britain and Turkey . . . His Excellency the Viceroy is authorised by His Majesty's Government to make the following public announcement in regard to the Holy places of Arabia, including the Holy shrines of Mesopotamia, and the Port of Jeddah, in order that there may be no misunderstanding on the part of His Majesty's most loyal Moslem subjects as to the attitude of His Majesty's Government in this war, in which no question of a religious character is involved.
>
> " These Holy places and Jeddah will be immune from attack or molestation by the British naval and military forces as long as there is no interference with pilgrims from India to the Holy places and shrines in question.
>
> " At the request of His Majesty's Government, the Governments of France and Russia have given like assurances."

On November 4 a Berlin newspaper stated that " a headquarters report from Constantinople informs us that the British fleet bombarded Akaba on November 1, and attempted to land troops near the Egyptian frontier. After four Englishmen had fallen, however, the remainder of the party returned to the boats. Although the British fired thousands of rounds of artillery, our losses amounted to only one gendarme."

This was followed by another Berlin report, on November 9, to the effect that " Turkish gendarmes belonging to tribes fighting on the side of the Turks destroyed the English troops landed at Akaba."

A British official account three days later brought the "attack" into due perspective. Owing to reports of mine-laying in the Gulf of Akaba, the cruiser *Minerva* investigated the position. Akaba was found to be occupied by a small detachment of troops, and negotiations for a surrender were attempted, but these were frustrated by German officers present. A few shells were fired, a reconnoitring patrol posted a proclamation, and re-embarked. "There were no casualties."

However, as Akaba was a port in the Holy Hejaz, the British authorities found it necessary to reassure their Moslem friends, and the next day Reuter's News Agency carried the following message to all interested countries :

"His Majesty's Government have no intention of undertaking any military or naval operations in Arabia, except for the protection of Arab interests against Turkish or other aggression or in support of attempts by Arabs to free themselves from Turkish rule."

Liman von Sanders, the German commander, himself decried the Turkish efforts to raise a Holy War. He wrote :

"Towards the middle of November 1914, the Turkish Government threw into the scales of war what formerly was the strongest arm of Islam, and solemnly declared a Holy War . . . It bore an appearance of unreality because Turkey was allied with Christian states, and German and Austrian officers and men were serving with the Turkish army.

"It received expression in Constantinople . . . .processions paraded the streets with green flags, appeared before the embassies of Turkey's allies and wound up on November 20 by breaking all the windows of a man who, Armenian by birth, had recently become a Russian."

The entry of Turkey into the war quickly led to demands for specialists. General Maxwell, then commanding in Egypt, asked for increased staff. Colonel G. F. Clayton was his G.S.O. (Intelligence), and to him were sent Major Newcombe (who had surveyed Sinai and South Palestine, and had travelled in Syria), Captain George Lloyd (later Lord Lloyd), who knew Anatolia, Palestine and the Yemen ; Aubrey Herbert (well known in the Balkans and Turkey) ; and

Lieutenant Leonard Woolley and Second Lieutenant T. E. Lawrence.

At that time Lawrence was little known outside the scholarly circle of archæologists, of whom Hogarth was the leader, though the survey with Newcombe in South Palestine had brought his and Woolley's names to the notice of the British War Office. Hogarth, now a commander in the Royal Naval Volunteer Reserve, had mentioned Lawrence as a man who " had travelled much in Syria, and knew its people, country and languages."

"OF LITTLE USE TO HAMMER COLD IRON"

At the end of January 1915 a report reached the Cairo office from Captain W. H. I. Shakespeare, a man who was, in many ways, as unique a personality as Lawrence.[1] He had made the desert his home, and had earned a reputation among the Arabs which remains unrivalled to this day.

"A messenger arrived at my camp on the night of January 17th, 1915 (wrote Shakespeare) with letters from the Sherif of Mecca and his son Abdullah, inquiring from Ibn Saud[2] as to his future attitude towards the Turks and the British. Ibn Saud read aloud the letter from Abdullah[3] who, owing to his father's age, leads the tribes. Its purport was to the effect that he had reached Medina in response to urgent and reiterated requests from the Turkish authorities, who desired him to call up his tribes and proclaim a 'Jehad,' and that he was temporising pending a reply from Ibn Saud as to his own attitude. Ibn Saud inquired what he should reply, and what reply would be most advantageous to His Majesty's Government.

"A 'Jehad,' especially if proclaimed at Mecca by one of the Sherif's standing in Islam, is a contingency of which the consequences are unforeseeable and incalculable. Such a proclamation would, at least, raise the whole Arab world, and Ibn Saud himself would be compelled by the circumstances of his faith, his prestige and position as an Arab chief to follow with all his tribes. This contingency—a 'Jehad,' proclaimed by the acknowledged and accepted descendant of the Prophet at Mecca—I venture to submit needs the most serious consideration, and to be constantly kept in mind at the present critical time in all our dealings with Arab chiefs in general and Ibn Saud in particular. Fortunately, through Ibn Saud's commanding influence in Arabia (and if His Majesty's Government are prepared to

---

[1] Shakespeare had been appointed Political Officer in the Nejd in 1914.

[2] The present ruler of Arabia, but then Emir of Nejd.

[3] Now Emir of Trans-Jordania.

meet his desires generously) we are in a position to limit the danger as to make it almost negligible. It was with these thoughts in my mind that I proceeded to discuss the Sherif's letter with Ibn Saud.

" I told him that His Majesty's Government had been forced into war by Germany, and that Germany had then forced war between Turkey and Great Britain, as had already been explained to him, and that the last thing which His Majesty's Government desired, was any further extension of that war. He had seen the British attitude towards Islam and its Holy places explained in the Viceroy's proclamation, and must be aware from his own previous knowledge that non-interference with any religion was a cardinal feature of the British policy. He had himself been sufficiently convinced of British sincerity in this war to help materially, by temporising with the Turks, to prevent further extension of it in Arabia, and by his lead and example to assist our campaign in Mesopotamia.

" While certain assurances had been vouchsafed to him, I had no authority to offer anything of a similar nature to the Sherif. However, Great Britain, on behalf of the vast number of her Indian Moslem subjects, on whom pilgrimage to the Holy places was as incumbent as on all Islam, could not remain uninterested in the attitude of the Sherif of Mecca. Consequently it was obvious that her benevolence or indifference would probably be commensurate with the treatment accorded to Indian Moslems at Holy places. I believed (and Ibn Saud concurred in this) that in Mecca and Medina the Sherif's word probably carried far more weight than that of the local Turkish authorities. Therefore, it behoved the Sherif to use his best influence for peace, if he desired the benevolence or countenance of His Majesty's Government.

" So far as one could guess, the future of Turkey as a great power was doomed ; whether the Sultan's rule over Arabia and the Holy places was also doomed was a matter for the Arabs themselves, but it was clear from the Viceroy's proclamation that the British Government had no designs on the Holy places, and had even bound themselves as well as the French and Russian Governments, to take no military action against them and Jeddah, provided that Indian Moslems were not molested. It seemed to me, therefore, advisable for the Sherif in his own interest to continue to temporise with the Turks, while Ibn Saud would be further assisting His Majesty's Government and improving his own chances of a satisfactory arrangement with them if he advised him accordingly.

" Ibn Saud said that he agreed with me, and that, as he had been at pains to convince the Sherif already that the Turks were not his true friends, he would reply that a temporising reply should be made with excuses of apprehension of reprisals on Jeddah and the like ; he would also assure the Sherif that, as he himself saw no advantage in siding with the Ottoman government at the present juncture, he had also returned a deputation just sent by the Porte to him, alleging his campaign against Ibn Rashid and the fear of a British attack on the Hasa and Qatif coasts as his excuse for an inability to move. . . . .

" It will be noted from the above that Ibn Saud is doing all in his power, short of an open rupture with the Turks, to further British interests. It will be said that he seeks the betterment of his own position, and that this is true he himself frankly admits. I would venture to urge that the co-operation of Ibn Saud as furnished by his own attitude and his influence with other Arab chiefs has been of no less value than the active support asked for, and deserves generous response from His Majesty's Government to his wishes for a close and binding understanding."

Shakespeare's letter was extremely valuable. As always, he rather understated his arguments, and so clear a presentation of Central Arabian opinion threw valuable light on what were very critical relations.

The preparations for the attack on the Suez Canal were stirring the pan-Islamic agents into a frenzy of activity. The " Jehad " was an open proclamation. All Arab eyes looked to the Holy places, and their ears strained for the signal from Mecca which would send them leaping at the throats of the enemy.

But the Sherif remained silent, and the talk Shakespeare[1]

[1] Shakespeare was killed shortly after, during a clash between Ibn Rashid and Ibn Saud, in which the latter heavily defeated his enemy. It was afterwards reported that the British officer, wearing British uniform, was watching Ibn Saud's artillery in action, and was such a conspicuous mark that he was " picked off " at long range. His sun-helmet was afterwards exhibited by the Turks at Medina as proof that Ibn Saud was a traitor to Islam.

17

had had with Ibn Saud hinted at influences which were sufficiently strong to ensure neutrality rather than action from Mecca, at any rate for the time being.

"EAT WHATEVER THOU LIKEST, BUT DRESS AS OTHERS DO"

THE British Intelligence Staff persevered. Reports were sifted, collated and signed,[1] but Lawrence appeared at varying times over the titles of " Second Lieutenant," " Captain " and " Major." There was no sign of the authoritative " for."

Profiting by his own experiences, Lawrence, early in 1915, drafted a general review of Syria, which was circulated among the British General Staff as a guide and reference. (It is used in the " Seven Pillars of Wisdom " as if it were written in 1917. Its existence two years before, therefore, makes the survey the more remarkable for its accurate diagnosis of a country with so many ills).

Syrian politics were beginning to assume a certain importance, while at home the position of Turkey in Asia led to a meeting of experts in April 1915, when Arabia loomed large in the discussions. The Sherif of Mecca had been approached by certain prominent Syrians with plans for a military rising in Syria, and he had sent his son, Feisal,[2] to Damascus to sound public opinion in the matter.

It had been in November of the previous year that Kitchener had given a very important assurance to the Sherif of Mecca. This, in effect, stated that if the Sherif and his Arabs would throw in their lot to assist Great Britain, the latter would not intervene in any way " with things religious or otherwise."

Kitchener also promised to guarantee the Sherif against all external aggression, but one suggestion lifted the assurances above any ordinary " arrangement." It was a promise to help in the creation of an Arab caliphate at Mecca, and in securing the freedom of the Arab race. Kitchener had been circumspect in his approach, which he had made when High Com-

[1] Lawrence and Graves (Sir Robert Windham Graves) had been engaged in the correction of the Turkish in the Intelligence Manual which was to be issued to British officers.

[2] Feisal had been put to a military career, commanded an Arab contingent in three Turkish campaigns, and sat for two years in the Turkish Parliament, as member for the Jeddah division.

missioner of Egypt, but whatever Hussein thought of it, he refused to consider it at that time.

It was, however, the beginning of an idea—Arabia for the Arabs—and had little to do with any suggestion of British occupation.

On the eastern side of Arabia there was another idea—sponsored by the Indian Government. Here, an underlying belief in Turco-British friendship, as a safeguard to Moslem interests, led to propaganda that Britain was not actually at war with the Ottomans as such, but with their corrupt government.

The Mesopotamian force started its campaign, in which the British-Indian force was to be the liberator of the country, the general tendency being to discourage Arab co-operation in the fighting, and with this offensive starting in the East, the western side of Arabia slumped into a lethargic " wait and see."

The projected British landing in the Gulf of Alexandretta, then a very weak spot in the Turkish defences, was considered to be an indispensable preliminary to the raising of Syria against the Turks, but France, with her hands too full in the west, could not even relish the rescue of her adopted Syrian child by other arms than her own.

France's natural sphere of interest in Turkey was in the Syrian vilayets. Since the dawn of history the Mediterranean had linked the southern French coast to Syrian harbours. Phœnician oversea trade in the first millenium before the Christian era had reached the coasts of Provence and Languedoc. Marseilles, a city born of this intercourse, had maintained commercial relations with Syria uninterruptedly down to the present time.

Franco-Syrian ties were strengthened considerably during the Crusades. The conquest of Syria and Palestine by the Arabs diverted the thoughts of Christendom from the economic importance of these lands to their religious appeal. France, " the eldest daughter of the Church," took the lead in the attempt to wrest the Holy Land from its Mohammedan conquerors. Many of the petty states founded by noblemen who took part in the Crusades were ruled by Frenchmen. Antioch and Tripoli had French princes, Jerusalem a French king. The title of " Protector of Oriental Christians " conferred by the Papacy on French kings had its origin in the active part played by France in the Crusades.

France therefore could still shout " Hands off Syria,"[1] and Britain, for political reasons, could not do more than assent to the shelving of a plan which had in it the possibility of a quick end to the war against Turkey.

Russia was planning for concessions, " as a result of the present war," which would have given her practically the whole of Turkey in Europe, and after she had been informed that Britain and France were ready to regard, " in the most benevolent manner," the realisation of her wishes, the field of negotiations shifted to Italy. These resulted in the signature, on April 26, 1915, of the pact known as the Treaty of London, which brought Italy into the war on the side of the Allies. It contained among others, the following clauses :

Article 8.—Italy will receive complete sovereignty of the Dodecanese Islands (a group of islands off the north-east coast of Asia Minor) which she occupies at the moment.

Article 9.—France, Great Britain and Russia recognise in principle *Italy's interest in the maintenance of the political balance of power in the Mediterranean* (my italics.—E.R.) and her right to receive, in the case of total division or partial division of Turkey-in-Asia, an equal share with them in the Mediterranean basin, viz., that part adjoining the province of Adalia over which Italy has already acquired rights and interests which have been the subject of an Italo-British convention.

Article 10.—Italy will receive in Libya the rights and privileges at present belonging to the Sultan, by virtue of the Treaty of Lausanne. . . .

Article 12.—Italy associates herself with the declaration made by France, Great Britain and Russia, leaving Arabia and the sacred Moslem places under the authority of an independent Moslem power.

Article 13.—In the event of the enlargement of the French and English colonial possessions in Africa at the expense of Germany, *France and Great Britain recognise in principle Italy's right to demand for herself certain compensations in the sense of an extension of her possessions in Eritrea, Somaliland, Libya, and the*

[1] In March 1915 the French Government explained that France would claim the control of Syria, including (as the term had long included) Palestine. This proposition was discussed by a governmental committee, which reported in June 1915 that the French claim to Northern Syria should be conceded, but owing to the world-wide importance of the Holy Land, Jerusalem and part Palestine should be reserved for international administration.—British Government's report on Palestine, 1937.

colonial districts contiguous to the colonies of France and England (my italics.—E.R.).

Article 14.—England undertakes to facilitate the immediate realisation of a loan by Italy on the London market, on advantageous terms, for a sum of not less than £50,000,000.

Article 15.—France, England and Russia undertake to support Italy in preventing the representatives of the Holy See from taking any steps whatever in the matter of the conclusion of peace or the settlement of questions bound up with the present war.[1]

It was not easy to assign a place to Italy in the array of European claimants to Turkish territory. The trade between Italian and Turkish seaports had lost the relative importance it had acquired in medieval times. Italian pretensions to Adalia Bay and its rearland were of quite recent date, but beyond vaguely formulated promises for railway concessions from the Turkish Government, no ties bound the region to Italy. She had, however, created her own sphere of interest somewhat unintentionally, by the occupation in 1912 of the islands of the Dodecanese, and had outpaced by this act every other European country taking part in the race for a share in Turkey.

These larger considerations all had their repercussions on the situation in Arabia, and they did not help to clarify it. On the one hand Egypt and the British home authorities were now inclined to support the Sherif. On the other, the Mesopotamian campaign was in full swing, with the local Arabs aloof in some sort of neutrality, mostly suspicious and harmful. The British authorities had given due notice to the Turks that they were threatening the Dardanelles, and the stage was set.

But if little could be done with arms, there was no premuim on words, and the following proclamation was scattered throughout Arabia, Sudan and the Western African desert :

" It is already known to you that we, the English, went to war with Germany because she attacked, without warning, the small states upon her borders, whose independence she had solemnly sworn to guarantee.

" You also know that Germany, being hard-pressed, cunningly induced the Turkish Government to assist her.

[1] " Documenti per la Storia della Pace Orientale (1915–1932), by Amedeo Giannini : and *Izvestia*, 28.11.1917.

22

This she effected by a lavish expenditure of gold and by lying promises. Her real object was to obtain the proclamation by the Sultan of Turkey of a 'Jehad' against ourselves and the Allies ; for, under the protection of our Empire are many millions of Mohammedans, of whom thousands are now actually fighting in our armies, and Germany hoped they would be induced to attack us, and so afford her help. Surely every true Mohammedan must regard with loathing this cynical employment of his religion as an instrument to be used by a foreign power for the furtherance of their own selfish ambitions.

" The Mohammedan subjects of the British empire, and of France and Russia and her allies, have shown their view of the matter by supplying thousands upon thousands of troops to help us in fighting the Turks and their deceivers, and even the more honourable of the Turks must realise the baseness of what has been done.

" Perhaps, however, there are those among you who ask what may be our intentions after the war is over.

" Lest there be any misconception, let the following be known :

" The Government of His Majesty the King of England and Emperor of India have declared that when this war ends it shall be laid down in the terms of peace as a necessary condition that the Arabian Peninsula and its Mohammedan Holy Places shall remain independent. We shall not annex one foot of land in it nor suffer any other power to do so. Your independence of all foreign control is thus assured, and with such guarantees the lands of Arabia will, please God, return along the paths of freedom to their ancient prosperity.

" Surely this is sufficient !

" Certain Arab chiefs have already assured us of their desire to be rid of the Turks, and some are assisting our troops with their swords.

" To those of you who wish us well, but are perhaps afraid to show their feelings, we say ' Have no distrust of us. Wait for the favourable opportunity, and when it comes shake off the oppressor's yoke, and we will support you to the full extent of our ability, and will, with God's help, make you a truly independent people.' "

" HE HAS AN EYE UPON THE CUPBOARD AND AN EAR TOWARD THE SELLER OF FOOD "

IN July, 1915, Ronald Storrs[1] received two letters from the Grand Sherif of Mecca. One contained bitter complaints regarding the treatment of Syrian notables by Jemal Pasha. There was a reference to support from the Central Syrian Committee—a committee which hurled denunciation at odd moments against Turkish oppression, and which generally succeeded in little more than losing lives through betrayal, and all civic interests through imprisonment.

The other was the beginning of an amazing correspondence, fated to become notorious as the McMahon correspondence.[2] This exchange of letters, reduced to generalities, resulted in an agreement by the British to recognise Arab independence throughout an area bounded in the north by about latitude 37 degrees, east by the Persian frontier, south by the Indian ocean, and the Persian Gulf, west by the Red Sea and up to about latitude 33 degrees by the Mediterranean ; and beyond that by an indefinite line drawn inland west of Damascus, Homs, Hama and Aleppo. Between this last line and the Mediterranean, the French and the Arabs would have to come to some agreement as to future administration, though the British omitted to acquaint either of them to that effect.

Great Britain was to hold Iraq, with Arab permission, while Aden and district were to remain entirely British.

In return, Britain agreed to help in the establishment of suitable autonomous governments in the agreed areas, to support an Arab caliphate, and to help the Arabs secure their desired independence.

The British authorities were, however, not now so free to make these promises or pledges. Guided by Indian administration, there were other ideas for Mesopotamia. Britain knew that Hussein had no actual warrant to speak for all Arabia ; in fact, they knew too well how many of Arabia's important

[1] Then Oriental Secretary to the British Agency, Egypt.
[2] Printed in full by the British Government, but not until 1939.

chieftains would emphatically repudiate Sherifian leadership.

Messengers had brought letters from Ibn Saud which seemed to infer a hardening of the Wahabi leader's attitude to the Sherifians. He had been pleased to hear of the suggested Arab revolt, and he was at one with the Sherif of Mecca in his effort to free the Arabs from Turkish dominion, but he would never tolerate any control or interference from Hussein within his own boundaries. What did the official report mean—would Hussein have some control over all Arabia in the future?

It was obvious, said Ibn Saud, that Hussein meant to play the British off against the Turks, and thus get the Turks to grant him the independence which Germany had guaranteed in bringing Turkey into the war.

Finally, Ibn Saud remarked that he had no personal desire for an alliance with Hussein. He had entertained the proposal because Britain desired it, and in the hope of expelling the Turks. As to his future action, if relations between him and the Sherif merely concerned themselves, he would comply with the request for an alliance only in the event of a satisfactory reply being received. If, however, the reply gave the impression that the Sherif's aim was to deceive him and to obtain control over him, he would take steps to protect his own interests. If his relations with the Sherif were of importance to British policy, he would be guided by her wishes.

The Saudi chief, as a result of this correspondence, was advised to come to a full understanding with Hussein, and if possible to afford him active assistance. In turn, the Sherif was told of the terms of the British treaty with Ibn Saud, and pressed to meet him half-way.

"DO NOT COUNT THE DAYS OF A MONTH WHICH MAY NEVER BELONG TO THEE"

DESPITE the Anglo-Sherifian agreement, Hussein was most unwilling to fix any date for action. He was not even prepared, and such reports as he was receiving from his sons, whom he had sent to Constantinople to obtain " reactions," were not at all favourable to British prospects. They reported also that the British were not doing well on the western front.

Feisal, from Damascus, had written of a talk he had had with Stotzingen[1] in which the latter had said that arms and ammunition were to be shipped from the Yemen across to Abyssinia, and an anti-foreign war begun in that country. Stotzingen himself was going afterwards to East Africa.

Jemal Pasha had also taken Feisal to a cinema in Damascus. The star film showed the Pyramids, with the Union Jack on top, and beneath them Australians beating Egyptian men and raping the women ; in the foreground was an Egyptian girl in an attitude of supplication.

The second scene showed a desert, with camel convoys and a Turkish infantry battalion marching on for ever and ever. The third returned to the Pyramids, with a sudden appearance of the Ottoman army in review order, the killing of the Australians and the surrender of General Maxwell, the joy of Egypt, the tearing down of the Union Jack and its replacement by the Turkish flag.

Feisal said he asked Jemal why he troubled his father and himself for recruits if the film were true, to which Jemal's reply was : " Well, you know, it encourages the people. We do not expect to try to conquer Egypt, yet."

From Kabul came reports that German and Turkish missions had already penetrated Persia and were plotting in Kabul itself to unite all Islam against the British Empire. They had their eyes on the Hejaz. Emissaries were to be sent to Hussein to bring the Sherifians and all the Hejaz Arabs into the revolt.

[1] Major Freiherr Othmarvon Stotzingen—see p. 37.

Already Turkey, and all Islam which Turkey could influence, were open enemies, and it was believed that if the Arab nations could be brought under the lead of the Sherifian family in opposition to the British, the combination would be complete. They saw so clearly that Britain must retain her stewardship of the Arabian peninsula if she wished to keep India and Egypt.

In February 1916 the British Government formally recognised the work of the little band of Middle-Eastern experts in Cairo, and accepted its existence under the title of " The Arab Bureau." (Hogarth had been there since June 1915, and Miss Gertrude Bell arrived in November of the same year.)

Lawrence had been busy with a plan for raising the Mesopotamian Arabs in open revolt against the Turks. He suggested that he and other agents should be sent to win them over, even those serving with the Turks, and made his argument sufficiently strong for his dispatch on a " special mission." He left Cairo on March 21, but events moved too quickly for him.

The Expeditionary Force " D " was stretching out in a line which grew longer and longer, and yet thinner and thinner, in its sensational attempt to reach Baghdad in one dash. Lawrence's fears, expressed so audibly in Cairo, were being fast transformed into actualities. The apparent hopelessness of Townshend's position at Kut began to fill Headquarters with ominous activity, and less than a week after Lawrence left Cairo he was informed that his special mission had another, more awkward angle to it.

General Officer Commanding Force " D " had been informed that Lawrence would undertake negotiations with the Arab elements in the Turkish Army, with a view to encouraging them to side with the Arab movement and detach themselves from the Turks. Emissaries were being sent to Mesopotamia, who would learn from Lawrence, or from the G.O.C., what political promises could be made to the Arabs, but even then the Intelligence branch in Egypt thought they would be too late to influence Townshend's position. Lawrence and an independent officer were also to approach Khalil, or another of the Turkish leaders, to negotiate terms for the prisoners of war in Kut and for Townshend.

Arrangements had already been made through Cairo for certain Arab officers to be released from India, and sent to Basrah under urgent orders to report to Lawrence, and when the latter arrived at Basrah[1] the news regarding Kut and General Townshend came as a blow, the more heavy because its beginning had been seen.

There is scant record of Lawrence's share in these negotiations. Aubrey Herbert, in his diary of the Kut campaign filled in a few gaps :

"April 19 (he wrote) Lawrence arrived at Wadi on Wednesday. Had some talk with him. I am very glad to see him . . . but he has gone and got fever. . . .

"April 24, 1916 : This morning Colonel Beach came aboard . . . He proposes to go out and see the Turks with Lawrence and myself. . . ."

On April 28 the Force " D " Commander reported to London :

" To-day an endeavour was made to negotiate with Khalil by Townshend, on the basis of the release of the Kut garrison on parole not to fight during the continuation of the war, in consideration of the release of an equal number of Turkish prisoners, plus the surrender of all arms and guns in Kut, plus the payment of £1,000,000.

" These terms were telegraphed by Khalil to Enver. He rejected the terms, and only offered to exchange for the surrender of Kut and all guns, personnel and warlike stores, the release on parole of Townshend himself.

" Naturally, the conditions were rejected by Townshend and he telegraphs : " If Government wishes to save lives of quite forty-fifty per cent. of my force, I would suggest to offer Khalil an equal number of Turkish combatants and £2,000,000, and to allow us to be despatched to India." Enver telegraphed in reply " Money is not wanted by us, and over Kut we lost 10,000 men."

The next day, the Force " D " Commander sent another wire to London :

[1] The presence of Miss Bell in Basrah came as a pleasant surprise to Lawrence, and she wrote on April 9 to Lady Richmond (her sister) : " This week has been greatly enlivened by the appearance of Mr. Lawrence, sent as a liaison officer from Egypt. We had great talks and made vast schemes for the government of the universe. He goes up river to-morrow where the battle is raging these days."

" Following has been received by me from Townshend :
" My guns have been destroyed and I am destroying most of
munitions. Officers have been sent to Khalil to say I am
prepared to surrender . . . I am unable to hold out any
more and must have some food here. Khalil was told by
me to-day and a launch has been sent with a deputation
to bring some food from the *Julnar*."

" Beach, with Lawrence and Herbert, have been sent by
me to Khalil to try and get permission to take over T's.
sick and wounded so that they may be sent to India."
Aubrey Herbert's story continued

" 30.4.16 . . . We (Herbert and Beach) left General
Younghusband and went up to the trenches . . . where
Lawrence joined us . . . We went out with a white flag
and walked a couple of hundred yards, where we waited
with all the pestilential smells around us. . . ."

After describing the arrival of the advance deputation
from the Turks, the narrative continued :

" Lawrence had hurt his knee and could not ride. He
got off and walked (they had been given horses) a
Turkish officer being left with him . . . I dictated a letter
in French to Lawrence, asking for permission for me to
stay and go across to Kut. I cannot think how he wrote
that letter. The whole place was one smother of flies,
and I kept them off Lawrence while he wrote. . . . ."

Jemal Pasha apparently still thought Hussein would not
declare himself against Turkey, and on April 2 he wrote
him telling him that he was sending a picked force of 3,500
men, under Khari bey, with a wireless mission under a
German officer, von Stotzingen, which was to work in the
Yemen. " German and Austrian troops," he added, " are
coming to participate in the Jehad under the sacred banner of
the Caliphate."

The Sherif of Mecca replied at length, but what he felt
was contained in one sentence : " the arrival of Austrian
and German forces will inauguarate a new chapter in the history
of Islam ! "

Meanwhile the already troublesome embarrassments which
had been brought into existence with Hussein's offer of help
were being further complicated.

Hussein wrote in February, giving the High Commissioner details regarding the suggested revolt, means of raising the tribes, times, etc., to which McMahon replied on March 10 :

"Your letter dated February 18, 1916, has been received. We are pleased to hear of the preparations you are making to meet the present situation to which His Majesty's Government give their approval. . . . We trust you will inform us officially when the movement begins. . . . . "[1]

[1] See pp. 38- .

"SELLING AND BUYING AND NOTHING
UPON THE BOARD"

Britain, it must be remembered, had now promised that the Arab state under Hussein should include the territory south of the 37th parallel, with the exception of Baghdad and Basrah and those districts where French interests predominated, but the India Office had promised a part of these territories in Central and Eastern Arabia to Ibn Saud. Neither chieftain knew of the exact engagements of the other, and the French apparently were not informed of the arrangements.

Sir Mark Sykes' *pourparlers* with M. Picot had continued, and as the talks proceeded, the difficulties of the situation were evident. What were to be the future boundaries of the prospective Arab state or states? In what direction were the respective spheres of British and French influence to be delimited? What was to be done with regard to Russian interests? What about Jerusalem?[1] What would satisfy Italy?

[1] "A telegram has been received from Sir Edward Grey to the effect that the question of settling Jews in Palestine has been brought to the notice of His Majesty's Government. Although many Jews are rather indifferent to the Zionist idea, a very great and influential part of Jewry in all countries would greatly appreciate the proposal of an agreement relating to Palestine which would satisfy the aspirations of the Jews.

"If the above is agreed to, it is clear that by utilising the Zionist idea important political results can be achieved. One result would be the conversion of the Jewish elements in the East. . . .

"If as a result of the war Palestine comes under the sphere of the interests of of France and Great Britain, the French and British Governments will not fail to take into consideration the historic interests of Jewry in that country. Both governments will secure to the Jewish population equal political civil and religious rights with the other inhabitants, municipal rights in colonies and towns which may appear necessary, as well as reasonable facilities for colonisation and emigration.

"The only aim of His Majesty's Government is to find some scheme which would prove an inducement to the majority of the Jews and would facilitate the conclusion of an agreement to secure Jewish support.

"Having this view under consideration His Majesty's Government is of the opinion that a project which would grant the Jews—when the colonisation in Palestine has attained a position which will enable them to rival the Arabs in strength—the administration of their internal affairs in that country (with the exception of Jerusalem and the Holy places) such an agreement would be a greater inducement for the majority of the Jews."—March 13, 1916 (Russian State Archives).

A basis of agreement was suggested in a letter from M. Paul Cambon to Sir Edward Grey, dated May 9, 1916, in which paragraph 10 is worth emphasis.

"(10) The British and French Governments, inasmuch as they are protectors of the Arab state, will agree not to acquire, *and will not consent to a third power acquiring territorial possessions in the Arab peninsula or construct a naval base in the islands on the coast of the Red Sea.*"—(My italics.—E. R.)

Replying to a further note from M. Paul Cambon, Sir Edward Grey clinched the pact, remarking that the British Government recognised its advantages to the general cause of the allies. There was one condition to its acceptance— "that the Arabs joined in the war and that the cities of Damascus, Homs, Hama, and Aleppo should be given to them."

The whole agreement,[1] which in effect meant that France would be able to curtail any ultimate Arab independence by her own administration, and that Britain could not possibly make good her promises to the Arabs beyond helping with the Hejaz movement, laid the foundations for future trouble. Already pledged as the champions of Arab nationalism, Britain's signature of the Sykes-Picot treaty meant that she must go on knowing she could not possibly reconcile her promises. (The treaty was absolutely secret : not only was there no hint of it to the Arabs, but the Italians knew nothing of it at this time.)

There were other considerations. The agreement violated all the natural features of the country. It ignored popular desire, cut across railways and communications regardless of present frontiers, cut towns and cultivated districts of the interior from the sea, divided local tribal groupings, and in the end would confine the Arabs to a ribbon of inland territory along the edge of the Syrian desert. It was a sowing which promised a ruinous harvest.

On the Sherif's part, he remained obdurate on three very

---

[1] On the day on which the agreement was signed, the *London Gazette* published the following :

Croix de Chevalier : tempy. Second Lieutenant Thomas Edward Lawrence, special list.

It was the publication of this award coincident with the signing of the Sykes-Picot agreement, which later led to Lawrence's name being connected with the negotiations. At that time he knew nothing of the terms, and very little of their purport.

definite points, and it is evident that when he raised the standard of revolt he believed the British understood his position quite clearly.

The Arabs—or Hussein speaking for them—would not permit the exclusion of Alexandretta (in the vilayet of Aleppo) or any other part of Syria from the area over which Arab independence should operate. Hussein's letter of January 1 had merely hinted that they were " averting their eyes " from the position. Whether the French knew this is uncertain : what is certain is that it is ignored in the Sykes-Picot agreement.

Basrah was the only vilayet in Iraq to which the Arabs would cede British rule ; any other concessions affecting other areas in Iraq would be temporary only.

Finally, and affecting the whole area of Arab independence, the Arabs would want neither Ottoman nor any other form of foreign sovereignty. Whatever understanding may have been given by McMahon to Hussein regarding Haifa and the country to the south now called Palestine, the only Government expected by the Sherif, or other Arabs, was a paternal British control over the existing population. There was no hint or suggestion of a Zionist movement.[1]

[1] " In the first place, it is not the case, as has been represented by the Arab Delegation, that during the war His Majesty's Government gave an undertaking that an independent national government should be at once established in Palestine. This representation mainly rests upon a letter dated October 24, 1915 from Sir Henry McMahon, then His Majesty's High Commissioner in Egypt, to the Sherif of Mecca, now King Hussein of the Kingdom of the Hejaz. That letter is quoted as conveying the promise to the Sherif of Mecca to recognise and support the independence of the Arabs within the territories proposed by him. But this promise was given subject to a reservation made in the same letter which excluded from its scope, among other territories, the portions of Syria lying to the west of the district of Damascus. This reservation has always been regarded by his Majesty's Government as covering the vilayet of Beirut and the independent Sanjak of Jerusalem. The whole of Palestine west of the Jordan was thus excluded from Sir H. McMahon's pledge."

To this the Palestine Arab Delegation replied to Mr. Churchill on July 17, pointing out that :

" The only reservation made by the British Government was the portion of Syria lying to the west of the districts of Damascus, Homs, Hama and Aleppo, and a glance at the map shows that by this was meant the Syrian littoral, Palestine which lies far to the south clearly not coming in this reservation. . . .

" By the word ' district ' His British Majesty's Government allege that the word ' vilayet ' is meant. But there were never any ' vilayets ' of Homs and Hama, and from this alone it is clear that the word ' district ' was never intended to mean ' vilayet ' . . .

" If ' vilayet ' was intended, we should like to know where is the territory to the west of the vilayet of Aleppo. There is nothing as far as can be seen on the map except the Mediterranean. . . ."

British White Paper, Cmd. 1700 June 3, 1922.

c

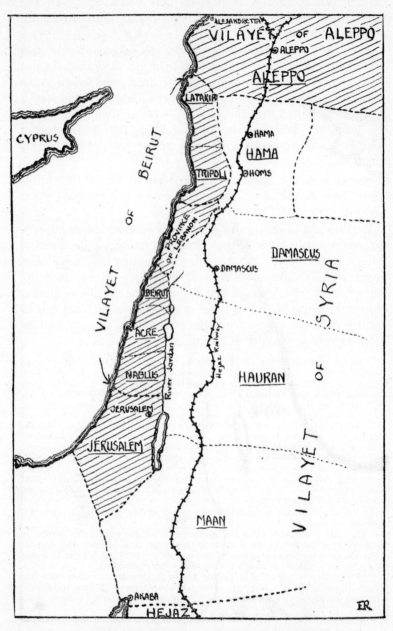

British interpretation of "West of Damascus."

34

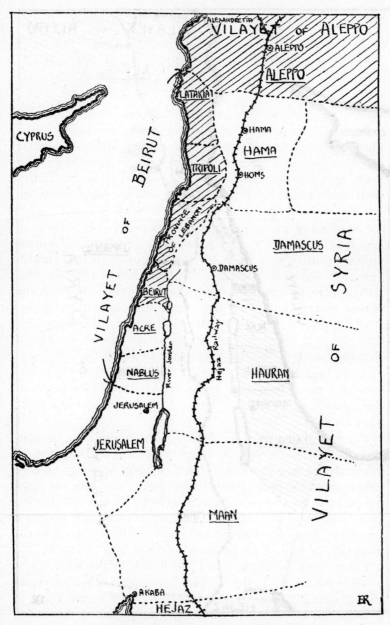

Arab interpretation of "West of Damascus."

"SHUT THE WINDOW THROUGH WHICH
A BAD SMELL COMES"

WHILE Britain and France were engaged in their treaty-making, Germany was steadily developing her hold on the Ottoman empire. It was an acceleration of the Germanic ascendancy over Turkey which had been in operation many years, as a counter to what they considered to be the British project of uniting Egypt to India by a broad band of British territory.

Conscious of the power they had gained in 1870, German eyes had naturally turned eastwards. In 1872, a German military mission undertook the reorganisation of the Turkish army. Seven years later the Deutsche Banke obtained important railway concessions throughout Turkey. In 1898, the Kaiser visited Damascus, proclaimed with due solemnity his "unalterable goodwill to the millions of Mohammedans scattered over the surface of the earth," and laid a wreath on Saladin's tomb—" from one Emperor to another."[1]

At the beginning of the twentieth century German capitalists secured a majority holding in the development of the Baghdad line, and from that time all big industrial concessions in Turkey were exclusively German.

Teutonic aspirations aimed at an imperialist domain spreading through Asia to Turkey, down to the Gulf of Alexandretta and the Persian Gulf. There was also need of colonisation for over-crowded Germany. She had no large agricultural area to meet the requirements of her fast-growing population, and her experts had estimated that with adequate irrigation Asia Minor could turn out a million tons of wheat annually, as well as an estimated 200,000 tons of cotton.

Everywhere Germany found the British in the way.

With the failure of the Turkish declaration of a Holy War, the German high command saw that it was an essential part of a successful campaign to secure the adherence of Arabia to the cause of the Central powers. Early in 1916, Jemal

[1] See p. 186.

Pasha's picked force was formed in Constantinople and sent down to Medina. It planned for a march through the Hejaz, and then on to the Yemen to join the Turkish force operating against the British in Aden.[1]

At the same time the Germans placed Stotzingen at the head of a party of wireless experts. His orders were (according to captured papers) " to establish an information post in the neighbourhood of Hodeida, for the purpose of opening communications with the German troops in German East Africa."

The wireless was also to be used for propaganda in Somaliland, Sudan, Abyssinia, and Darfur. Stotzingen knew a little Arabic, and he and Lieutenant Grobba—the latter attached as an interpreter—spoke English and French. They had an Indian servant who apparently knew English besides his own languages. Included in the party was a low-born, but extremely clever German-Jew, Karl Neufeld, who was known throughout Egypt, particularly in Assouan. He had been a prisoner for twelve years in the hands of the Mahdi, but had secured his release through the orders of Kitchener. He then returned to Germany, but he was back in Arabia again at the end of 1914, intriguing in German interests.

The first object of the party was to communicate with Muanzam, the German station in East Africa. This was over a distance of 1,500 miles. Stotzingen was to transmit the information obtained from East Africa direct to Medina or Damascus, for Constantinople. He was to pick up Berlin news direct. The great interest shown in the communications by telegraph and road between Hodeida and Sanaa, and a note about choice of sites, indicated that the station was to be built on this line. At either place there was sufficient power, but Hodeida was the more exposed.

Two of Hussein's sons were at Medina and saw the Turkish column arrive. Knowing their father's mind, and alarmed and uneasy at this sudden activity on the part of the Turks, they sent a warning to him ; from other sources he heard at the same time of the Stotzingen mission.[2]

The Sherif acted promptly by sending instructions to Yenbo for Stotzingen to be held up, but a little too precipitately for

[1] See p. 26

[2] The real merit in the Sherif's action lay in the fact that the Stotzingen plan was most effectively blocked. If the German propagandists had succeeded in making their contacts, Britain's position in Africa and the Middle East would have been dangerous, if not untenable.

Britain in his reaction to the other menace. He sent an S O S to a British patrol ship in the Red Sea, saying he was forced to rise " now or never."

"WHEN YOU ARE AN ANVIL, BE PATIENT; WHEN A HAMMER, STRIKE"

MORE than any other country in Arabia, the Hejaz was suffering from the effects of the war. The pilgrimage had ceased, the ports were blockaded[1] and foodstuffs could only keep the country going a little while longer before actual famine threatened. There had already been many deaths through starvation.

The Turks, long determined to drive the Sherif from his Caliphate, were obviously prepared to sweep away the stumbling block to complete rule in Constantinople. If the Arabs did not rise now, they would be crushed with the final blow of centuries of oppression.

Early on the morning of June 2, 1916, Hussein stood on his palace balcony and literally fired the first shot of the Arabian revolt.

It was the signal for a thin cordon of Bedouin tribesmen under Feisal and Ali to close their ring round Medina.

Feisal raised all the tribesmen about Medina and occupied the suburbs, but shrank from an attack on the Holy City itself. The tomb of Mahomet made Medina very sacred to all Moslems, and especially to members of the Prophet's own family, and the Arabs were new to this warfare. They had not yet heard of the example of the Turks, who shelled the Ka'aba at Mecca.[2]

Whatever the cause, the Arabs lost their opportunity. They cut the railway to Syria, tearing up lengths of metal with their bare hands and throwing them down the embankments, but they refused to cut the precious water conduits. They had never before met artillery fire and, in comparison

---

[1] Commander of man-of-war *Suva*, in the Red Sea, to the Arab Chiefs and the Sheikhs of Jeddah, order as follows :·
"On Monday May 15, 1916, I declare the blockade of all the Arabian coast in the Red Sea. No ships or sailing vessels are allowed to be on the sea. . . . All should know that this blockade ordered by Great Britain has been done against the Turks that are found in Arabia and not against the Arabs."

[2] The House of God, in the Court of the Mosque at Mecca. The famous Black Stone, or Hajr-el-Aswad, is built into its wall.

with the Turks, were woefully short of arms and supplies. What guns they had either did not fire at all or fired shells which, when they did explode, burst hopelessly and harmlessly far short of the Turkish lines. While the Turkish guns splashed death amongst the angry, though helpless tribesmen, the Sherifian attack was like the popping of corks from pop-guns.

Ronald Storrs was asked to go down to the scene of the revolt, and his later report to the High Commissioner, together with Hogarth's own appraisal of the situation, disclosed two definite facts : one, that the revolt was genuine and inevitable ; two, that as so much had been left to a last-minute impulse, and to luck, the rising was being handled with poor forces, poorer weapons, and that incalculable Arab fatalism the will of Allah.[1]

As McMahon informed the British authorities, in his first report, " success will depend more on the Sherifians' over-whelming numbers, but it will also raise problems demanding our assistance."

On June 9, Mecca—with the exception of the forts and entrenched barracks, held by small garrisons—fell into the Sherif's hands, and Jeddah surrendered a week later.

The first effects of the revolt were not seemingly important. The Turks published leaflets, some of which were dropped by aeroplane in Aden, appealing to all Arabs to join in the " Jehad," and advising them that Ali Haidar had been appointed Sherif of Mecca.

In Syria, both north and south, Jemal Pasha had already hanged the leading Nationalists and exiled others, so that the Syrians from Aleppo to Gaza could only express hatred in secret, while fear of the Turks was open and unashamed.

Germany took little note, publicly, of the revolt. There was a reference to it in the *Kolnische Zeitung* on June 23 which concluded : " A common attack by Arabs and shiahs upon the Turks seemed out of the question. The whole report must be taken as an attempt to damage the religious position of the Sultan as spiritual head of the Shiah. Success is likely to be small."

---

[1] " Thus began the Arab revolt against Turkey, a remarkable help to the cause of the Allies. Despite the reverses, disappointments, and periods of lethargy, it was to have far-reaching effects throughout the rest of the British campaign in Sinai and Palestine, a steady drain upon Turkish reserves and a powerful threat to the Turkish flank." (Official History of the War.)

Four days later the German wireless broadcast the following :
" We are in a position to deny absolutely that there has been
any rebellion in the Hejaz at all."

In Egypt the news of the revolt produced among the
intellectuals a feeling of stupefaction, mingled with uneasiness.
The local Islamic press, after maintaining a frigid silence for
several days, warned its readers to await confirmation of the
reports. Some papers theorized that the Sherif was playing
with the English as " did the Senussi last year," and that he
had already extracted from them some £3,000,000 in gold !
Among the lower classes, the news was received with
incredulity.

A report from India was not too encouraging. " The
Sherif's revolt " it stated " exploded with the effect of a
bombshell among the Mohammedans. . . . It is reported
that its effect on the north-west frontier is very bad : the
Sherif is universally suspected of being instigated by us. . . .
This is not due to Turco-German propaganda, but to the
pro-Turk feeling of educated Indian Moslems, and the feeling
that the Sherif has jeopardised the safety of the Holy places.
We do not anticipate any outbreak of violence, unless news
gets out of our naval action at Jeddah, or of a British landing
in the Hejaz."

By the end of June it was certain that the Arabs would
have to have the support of some disciplined troops. The
Sudan was the only available source which could be tapped,
but as impending troubles in Abyssinia, the garrison necessities
of the Sudan, and the Darfur expedition limited the numbers
that could be spared, six mountain guns and six machine-guns
with the necessary officers and men of the Egyptian Army,
were formed into two batteries and rushed off to the Hejaz
by Sir Reginald Wingate, Governor-General of the Sudan,
who had been in close touch with Sherif Hussein before the
revolt started.

" LOOSE ME FROM PILLAR TO PILLAR, AND PERCHANCE IT MAY FREE ME "

So far as British military circles were concerned, the authorities were hampered by confusion as to responsibility. In order to evolve some system of co-ordination, there was a discussion in the E.E.F. Headquarters, Murray going over the whole question of the revolt with McMahon, Hogarth, Storrs and others, dwelling particularly on the point of military co-operation, and it was decided that the Sirdar should supervise this side of the revolt.

Murray was asked directly what help he could give the Sherif, and whether he could undertake operations at Akaba and in Syria, but he was quite definite in his refusal to undertake such expeditions. His force had been reduced, he said, and he could only " hold his own." He left London in no doubt as to what he thought of the Arab rising. " We are in for a long and difficult business," he informed them, " and demands will increase. It is most important, not only for Egypt, but for the whole of the East, that the Turks should not crush the Sherif."

However, despite the agreement in Egypt that the Sirdar should supervise military commitments, in connection with the revolt, Wingate himself, knowing that France, Russia and even Italy were all involved in the matter, wanted to know whether Britain had promised the Sherif any military assistance.

He knew—even better than Murray—that in the absence of immediate help, the Turks could, with German assistance, effect sufficient repairs to the Hejaz railway to enable Medina to be relieved, and even to recapture Mecca itself. On the other hand, as he pointed out to Murray, immense advantage would accrue to Britain throughout the Moslem world if he helped the Sherif to success, while the displacement of the Ottoman Government from control of the Holy cities would have an incalculable effect on Britain's enemies.

Murray knew of no definite promise of military assistance to the Sherif, and told Wingate so. This did not help the latter, and he proceeded to sound the home authorities.

He emphasised to London, as he had done to Murray, the serious consequences in India and elsewhere arising from any failure of the Sherif's project. The stumbling block to any offer of military assistance to the Sherif was the very serious objection to the use of Christian troops in the Hejaz, but Wingate argued that any counter-move by the Turks would force Hussein to one choice only—that between accepting such assistance, or certain defeat.

At that time, Turco-German propaganda was meeting with considerable success in India, and the success of the Arab movement headed by the Sherif was absolutely essential to secure the necessary revulsion of Moslem opinion. There was, however, no immediate response from the home authorities.

Meanwhile, the Arab Bureau, on July 4, received a very sharp reminder of the widening circle of interest in the Sherif's revolt. Captain Picart, of the French army, paid them a visit. He had been sent by the French Admiral, he said, to urge—" quite unofficially "—that speedy help should be given to the Sherif of Mecca, by means of some French action in Syria !

Asked what help the French had in mind, Captain Picart suggested that the natives, helped by money, material and French technical assistance, could create a diversion.

It was pointed out that such a diversion would only create more danger than help, and in the end it was evident from the French captain's arguments that he, or rather the French themselves, envisaged a considerable force of allied troops operating in Syria.

The Arab Bureau were non-committal, and Captain Picart left with the hint, to him, that it was a matter of principle which should first be dealt with by London and Paris. His departure was marked by a very serious discussion. This was no chance visit. Why this sudden French interest in the revolt, this talk of action in Syria ? The Bureau immediately filed a report to Clayton, asking for information as to whether London knew anything of this French interest in the Sherifian revolt.

On July 7, a sheaf of letters arrived in Cairo for the Sherif, chief of which was an official request for the blockade on the coast to be raised. The messenger also brought with him a copy of Hussein's proclamation to the Moslem world, in which the Sherif of Mecca, after setting forth the grounds on which he had called his people to revolt, wrote :

" God (blessed and exalted be he) has vouchsafed this land an opportunity to rise in revolt . . . her peoples are to defend the faith of Islam, to elevate the Moslem peoples, to found their conduct on the holy law, to build up the code of justice on the same foundations in harmony with the peoples religion, to practice its ceremonies in accordance with modern progress, and to make a genuine revolution by spreading education among all the classes according to their station and needs.

" This is the policy we have undertaken in order to fulfil our religious duty, trusting that all our brother Moslems in east and west will pursue the same in fulfilment of their duty to us, and so strengthen the bonds of Islamic brotherhood."

Another letter asked for international recognition, and the formation of a standing Army.

Lawrence's interest at this time was centred in a report on Rabegh and Jeddah, which emphasised a curious state of affairs. There had been trouble at Rabegh, for misunderstanding, and an officer's ignorance of Arabic, had led to a sudden animosity against " infidels " and it seemed obvious that there was going to be difficulty in persuading the Arabs to accept British help.

The townsmen of Jeddah itself were definitely anti-Arab, and were really anxious for the British to do with Jeddah what they had done with Aden.

"YOU ARE LIKE THE BEAR, NEITHER TO BE MILKED, LED IN THE PROCESSION, NOR RIDDEN"

THE Press in Turkey and throughout the Central Powers generally discounted the revolt, and they went to some pains to explain how unimportant it was. The *Norddeutsche Allgemeine Zeitung*, on July 27, enlightened its readers :

"Considerably exaggerating the unimportant local incident in Jeddah and Mecca, the English and the French have fantastically elaborated it and made out that the whole Arab world has risen against the Ottoman Government. . . .

"It is absurd to talk of the rebellion of one of the Emirs as a revolt of all the Arabs and Moslems against the Ottoman Government. Our enemies are attempting by these means to set aside the fact that the Moslem world has declared in favour of the Holy War.

"The whole world knows that the English are secretly endeavouring to secure dominion over the whole Mohammedan world by seizing the Holy places and then to put into practice Gladstone's declaration, ' as long as the Koran exists there will be no peace in the world. . . .' With the help of God the Ottoman Government will use every influence to put a stop to the English policy to destroy the Moslem world. They will deliver the Moslems from the claws of their enemies and the clutches of England, and create a free Moslem world !"

Meanwhile, Murray, Wingate and the Arab Bureau were in constant touch with each other. It was certain that the Sherif could not possibly carry through the revolt alone. He had shot his bolt, so far as his own resources went. Jeddah was his, and so was Yenbo, captured on July 27, but he had not done the British, or himself, much real good so far.

If the revolt resulted in ultimate disaster, it would have far-reaching and detrimental effect on British prestige in the Islamic world. Yet what could be done in a forbidden

45

land? There were no British troops, except the details supervising the landing and distribution of supplies from the ships, and most of these slept on board ship.

Considerable diplomacy was necessary to ensure such help for the Sherif as would not injure his religious scruples. Lawrence, in the Arab Bureau, took a deep interest in his affairs, and combined with it the persistent propagation of his own dislike of his " imprisonment " in the Maps section. He had long talks with Hogarth, but neither the authorities in Egypt, nor at home, were agreed as to what the next Briitsh step should be.

Hussein's oriental mind, boggling at the landing of Christian feet on his Holy Hejaz, saw no objection to the use of aeroplanes, so long as they did not fly over the sacred cities. If in their flight they bombed and destroyed towns on the railway, particularly in the neighbourhood of Ma'an, Allah be praised ! He was however averse to the destruction of the railway itself, because, he said, it had been built by Mohammedans and was a Mohammedan enterprise.[1]

Little had been heard of the suggested French intervention since Captain Picart's " unofficial " request through the Arab Bureau. But the French were busy. Following instructions from Paris, the French Minister in Egypt had a long talk with McMahon in August, in which the latter was informed that the French Government had already decided to send a mission to the Sherif of Mecca. Included in it would be a military delegation which meant to discuss with the Sherif what military assistance could be given to the revolt, particularly with Moslem units. The French Minister had been instructed to consult the British High Commissioner with regard to the establishment of the mission in the Hejaz, and to facilitate its safe arrival at Mecca.

All of this was enlightening to McMahon, but what he wanted to know was—were the British and French Governments aware of the exact aims of the mission ? It was taking presents and subsidies of great value to the Sherif.

The authorities in Egypt were extremely cautious in dealing with any French approaches, and it was no surprise to McMahon when he learned that, while he should give every assistance

[1] Construction of the railway was begun in 1901, the capital being raised by contributions from Moslems all over the world. Its purpose was religious, but the Turks also used it to strengthen their hold over Arabia.

to the French Mission, the French Minister had actually been a little too enthusiastic in his interpretation of his own Government's wishes. As McMahon put it to the French : the Mission's interest in the pilgrimage was the only particular phase in its work which needed emphasis. Otherwise, the French interest in the Sherif of Mecca and the Hejaz, while it might profess no desire to interfere in the caliphate was—like that of the British—liable to suspicion, coming from a Christian nation. The French Government could show its sympathy with the revolt, and the Mission could congratulate the Sherif on his fight for freedom. Beyond that it was dangerous to trespass.

A week later a long and interesting letter from Ibn Saud presented yet another angle to the Sherifian problem. It was dated July 25, and contained news regarding the position between the Wahabi leader as a supporter of British interests, and pro-Turk Ibn Rashid. Reports of the Sherifian revolt had now reached Ibn Saud, and, commenting on them, he remarked on the " severe blow " to the Turks and their probable expulsion from Arabia. He did not however like the inclusive phrase " the Arabs." If the British authorities wanted his (Ibn Saud's) opinion on the matter, Hussein had originally intended to play the British off against the Turks and thus get the Turks to grant him a measure of independence. This intention had developed into his definite committal to British interests, and he was now in an awkward situation. If he went back to the Turks they would hang him, and if he supported the British he was liable to lose the whole of his religious authority, which was the only really important thing in his life.

Ibn Saud's position was now clear. He was definitely committed to the British side. He was at war with Ibn Rashid, not actually because the latter was in active alliance with the Turks, but because they were bitter enemies. His relations with the Sherif were however difficult. Nominally, as an ally of the British he was also an ally of Hussein, but he was undoubtedly jealous of the then growing strength of the Sherifian party, whose aim of ultimate supremacy over the whole of Arabia he could not regard with complaisance.

Following the receipt of this very clear indication of a partition in Arab opinion, Murray was favoured with a visit from Colonel Bremond and the members of the French Mission, which had arrived in Egypt on their way to Mecca.

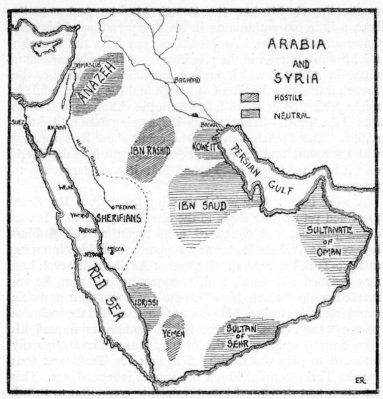

Labels on map:
ARABIA AND SYRIA
HOSTILE
NEUTRAL
DAMASCUS
BAGHDAD
ANAZEH
SUEZ
AKABA
IBN RASHID
KOWEIT
BASRA
PERSIAN GULF
HEJAZ RAILWAY
WEJH
MEDINA
IBN SAUD
SULTANATE OF OMAN
YAMBO
SHERIFIANS
RABEGH
MECCA
JEDDAH
RED SEA
IDRISSI
YEMEN
SULTAN OF SEHR
ER

Tribal sympathies at the beginning of the Revolt.

The Frenchmen were encouraged to be frank, and Bremond
stated quite blandly that the objects of the Mission were both
political and military. They intended to acknowledge the
Sherif as a ruler, and to ask his protection for such French
Moslems as would make the pilgrimage. In addition, however, they were going to offer him assistance in the way of guns,
quickfirers, rifles and instructors.

Murray was quick to inform London of the significance of
this offer. He knew McMahon's feelings on the question of
French assistance, and warned London that in his opinion
Britain would eventually have to pay a very high price
politically for all the military assistance France offer to the
Sherif. They had the advantage in being able to save purely
Moslem units, and if the use of such troops could save the
Sherifian cause, it was difficult to see how Britain could object

48

to such an offer from their ally. Personally, he would prefer that every effort should be made to minimise the French offer, and to make it possible for the Egyptian forces to supply what personnel and material was necessary.

The home authorities, however, being closer to the French Government and far removed from the actual operations, evidently thought Murray was exaggerating the situation. The French Government had, they informed the Egyptian commander, given an undertaking that they would not use any assistance they might give the Sherif as a lever to obtain advantages for themselves in the Hejaz. In the circumstances Murray could accept what French assistance he thought suitable.

In London, the French Ambassador underlined the concession. From the latest news reaching Paris, he reported to the British authorities, that it would be important to give the Sherif of Mecca, as soon as possible, the aid of the technical experts for whom he had asked. France was disposed to lend to the Sherif, within limits, and in consultation with the British authorities in Cairo, any aid he might wish for, without interfering in any way with the administration of a country whose complete independence was to be respected by the British and French governments.

Sherif Haidar, definitely established in Ottoman eyes as Sherif of Mecca, issued a proclamation to the Hejaz on August 9, as a counter to Hussein's justification for revolt.[1]

" The English," he said, " have severed India, Egypt, the Sudan, Zanzibar, Somaliland, and a part of Arabia from the body of Islam and occupied them. They turned the strength of their inhabitants into weakness. They were not satisfied with that, but helped the French to occupy Morocco and Central Africa, helped the Russians to occupy Persia and the Italians to occupy Tripoli. There remains nothing they have not done in order to destroy Islamism. . . ."

Wilson had been down to Yenbo to see Feisal, and had spent two days with him. It was his first meeting with him, and Wilson was favourably impressed. He heard of the beginning of the revolt, of the tribes who joined armed with " old guns and flint locks," of men pulling up the railway with their bare

[1] See page 44.

49

hands, of vain efforts against Turkish machine-guns and armoured trains, of lack of ammunition. "I sent messages to the sheikhs," said Feisal, "that arms would surely come this week, next week, until they at last replied, 'You promise arms, and you promise food, and none come.' Now most of them have gone home."

The Arabs wanted more arms, he said, more evidence that the British promises of assistance were going to be kept. While they looked, apparently in vain, for help, the Turks were lavishing gold right and left among the tribesmen, and it was now impossible for him to push them back. If they did attack him now, they would break through, the revolt would be smashed, and the Arabs enslaved for ever.

Feisal was not at all complimentary to his father, and Wilson did not improve the opinion when he told him that the Sherif had stopped the dispatch of trained men, held up thousands of bombs, and had even sent back dynamite—backing his actions with religious objections.

Giving a more up-to-date review of the situation in Rabegh —which was still bristling with difficulties—Feisal, disagreeing with his father's wishes, appealed for British troops to be landed there to give support and confidence to the Arabs.

"LET US QUARREL WITH OUR FRIEND RATHER THAN BE TOO LONG FRIENDLY WITH OUR ENEMY"

FOLLOWING the exchange of assurances between the British and French governments, the French Mission left Suez for Jeddah on September 12 under Colonel Bremond, but the High Commissioner thought it necessary to strengthen Murray's representations to London on the subject.

Wilson resumed contact with the Sherif and the latter, dismayed on the one hand at the Turkish threat and on the other at what he considered the "luke-warmness" of the British offers of help, told the Colonel that he did not believe the British intended to support him. The Turks, if they succeeded now, would smash the Arab movement, and his family would be wiped out.

McMahon supported Hussein's views. Any forward move by the Turks would mean the recapture of Mecca, and the opening up of the whole of Arabia to the Turks. But the effect would not end there, he added. The situation in Abyssinia and Somaliland would also be seriously affected and the whole political and military situation east of Suez would be jeopardised. He appreciated the religious and political objections to the landing of British troops in the Hejaz, but even this was preferable to the alternative—the acceptance by Hussein of the French offer of help. It was essential that the very great political advantages accruing to a Sherifian success should remain with the British.

Murray supported the High Commissioner's general argument, but, as always, he disagreed with any plan that would mean the dispatch of British troops.

McMahon added another argument to those he had already used in his attempts to educate distant London in the political and military situation. He repeated the story of the Stotzingen mission. Notebooks captured from the German officers showed that the enemy " intended to threaten Aden, organise attempts at destruction of British commerce and stir up rebellion

51

on African coast, Abyssinia and Somaliland protectorate" (so ran McMahon's message to London). " It was arrival of this force that compelled Sherif in self defence to revolt sooner than he intended, and his action has undoubtedly saved us from serious trouble, especially in view of previously prepared situation in Abyssinia and Somaliland Protectorate. Should Turks and Germans succeed in regaining Hejaz, they will resume these attempts and hence another cogent military reason for assisting Sherif to best of our ability."

London began to assess values. Britain's hands were full. Troops could not be spared either from Egypt, Salonika, Mesopotamia or East Africa, without endangering the position in each of these theatres, and in any case, whatever surplus troops became available ought to be sent to France. In addition, Britain might be compelled to send troops to India at any moment.

Robertson, Chief of the General Staff, did not mince matters. His opinion was that the only way to win the war was to beat the German armies. " As I have consistently held," he wrote, " ever since I became Chief of the General Staff, we must accordingly concentrate every available man against those armies. In forming this opinion, I give full weight to what is called the political side of the question, and in war there is no difference between political and military considerations. It is a commonplace that policy and strategy must be in harmony. Strategy is bad if it aims at results which are politically undesirable, and the converse is equally true. In a war of this magnitude, neither policy nor strategy should be local in their aims ; every proposal, whether political or strategical, must be examined as regards its effect upon the war as a whole, and I have examined in that way the proposal to support the Sherif with British troops."

The General Staff's opinion was definite. Troops could only be found to the detriment of the main theatre, and even if a force were landed at Rabegh, or elsewhere on the Hejaz coast, merely as an indication of moral support, circumstances might drive the allies into an undertaking beyond their present power. There were lessons to be learned from the Dardanelles and Mesopotamia.

In Cairo, the Arab Bureau—and Lawrence in particular—felt that the High Command was not fully aware of the significance of the situation. Lawrence had been against the sending of any British expeditionary force. What was wanted he argued, was that the Arabs should be given a backbone, mainly of ammunition, arms, supplies and money, which would help them immobilise the Turks in the Hejaz. The railway could then be rendered ineffective, the Turkish forces harassed, they would not be able to concentrate in dangerous strength either in Arabia or Syria, and the Arabs themselves could fight for their own freedom.

Argument went full circle. The Sherif could not carry the revolt through. British troops could not help him because of religious difficulties. The Arabs would go home, and the British would have to fight the Turks in a hostile country—with the possibility of another failure being added to the Dardanelles and Kut disasters. French troops could help, because they had completely Moslem units, but this would defeat the British need of being paramount in this part of the world.

The French through Bremond kept up a pressure of report, telegram and visit on Wilson and other political officers in the Hejaz, advising the Rabegh proposal. The British Government began to yield, and, faced with the strong recommendations of McMahon and Wilson, renewed their demands on Murray.

Murray would not alter his mind, and India was emphatically against Mohammedan troops being sent to Rabegh. It would be construed as a deliberate breach of the British pronouncement regarding the Holy places.

It was an awkward situation. The Turks in Medina had pushed their lines further and further afield, and by seizing the only wells in the countryside began the long awaited move on Rabegh. Feisal flung himself into the tangle of difficult sandhills that flanked the Turkish defences, and while his brother Ali at Rabegh was striving to form the beginning of a regular army, set himself with little bands of ravaging Bedouin on camels, to make impossible a serious advance of the Turks by raiding their lines of communication.

It was risky work, since the Arab parties—because of difficulties of water supply—could not exceed ten or fifteen men, and these had to dash in on the main route, killing or carrying off what they could, and to regain their camels and escape before the garrisons of the blockhouses—all within rifle shot of each other—could turn out.

53

At the end of September Storrs paid a visit to the Grand Sherif. He went down to Jeddah by the *Euryalus* and on landing he and Admiral Wemyss were greeted by a grand salute of eighteen shots, fired, hazardously, from eighteen ancient mortars.

Wilson was there to greet him, and soon a miscellaneous cavalcade was doing the rounds from the Arab Governor's house to the French Consulate, and from there to the British Consulate. Wilson was obviously delighted with the reception afforded to the visitors by the Arabs, and told Storrs that the magnificence of his arrival had elevated the British to heights of unimagincd splendour !

Later in the morning, Storrs rode round the bazaars, chatting here and there with the merchants, and then, after lunch at the British Consulate, went back to the *Euryalus* in company with all the Sherifs, sheikhs and sub-chiefs who could inconveniently crowd on to the then spotless decks of the British ship. It was the big guns that fascinated the Arabs, guns which in themselves must be signs of ultimate victory. Nothing but a winning cause could own such weapons ! The Arabs prostrated themselves for evening prayers on the stern walk, and then left the boat in a daze of pride that augured well for future British co-operation. So great was the impression created by the " iron ships afloat on the water " that Admiral Wemyss was officially invited to ride at the head of the procession of the Holy Carpet, an offer which was prudently declined.

Jeddah had been dazzled by this more or less ceremonial visit of the *Euryalus*—the *Fox* and the *Hardinge* were there also—but the British naval folk were themselves amused and amazed when the General in charge of the Pilgrimage received them " officially." He and the military band which played the " salute " were dressed alike in pilgrim bath towels, costumes, and sandals, the only difference being a gorgeous " officer's belt." round the portly waist of the General.

A wonderful day ended when the British warships flooded the harbour, the town and distant hills with their searchlights, completing hours of mutual surprises with the final miracle of turning night into day.

" LIKE A STORM IN THE SHOP OF A
GLASS DEALER "

THIS interval of ceremony was but an interruption to the serious business of extricating the Sherif from the consequences of his precipitate revolt. The Turks still wanted Mecca. Its retention by the Sherif was a blow to all their political and religious objectives, and until they were definitely cut off from Syria or routed in the field, they would remain a menace to the Sherif's—and incidentally, the British—operations.

Rabegh was the obstacle to any advance on Mecca, and the home authorities asked for, and at last insisted on, at least a brigade being concentrated for urgent dispatch to that port. Under protest, Murray put a brigade in reserve.

Wingate[1] while he recognised Murray's difficulties, argued it was better that British troops should be at Rabegh than a suggested French force from Algiers. For three or four days there was no hint from London as to what decision had been reached. Then, on October 19, Murray was informed that no brigade would be sent to Rabegh.

Murray, having won his point, turned all his attentions to El Arish. The French, deprived of British co-operation, began to urge for the dispatch of an all-French Moslem force. The Sherif, desperately in need of help, and inclined more to the British than the French, still erected his religious " barrier."

It was into this conflict of motives, or lack of them, that Lawrence, having asked for ten days' leave to go down the Red Sea with Storrs, made his plunge.[2]

On October 18 Lawrence and Storrs sailed from Suez in the *Lama* for Jeddah, and for some days the Hejaz pot merely

---

[1] On October 3 the War Office made Wingate responsible, in his capacity as Sirdar, for the military control and superintending of all arrangements for assisting the Sherif.

[2] " In October 1916," writes Mrs. Stuart Erskine in her book *King Feisal of Irak,* " news came of the visit of an old friend of the family to Jidda, Mr. Ronald Storrs. . . . With him was a member of the Arab Bureau in Cairo, a man named Lawrence, who desired to ride up to visit Feisal's camp. . . . The fact that the visit of the enterprising stranger had been sanctioned by his father made the Emir (Feisal) think that it must have some political significance. This Lawrence was not a trained soldier : he was an archæologist."

simmered. Then Hussein, despite his precarious position, added another complication to the Allies' problems. He announced himself as " King of the Arab Nations." Telegrams were despatched to the Allied governments and to some neutrals, announcing the " coronation."

Influential deputations from Syria were in Mecca at the ceremony, as were Mohammedan leaders from French Northern Africa—although the latter did not know at first that they were attending such a ceremony. French opinion was none too pleased with the fulsome support given Hussein's interests by *L'Orient Arabe*, edited in Paris. " This day is a great festival for the Arabs," said the paper. " We now see at the head of the Arab kingdom the reigning house in the world, acknowledging no superior but God, and no banner but the Arab flag."

The authorities in Egypt, particularly the Arab Bureau, were quick to see the danger of Hussein's adoption of such crown, and on their recommendation Wilson was asked to convey as delicate a warning as possible to the Sherif. He was to congratulate the King " on his expression of the wishes and the confidence " of his people, but the moment was " inopportune." The Allies were unable to recognise the " presumption of any sovereign title which may provoke dissension among Arabs at this moment and thus prejudice the final political settlement of Arabia on a satisfying basis."

The French, stirred by the British refusal to send a force to Rabegh, managed to influence London again sufficiently to secure an ambiguous modification of the original instructions sent to Wingate. He was told that if the Arabs could not hold Rabegh, naval assistance should be sent, with whatever French, British and Sudanese military aid was immediately available. This, however, was not to be construed as an authority to send an expeditionary force.

Approval was actually given on October 30 for the dispatch of a flight of aeroplanes to Rabegh, with the avowed object of " stimulating the morale of the Arabs and stiffening their resistance to the Turkish advance " ; and Major P. C. Joyce was sent from the Sudan, by Wingate's orders, with two hundred Egyptians, to guard the flight.

In the meantime, Lawrence had seen Feisal on the Medina road, visited Rabegh, and had then spent four days at Yenbo, writing his reports. On November 1 he was picked up by

56

the *Suva* and taken to Jeddah, and there he met Wemyss, who was on his way to see Wingate at Khartoum. Lawrence was anxious to see Wingate. He knew that the latter had been mainly instrumental in backing the Sherif at the beginning of the revolt, and had sent guns and troops of the Egyptian Army to Hussein's assistance when he could ill spare them. So Lawrence went with Wemyss, and gave Wingate a first hand report of his visit to the Sherifians, and his strong views on the situation.

Wingate was so impressed that he wired to Murray :

" Following observations of Lieutenant Lawrence an officer of great experience and knowledge who has just returned from visit to Feisal's camp and also to Rabegh are very pertinent to the question of dispatch of brigade to Rabegh which seems again to be under consideration of government. . . .

" Sherif entirely dependent on tribesmen for success of his movement and it is they who have held up the Turk for last five months. Assistance in material especially quickfirer guns and machine-guns is vital if they are to be kept in the field. If given this there is no reason why they should not continue to operate successfully for an indefinite time. Their morale is excellent and their tactics and leadership well suited to present objective.

" A successful advance on Rabegh will mean that tribal resistance has ceased and the Sherifian movement no longer has any military strength. Spirit of troops intensely national and suspicious of foreign interference. They welcome every sort of technical assistance even if some European personnel involved. The landing of a considerable force however would undoubtedly alarm them and might well result in the return of many tribesmen to their tents, in which case we shall have contributed to the very result which we wish to avoid. Moreover, once tribal resistance ceases Turks are free for advance on Mecca."

Wingate on November 7 informed the British authorities in London that he had reviewed the situation after a talk with Wemyss and Lawrence. He was of opinion that the Rabegh position, if strongly attacked by the Turks, would not be tenable even with naval assistance. No regular troops with artillery were available to hold the place, having been denied by the authorities, and the only alternative—a trained

Arab force of about five thousand men with artillery—could not be possible without time for organisation.

He amplified what he said to Murray, pointing out that he had already asked India to send Arab military prisoners, who volunteered for service with the Sherifians, to Egypt to join the Sherif as soon as possible. He would also like Newcombe sent out again, with assistants who had had previous experience with Arabs, to help in their organisation.

Murray kept to his course. He was going to harass the Turks in Syria with his mobile forces, to the full extent of his strength. " I thus hope to attract to myself Turkish forces which would otherwise be engaged against the Sherif or the Russians or in Mesopotamia. . . . The sending of any detachment to Rabegh would menace this offensive."

The next day the London authorities examined the Rabegh question once more. The political side had been discussing the Sherifian revolt, and had come to the conclusion that it was " of the highest importance to deny Rabegh to the enemy." The General Staff had to report " what force is necessary to secure that place against attack."

French pressure on London had something to do with this. They talked about constant requests for a Rabegh expeditionary force being " without acknowledgement " from the British Government. The Sherif, they said, had threatened to enter into negotiations with the Turks if we did not send aid.

Robertson attacked the French arguments. If the security of Rabegh was a matter of highest importance to Britain, it followed that the Turks attached the same value to its seizure. The British had had sufficient experience of the folly of embarking upon expeditions with minimum forces. Fifteen thousand at least would be needed to defeat any Turkish attack. Such troops could only come from Egypt, and Murray had persistently pointed out that the detachment of effectives from his forces would render impossible any chance of carrying out his orders for an attack on El Arish.

Such an expeditionary force would, he continued, involve the loss of many valuable lives, and at best it would not afford any effective contribution, either directly or indirectly to the successful conclusion of the war. The Germans would be pleased to see Britain frittering away her troops in secondary operations, he concluded, and that of itself was sufficient reason for not embarking on still another campaign.

"IF THE WIND BLOWS IT ENTERS EVERY CREVICE"

MOMENTARILY, French pressure held the upper hand, and it was decided to ask in what way Murray's prospective operations would be affected if his force were reduced by an infantry brigade, or, alternatively, two artillery brigades and two camel corps companies. Murray's reply—by now an almost automatic one—was to the effect that any reduction would nullify his El Arish operations, and that the Egyptian force would become a defensive unit only.

On November 17, Lawrence saw Murray, and the latter reacted to his information exactly as did Wingate. He suggested to Wingate that London be informed that " expert opinion " was definitely against the dispatch of white troops to Arabia.

Murray himself sent Lawrence's report on to London, and backed it with the following comment :

" Although the question of the advisability or otherwise of sending British or foreign troops to Arabia is out of my province, I think I ought to ask you to read Lawrence's views on the Hejaz question. He has just returned from a visit to Feisal's forces and his strongly expressed opinion, that no British or foreign forces should be sent to the Hejaz, is supported by soldier and civilian residents in this country who are intimately acquainted with the peculiar feelings of the Arab Moslems towards foreigners, and the delicate nature of the Sherif's position as a religious chief.

" Put shortly, the views held by the Moslem experts who have spoken to me on the subject entirely confirm Lawrence's views that the moment foreign troops land in Arabia, the Sherif as a religious chief ceases to exist, and that the occupation of Rabegh by a force acting on the defensive is useless."

Murray sent a copy to Wingate " for his information." But the latter replied pointing out that his own telegram to London of November 7 was drafted while Lawrence was in

Khartoum. In the circumstances he considered that London had the true facts of the situation before them, and to complicate them further by such remarks as Lawrence's would be " highly undesirable." The Sirdar's " would be " was too late, for Murray had already cabled the report.

Robertson told the home authorities that the report had been submitted by " Captain Lawrence, of the Intelligence Staff, Cairo," remarking that he had lived for several years in Asiatic Turkey, and was said to have an intimate knowledge of the Turks and Arabs.

It was evident from the telegrams which had been passing between London, Egypt and the Sudan, that the insistence on the Rabegh proposal, after London had definitely turned against it, had puzzled the military authorities in Egypt not a little, but a message to Murray at the end of November put the position in a very clear light—a light that was, perhaps, too dazzling for military minds.

The politicians had not been too happy about the business, Murray was told, and had " taken advantage " of Robertson's absence to re-open the Rabegh subject. That had led to the contradictory instructions, and the situation had got " a little out of hand," but with Lawrence's report to hand, and the Chief of the General Staff back, the French move had been countered. The value of Lawrence's report had been discounted somewhat because the Sirdar had said nothing about it. What was Wingate's opinion ? Robertson himself objected emphatically, once more, to the dispatch of French and British brigades, or a Franco-British force, preferring anything to a repetition of the Salonika muddle.

When Murray saw the copies of the reports London had received, from French and British sources, amplified by voluminous opinions of home experts, he fully appreciated the remark of his London correspondent : "The Sherif and his Arabs take up more time than most of the other theatres of war."

Wingate, faced with London's request for an opinion on Lawrence's report, asked Murray for the full text. Having read it, he gave it a general blessing, but added " Colonel Wilson and Colonel Parker, who were on the spot and have had much more experience and whose knowledge of Arabs is considerable, are of opinion that Rabegh could and should be held if the Turks advance in force." The reply concluded :

" I fully understand objections to landing British troops in Hejaz on account of opposition and in view of my military operations against the Hejaz railway which Murray is initiating very soon. For these reasons I recommend dispatch of French troops in an emergency, as I am of opinion that they may avert complete collapse of Sherifian movement, which I understand to be main object of His Majesty's Government."

The next day came another request from Wingate to Murray. The situation was serious. Could a brigade, with supporting artillery, be sent from Suez to Jeddah ? At this moment the Sherif seemed disposed to accept the presence of British troops at Rabegh, but only so long as they did not leave " the fringe of palm trees." (In other words they had to stay on the sea-shore !) The next day he altered his mind, and said he would rather a British brigade be kept at Suez or Port Sudan " for any emergency."

Murray made no promise. He could not spare the troops, and, repeating this to London, Wingate pointed out the serious consequences of Hussein's latest indecision. He thought that as neither he nor Murray could send troops, the situation should be fully explained to the Sherif, and to Lawrence and Joyce, so that the latter two could be prepared for any emergency and the former be warned of the consequences of his folly. Wilson was given the very awkward task of telling the wavering Sherif that he must accept full responsibility for the military conse-quences of his indecision.

Lawrence, apprehensive as to the next move of the Sherif, had (as he had reported) seen Feisal, and the latter argued that the situation was entirely changed. The Harb and Juheinah tribes—who hate Christians and whose presence in and around Rabegh were the weights his father used in his scales of judgment—had dispersed, and with their departure the obstacle of public opinion also practically disappeared. Feisal considered it a good time to come down to Rabegh personally, and under the cloak of his protection negotiate the reception of British troops. Without such backing the revolution would probably collapse in about three weeks' time.

Feisal's opinion was passed on to Jeddah, where Wilson reported it to both Storrs (who was on one of his periodic visits) and the Sherif. The latter would not see reason. His objection to Christian troops was an obsession. Instead, he spent his time charging the British with " breaking faith." The Arab plan had, he said, been based on British promises to cut the Hejaz railway : " If I had known you were not going to do this thing other plans would have been made ! " (An oblique hint about changing partners.) He attributed his present position to the British failure in this respect, and then shifted his ground with the statement that if the Sinai offensive progressed quickly it would entirely ease the situation.

Murray himself left London in no doubt as to his unaltered opinion. " The moment British troops land at Rabegh the Arabs will withdraw from the contest and leave us to settle with the Turks. The situation is a difficult one because I fully realise the possible outcry at home if the Sherif's revolt is crushed. But in view of the practical certainty that if we should land troops at Rabegh we should be committed to a campaign in Arabia I would accept the risk of the Sherif (who, after all, is not backed by about half the Moslems in his own country) being deposed and Mecca captured by the Turks."

A report from Lawrence dated December 6th amplified some of the apprehensions which he had expressed in his rare " official " cables, and a week later Storrs went down to Jeddah for a personal survey. He arrived on December 11, seeing Wilson at the Consulate, and there learned that Hussein, already in the town, had received Wilson, Lloyd, Bremond and Barnabei (the latter the head of the Italian Mission), and had discussed at length the general situation, with special reference to Rabegh. (The Sherif had decided to request Britain to send troops to hold Rabegh, a decision on which he had gone back the next morning.)

After a brief and cordial greeting, Storrs was led into a small room, furnished with comfortable leather chairs of the club type, and lighted by an acetylene lamp of several candle power. The Sherif was dressed with an elegant simplicity in a plain black " evening " cloth kaftan of embroidered Persian silk.

He embarked upon an exposé of the general situation, which resolved into about two and a half hours of criticism and suggestion without chance of interrruption. By this time it was nine o'clock and Storrs, withdrawing, returned the following morning to spend another two hours in his company.

Having just received encouraging letters from his three sons, Hussein was inclined to view the position in general under a much more rosy light than on the previous evening. He subsequently favoured Storrs with an unsolicited explanation of the reasons for his assumption of a regal title. Storrs suggested that he might have consulted the British Government before taking so momentous a step ; and he replied that as he had already been officially addressed by the residency as Khalifa (a title to which he did not aspire), he had considered that " the greater including the less " it was superfluous to apprise Britain of his resolution.

Wingate had remained very apprehensive regarding the military situation, and had warned London : " The immediate question for decision is whether we shall make a last attempt to save the Sherif and his Arabs in spite of his refusal to have European troops." London was silent, and then Wingate recommended that the offer of British troops should be made to the Sherif for the last time. If he refused he should be told that the offer was absolutely final, and that in no circumstances could it be repeated. Actually this crossed with an authority from London to Wingate, telling him to " take the necessary steps with a British brigade and also with the French contingent."

At this time, a few medical, Ordnance, Army Service Corps and other details were on shore at Rabegh, together with a detachment of the Royal Flying Corps, guarded by Egyptian artillery. Captain Goslett ran the base. A London business man, it seemed nearly impossible that in the Arabian heat (with a normality of about 120 degrees in the shade) he could manage to look and to be so efficient. It was a lesson in deportment to see him pick his way in and out of the conglomeration of tents and mud huts, and in precise and orderly fashion reduce the oriental miscellany of stores into something approaching his requirements.

Lawrence was against Wingate's campaign. He maintained the views he set forth in his report of November. He knew and appreciated fully the shortcomings of the Arabs, but he was certain that the situation could be retrieved by the Arabs themselves—and therefore without any religious or political repercussions—if good material, serviceable guns and ammunition, and usable rifles could be rushed up to the tribes.

On December 20, Wilson met Pearson, Bremond and Lloyd

in conference at Jeddah. It was actually convened at Bremond's request, and he opened immediately with a demand that the British and French Governments should " insist " on the Sherif allowing Christian troops to land.

Wilson pointed out to Bremond that the Sherif was quite sincere in his belief that if Christian troops landed, all the Arabs would immediately desert his cause. " Given such a certainty," he asked Bremond, " do you still advocate the landing of such troops ? " The Frenchman replied in the affirmative. There were several Senegalese battalions at Marseilles, he said, which could be transported to the Hejaz, as they could not stand the French winter.

Wilson's rejoinder was to the point. If the Sherif was forced against his will to ask for Christian troops, the whole responsibility for the Hejaz would pass from his hands to the Allies, and the latter would be forced to meet any contingency which might arise. In the end Bremond temporised by agreeing to ask his government for troops to be placed at his disposal " for use in an emergency."

The Sherif, as involved as ever in his reasoning, sent a long letter to Wilson, reiterating his objections to the landing of Christian troops in the Hejaz, and concluded, in amazing fashion :

" I cannot believe that Great Britain is unable to spare fifteen hundred Mussulmans from five million soldiers mentioned in Reuters or from the Allied powers. . . . Meanwhile, I am sacrificing the lives of my sons and all dear to me and doing everything possible in the name of honour and dignity."

For two or three days there was an exchange of opinion between the authorities in Egypt, the Sudan and London, Wilson keeping in touch with the Sherif, and the latter wrote again on December 27. Neither the original Arabic nor the translation helped matters much :

" It appears that it is impossible to expect any use from Moslem troops, even supposing they can be found. . . . It also appears according to previous communications that European troops, if landed at Rabegh, must not go into the interior beyond the palms, a restriction which will not half repulse the enemy, for the enemy could avoid the position at

Rabegh and advance in any direction he wishes. Thus the desired result will not be attained.

" Consequently, I wish before everything to inquire from Your Excellency whether that result is still pending, as it was formerly understood to be. If it is it will not bring about the desired result, but will only cause great difficulty, materially and morally. Therefore, owing to the restriction I cannot naturally give the final answer until I understand your reply on the above-mentioned position. In any case, if it is the considered opinion that the case is such—that the sending of the above with the keeping of the town restriction would fulfil the desired object, and that it would ward off danger—then I submit and hand over for consideration the sending of it and its landing at Rabegh."

This did not satisfy Wilson, and he advised the Sirdar that he did not consider the decision was at all definite. In reply he was told to inform the Sherif that the troops would now have to be withdrawn from Suez, and " that he must stand on his own feet from now with regard to military operations."

Thus ended the year 1916, with Lawrence maintaining and proclaiming his belief in action by the Arabs themselves, equipped with sufficient arms and strengthened by expert military advisers.

The Sherif wanted to be saved, but hedged his possible salvation with impossible conditions.

The French wanted all the glory of a military campaign.

The British, committed up to the hilt in all the other theatres of war, could not spare any troops to help the Sherif, but at the same time could not afford the loss of prestige his collapse would entail. Neither could they afford the luxury of help from the French. The Turks themselves, fully aware of the Sherif's precarious position, dared not take advantage of it because of their fear of an Allied counter-attack.

The New Year began with a renewal of the squabble over the Rabegh base. The Sherif had sent Wilson a telegram which opened with the usual interminable preamble of argument and counter-argument and then ended :

" Consequently I beg of you to inform the High Commissioner immediately of my approval for landing the forces not only at Rabegh but also at Yenbo for the purpose stated."

This was so definite that Wingate hardly overstated his feelings in the reply he sent to the Sherif, in which he thanked him and said he " was much relieved in consequence." The relief was not shared by Murray. He considered the letter " a blow," and in expressing his opinion to London, underlined once again his long-standing opposition to the idea : " It is still my opinion that it is militarily unsound."

Wilson, not at all satisfied with the apparent permission of the Sherif, wired Cairo urging that action should not be taken in the matter until Hussein actually asked personally for the troops in a written and signed application, and took full responsibility for the consequences. Wingate stood by Hussein's telegram of approval, and Wilson again urged for delay, but it was the Sherif himself who finally exhausted Wingate's patience. He began to hedge again, and in yet another telegram said :

" . . . delay dispatch of troops until every necessity by us is justified by enemy retreat which just been established. . . . We quote well known proverb ' Your partner in business does not betray you.' "

Whatever Wingate thought of the proverb, he put an abrupt end to the negotiations for the troops. He instructed Wilson to inform the Sherif that the offer of military assistance was finally withdrawn, and would in no circumstances be repeated.

This, however, was no solution of the main problem—the revolt. Wingate had heard from Murray that the French had now turned their attention to an Akaba landing, but that he had turned the idea down " flat." Murray could only suppose it had been put forward as a continuation of French diplomacy, without consideration of the military problem.

In view of the lack of organisation in the Arab forces, Wingate recommended that further assistance in qualified British officers should be provided for Wilson on whom, he wrote, " up to date had fallen the whole of the difficult task of guiding and advising Arab leaders, both in military and political matters." Newcombe was sent for again, and he, Major Vickery (R.F.A.), Major Cox and Captain Marshall (R.A.M.C.) left Suez for the Hejaz at the beginning of January.

Although they were on the defensive, in the military sense, the Turks were adopting a rather broad outlook in their propaganda and all the bazaars were alive with the news of "peace."

An agent brought an official Turkish proclamation to the Bureau, in which were detailed all the Turkish " successes " in the Hejaz and elsewhere, and giving the terms of peace which were shortly to be ratified. These included, among other provisions, the cession to Turkey of Egypt, Aden and Basrah.

Another telegram sent to Hodeidah for publication announced :

" Negotiations have been passing during the past ten days between the various belligerents on the subject of peace, resulting in England being obliged to make large concessions.

" An armistice has been declared.

" Russia, France and Italy have been compelled to accept the conditions offered (by Germany) and have agreed to pay indemnities. The British have been forced to consent to evacuate Egypt, which is to pass into the hands of the Egyptian Khedive, as previously. The Ottoman Government is to dominate and control the Red Sea and Basrah, to which all the contracting powers have given their consent ; further that none of the enemy powers will be allowed to interfere in Arabian affairs, or such as pertain to the Arabian islands.

" Lahej and the nine cantons in Yemen, which have been conquered in this war, to be given up by England, together with Sheikh Othman and Aden, to the Turkish Government. British stocks of coal to remain at Aden.

" The French are being annihilated in the same manner as the Belgians."

" MAN AMASSES, AND TIME DISPERSES "

LAWRENCE did not seem to be so much worried now by the bickerings of the high commands. He was " submerging " himself in the Arab campaign, living with the Arabs, learning and fighting with them.

He kept Clayton and Wilson very closely informed as to his activities, and it was evident he felt that a definite change of plan was necessary if the Turks were to be prevented from regaining Mecca and crushing the Arab movement in its infancy. It was bad for the Arabs to think of possible failure, or of the time they were staying away from their families and pastures.

After consulting with the British naval authorities in the Red Sea, Wilson and Lawrence determined that if they would support Feisal to the limit, the Arabs could risk leaving the Mecca route undefended, and move the whole of their forces from Yenbo to attack Wejh, two hundred miles farther north along the Hejaz coast. They argued that by boldly taking the offensive against the Turkish communications—and Wejh covered a vital section of the Hejaz railway, the lifeguard of the Turkish forces—it would drive the Turks to concentrate considerable forces for defensive purposes, and yet so deceive them with the Arabs' apparent careless confidence in the strength of Mecca as to persuade them to abandon their march against it.

To take his place Feisal called up his younger brother Zeid and gave him all the men he thought not worth taking away, so that Zeid could make a semblance of resistance in the hills. He also asked his elder brother Abdullah, who was blockading Medina on the east, to move across the Hejaz railway north of Medina with the appearance of making a direct threat to the Turkish lines of communication.

Abdullah's force was more straw than substance, but he made a fine start. He managed to isolate some mobile Turkish units and cut them up, and, for the information of the rescuing patrols skirmishing out from Medina, left a message between the metals of the railway. It was a polite note to the Turkish commander, telling him of all and much more than all of what he meant to do.

Feisal's own operation was to be a flank march by an inferior fighting force to Um Lejj, parallel to the Turkish front for two hundred miles. It was a little coastal village about half way to Wejh, and the next move was another march of one hundred and fifty miles without a single spring of water, and only a few weak wells to suffice for what was, for the desert, an exceptionally large army. To aggravate this, there was little grazing for the camels, and the scarcity of baggage animals made it impossible to carry forage.

The Bedouin who acted as guides had no short unit of time such as an hour to inform the Sherifians of distance, and no longer measure of space than a span. They had no realisation of numbers larger than ten, and could not tell Lawrence anything of the roads or of the wells, or how much water they held. No man in the force could read or write.

(Vickery had reported for duty on the 16th and he and Lawrence were soon discussing the future. The latter talked of being in Damascus in 1918, but Vickery looked his doubts. He was a regular, and eyed the hybrid units of the Sherifians with amusement. He expressed open disapproval of the wearing of native headdresses by the British. It just wasn't done. He did not realise that any headdress other than this which was seen outside the limit of camp was a fair mark for any Bedouin, and it was rather troublesome if a head happened to be inside the offending headgear !)

The land army, owing to its many hindrances, got behindhand with its timetable, and when they did get to Wejh they found it already in the hands of the Sherifians.

The capture was mainly due to the navy. They scraped marines, bluejackets and stokers together, lumped them in with half a thousand Arabs, and after a hot piece of work by the naval guns, stormed and took the town.

It was during the bombardment of Wejh that the Red Sea fleet recorded its first casualty. One of the observers, Lieutenant Stewart, of the 7th Royal Scots and R.F.C., was hit by rifle fire while spotting for the gunners of one of the warships.[1] Lieutenant King, the pilot, and Stewart had been flying for an hour and a half over Wejh, and on their return

[1] H.M.S. *Anne* carried 'planes to be used as " spotters," while Captain Boyle conducted the operations from the *North Star*.

Stewart was found to be dead when the machine was hoisted on board.

Within a few days the few British personnel further south were moved up to Wejh, from Rabegh, and they soon found their hands full. Those in the Ordnance camp had to throw their regular army training into the discard and fall back on their own ingenuity.

Seaton, a slow-speaking obstinate man, already middle-aged, self-opiniated, with an habitual swearing grumble as he worked, was as much a craftsman as his comrade Bright, who was tall, thin, younger, and had a crisp sense of humour. Ill-paired as they appeared, they were always sure of an admiring gallery as they worked away in their marquee. They handled the mixed mass of Arab arms as if they had inherited the centuries-old skill of the oriental armourers.

Flintlocks, matchlocks, Japanese, Egyptian, German, French and British arms, daggers, old cavalry sabres, pikes, spears, scimitars—the dogged and sweating Englishmen cured them of their ills and handed them back to their marvelling and delighted owners. Twisted barrels, barrels tied with string and wire, barrels choked with the filth of years, smashed stocks, absent sights—they took all such in their care. Testing was always a risky matter. Arms were never oiled. Oil caught the sand and clogged them up. There were jammed cartridges, powder-clogged barrels, every death-trap known to armourers. Most of the rifles were certainly as dangerous to friend as to foe.

Daggers with leaden handles, some inlaid with silver, others —rare enough—with gold ; swords and scimitars which had seen the passing of many a sultan—all went through their hands. Some had been used much as man would use a pen-knife as a can-opener, with points and edges blunted to uselessness. One glorious, vibrating yard of steel, covered in grime, revealed itself as a rare blade from the Middle Ages, a weapon to gloat over, but the chopping stick of a sheikh of the desert.

"IF THE CAMEL GETS HIS NOSE IN THE TENT HIS BODY WILL SOON FOLLOW"

AFTER the capture of Wejh, the Arab operations had to take on a new phase.

Besides the labour of forming a regular army, Feisal, with Lawrence's discreet prompting, devoted himself night and day to securing the desert power to take the place of the British sea power that could henceforth only serve him indirectly.

In Cairo, Murray was still under French pressure. They had filed another request for the establishment of a military force, this time at Akaba. With combined Anglo-French forces, they said, a victory could be gained, with the capture of fifteen to twenty thousand enemy troops, which would ring throughout all their Mussulman colonies. British and French warships could be freed, and so soon as Medina was taken the military expenditure of the Sherif could be sensibly reduced.

Murray told Bremond that he was no less opposed than formerly to landing troops at Akaba. Bremond countered by telling him that the French intended to try to induce the Italians to land troops in Arabia in co-operation with the French—information which Murray very quickly passed on to London.

The Turks themselves, furious not only at the continued resistance of the Sherifians, but at their defiance of all Ottoman authority, continued a policy of calculated oppression, under the guidance of Jemal Pasha, which had as its ultimate end the dispersal of the pro-Arab element in Syria, and the complete subjugation of all those remaining under Turkish rule. They surrounded the whole of the Lebanon with a military cordon, and prevented food getting through, with the result that something like half of the infantile population of the Christian and Druse peoples in that zone died of starvation. The Turks denuded the country of its olive and orange trees, both for fuel and as a purely destructive measure. They deported large numbers of the more influential Arab families, and hanged, on all and any pretexts, those Arab leaders on whom they could lay their hands, no matter whether they were pro- or anti-Turk.

In the south an awkward position had been surmounted, during which Abdullah's area had been in a turmoil owing to tribal disaffections, war weariness and an increase in enemy propaganda. One raid by Garland was jeopardised by the disturbed atmosphere, but a force he took from Wejh on February 12 managed to reach the vicinity of the line eight days later. It was a daring foray, because the temper of the Bedouin, at the sight of an " infidel," was still an uncertain quantity, and Garland had not been in Arabia before.

The guides led him to a small two-span bridge, supposedly midway between two stations, but Garland had hardly been five minutes on the line, preparing a mine—it was midnight— when he was astounded to hear the whistle of an approaching train. (It appeared afterwards that he was no more than a quarter of a mile from Toweira itself.)

Garland left the mine hurriedly prepared, and scampered away into the desert, minus his boots, but the train hit the mine and went up in a burst of machinery when he was barely fifty yards away. It was the first time the Turks had had a train so wrecked in the Hejaz, but the guides' mistake nearly made it Garland's first and last effort.

It was now known that the Turks intended to withdraw their Hejaz forces. It was an embarrassing situation for the British, and everything was done to prevent the information leaking out, for the first hint of such a large-scale withdrawal would find the French pressing their long-shelved military expedition. It was also better for the Egyptian force that the Turks should be compelled to maintain their 15,000 men up and down the Hejaz line, than that they should transfer them to Palestine and thus become an ominous threat to Murray's reduced effectives.

At this moment the British home authorities drove near-Eastern experts into a frenzy of speculation. Agreements signed in 1916, to placate French and Italian opinion then, were now apparently not comprehensive enough in their possible rewards, if and when the Allies won the war.

Italy in particular had expressed her dissatisfaction at the comparatively meagre slice promised her of the Turkish empire, and Egyptian Headquarters were asked, quite casually : what opinion could they offer to the suggestion that

British Somaliland be given to Italy in return for the French ceding their part of Somaliland to Britain ? As an after-thought, they were also asked what they thought of the surrender of British Somaliland to Italy even if French Somali-land were not given up. As quickly as the request arrived, so did another follow, hinting that it could be conveniently " forgotten."

As Hussein and his sons were as yet ignorant of the Sykes-Picot agreement, and the Arab Bureau only suspicious about it, the latter—and Lawrence—began to wonder what other complications were likely to be introduced by the far-removed authorities in the West. Wingate suggested that it was high time that Hussein was informed of the general lines of any agreement that had been reached between the British and the French ; or alternatively, if it had to be kept secret, that representations should be made to him that a mission should be formed to consider the future of Arabia.

Since the capture of Wejh, Lawrence had been more or less concerned with improving his connections with the various tribes between the coast and the railway and, in order to keep their tempers sweet, indulged in raids on the line with a varying result of loot and fighting. Then a messenger arrived for whom Lawrence had been told to wait in Wejh, as he had urgent news. It turned out to be a copy of the Turkish instruc-tions for the immediate evacuation of Medina. Would Law-rence do what he could to see that the Turks were headed off, or destroyed ?

A section of the Abu Tayi tribe arrived on the outskirts of Wejh on February 17, an addition to Feisal's army which had interested Lawrence intensely, particularly when he heard that Auda abu Tayi, reputedly the greatest fighter of them all, was expected. In addition to the armoured car details[1] Joyce had joined as military adviser to the Sherifian troops. Over 6 ft. in height he had a very stiff-legged walk, was gruff but genial, and it was amusing to see him walking about the camp with the smaller Goslett.

Newcombe and Garland[2] had gone out to the line, the former leaving Wejh on February 21 with about 160 Arabs,

[1] A section of the Duke of Westminster's armoured cars, already famous for their work in the Siwa oasis, had been transferred to the Hejaz as a " moral help " to the Arabs.

[2] Garland had been training some of the Bedouin in the use of dynamite.

mostly mounted two on a camel. When they returned to the base on March 11 Newcombe reported that the Bedouin along the railway at this point were paid by the Turks thirty Turkish pounds and ten loads of corn per month to guard the line, " but," he added, " they are open to arguments from the other side, and generally get paid twice over."

" WRITE NOT THY PROMISES IN SAND "

CURIOUSLY enough, despite the request for " urgent action "
Lawrence did not appear to do much about it. He surveyed
the plain of El Khubt and then returned to Abu Markha about
the middle of March, where he was forced to remain for a
time, incapacitated by a succession of illnesses, first with boils,
then dysentery, and ending up with malaria.

Recovered from these, he rode in to Wejh, rested for
twenty-four hours, and then, with a force of thirty men,
started off for a raid on the railway at Abu Naam. There
was a lot of skirmishing, false alarms, and ineffective attempts
on the line, and in the end Lawrence returned to Abu Markha
with little accomplished except additions to his knowledge of
the Arabian countryside.

After a short talk with Abdullah, he went on to Wejh,
where Feisal held court to the Sheikhs of the Howeitat and
Beni Sakhr, and other Aneizah tribes. Lawrence kept well
in the background, but he had primed Feisal with a plan of
campaign, and he wanted to see the varying reactions of the
more important desert sheikhs, especially Auda abu Tayi.[1]

Twenty thousand rifles was the force Lawrence had in mind,
and they discussed the project of descending on the railway—
using the Druse mountains as base—between Damascus and
Ma'an, and from Deraa to Afuleh.

Having talked this over, Feisal expressed considerable alarm
at the rumour which had reached him to the effect that the
French were due to land " some 60,000 men in Syria." He
turned enquiringly to Lawrence, who took refuge in diplomatic
silence. He sensed Feisal's annoyance, not so much at the
rumour itself as its implications, and was not surprised when
he said, quite openly, that if there were any truth in the
rumour, it was evident that England would cease to supply the
Sherifians with arms and ammunition, and that the French
would take Syria without the assistance, or the permission, of

[1] Auda had come to Wejh to swear allegiance to the Sherif in the picturesque
Arab formula, and celebrated his first meal with Feisal by summarily ejecting
his Turkish-manufactured false teeth and smashing them on a rock.

the Arabs. " If this comes to pass," he concluded forcibly, " I will first fight the Turks, and then the French." The buzz of approval from the circle of sheikhs confirmed Lawrence's opinion as to Sherifian and Bedouin feelings regarding French interference.

The last Lawrence had heard about the French and their plans in Arabia and Syria was a complete refusal by Murray to permit any allied expeditionary force to operate in the Hejaz. Actually—whatever had been the source of the rumour which had reached Feisal—the French were still manoeuvring to get a footing on the Palestine coast, and the French War Minister even announced that they intended sending General Bailloud to Egypt to command the French contingent. Perhaps, they asked, the British authorities would be good enough to give the General command of some place on the line of communication, such as Gaza.

London very promptly cabled to Egypt to the effect that no place of consequence in Palestine was to be permitted to be occupied or garrisoned by the French.

Italy then proceeded to consolidate her claims to a share in the spoils, by securing the agreement of San Giovanni di Moriana, signed on April 20, 1917.

The outstanding article in the pact follows :

(8) It is understood that in the case of it not being possible at the end of the war to obtain for one or other of the powers mentioned all the advantages foreseen in the agreements concluded by the Allied powers regarding the apportionment to each of them of a part of the Turkish empire, *the maintenance of the Mediterranean equilibrium will be equally taken into consideration* (my italics—E.R.) in conformity with Article 9 of the Pact of London of April 26, 1915, in all changes or arrangements affecting the provinces of the Turkish empire as a consequence of the war.

(Actually, before any official signature could be secured from the then Russian Government, it was swept out of power by the revolution.)

The next hint of the growing Italian interest in Arabian affairs came from Wingate. The Italian Consul-General for Egypt told him that the Italian Minister for the Colonies purposed sending a special mission composed of Mussulman representatives from Tripoli, Cyrenaica, and Italian Somaliland to Jeddah " to make a study of the questions respecting Italian pilgrims." Of course, he had said, the mission had no political object.

As Britain had blocked several French moves which had "no political object" London told their representative to arrange for the mission to be postponed, if possible, " till the end of the war," as the proposal was regarded with " some misgiving."

Faced with these accumulating political and diplomatic moves, Wingate had a conference with his experts regarding the situation in the Hejaz, and the hope was expressed that M. Picot (who was proceeding with Sir Mark Sykes to Jeddah " to talk to the King ") would succeed in satisfying the Sherif in regard to the future of Syria, and also that he would subsequently succeed in persuading his own government to withdraw all French interests from the Hejaz.

The general tendency of the recent British agreements had been framed, obviously, with the object of securing their roads to the East, and in " assisting " the other powers to create spheres of interest remote from these roads, to divert their influences from the Red Sea and the Persian Gulf. Arab aspirations were being encouraged, and the British were doing their utmost to create a series of independent Arab states favourable to themselves and hostile to the Turks and to anyone else.

Once the French acquired political influence in the Hejaz, or the Italians in southern Arabia, the whole of the British plans would be jeopardised.

"THINK OF THE GOING OUT BEFORE YOU ENTER"

During the enforced period of idleness Lawrence had subjected the Sherifian situation to a close analytical survey which, in the end, prompted a change of plan. He saw in Auda abu Tayi and his men a force which under the necessary impetus, could strike sharply yet heavily at the Turkish forces. It was necessary to have a base other than Wejh, much farther north, and the only feasible one seemed to be Akaba, already stated by the experts to be too strong for frontal attack. Lawrence planned for a march through to Wadi Sirhan, where the Howeitat could be assembled, and then to rush to Akaba from the interior. He put it to Wilson, but the latter would have none of it. Lawrence, however, did not wait, but booked a passage on the *Arethusa* and proceeded to Cairo to win Clayton and the others to his side.

His reception was not too encouraging. There appeared to be too many obstacles, both physical and political, to so risky a scheme. It meant a five hundred mile detour, with strong forces of Turks between Lawrence and safety, a doubtful right of way through the Sirhan, no reliable knowledge as to water, and the almost impossible feat of reaching actually within striking distance of Akaba without being discovered by the Turks or being betrayed by the local Arabs.

Lawrence returned to Wejh, made his own arrangements—against Wilson's continued opposition—and left the base on May 9. Before he left he despatched a brief note to Clayton acquainting him of his decision to undertake the journey, and left it at that.

The force marched off through the Hejaz hills, across dreadful limb-breaking lava fields which crippled their camels and sometimes the men, and crossed the railway in a thunder of dynamite explosions which pleased the raiding Arabs and mystified and troubled the Turks.[1]

---

[1] The destruction of twenty-five bridges on the Hejaz railway line from May 1 to 19 shows how difficult it was to maintain the Hejaz railway in operation (German General Staff).

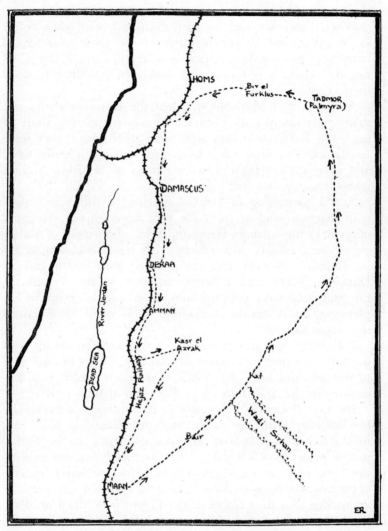

Lawrence's "Secret" journey.

Once across the railway they were in the pathless central desert of Arabia, where they wandered for days in a ceaseless torture of heat, thirst and hunger. Many of the party were lost and many more were disheartened and turned back for their homes.

When Lawrence and his men eventually did reach water in the Wadi Sirhan the majority of the force were saved, both men and beasts, but poisonous reptiles struck terror all round. Many were bitten, and three men actually died from their venom.

At the end of May they reached the Howeitat tents, and then spent many uneasy days. They were getting short of food, the Turks knew they were somewhere about, they were nearly four hundred miles from their nearest friendly base, and were still uncertain as to the temper of the tribes through whose country they had yet to pass.

At the beginning of June, Lawrence, a little dissatisfied with inaction, and at the same time eager to test the spirit of revolt in the northern Hejaz and Syria, slipped out of Auda's camp on a solitary trek which in the end took him as far as Tadmor (the old Palmyra), many miles north east of Damascus. The vast pillared enclosure of the Temple of the Sun may have tempted him, as it had no place in his planning, but it was the actual limit of his lonely five hundred mile reconnaissance.

Following the caravan route to Furqlus, he made his way down the line until he reached Ras Baalbek. Here he managed to damage the line—the origin of a report which was discounted in the Arab Bureau until the end of July.

He then slipped into Damascus. At this stage of the revolt, his influence with the Arabs and the damaging blows his roving bands of irregulars had already struck at the Turks, put a price on his head. " El Orrance " was the nearest the Turks or Arabs could get to his identity, and in the bazaars of the towns and the gossip centres of the village it was common knowledge that the capture of the Englishman, dead or alive, would secure a reward of five thousand golden sovereigns.

The amazing part of Lawrence's journey was that, as always, he made no attempt to disguise his facial appearance. Intelligence reports received later in the year confirmed that he had managed to get into the inner councils of the Turco-German commands. (He referred once to " a meal in the

Town Hall at Damascus, a gilded room with tables and carpets"!) It was learned from the same source that, as a merchant of obvious wealth but unknown origin, he sold non-existent grain crops, camels, stores, etc., on terms which were so favourable to the Turks that they actually cultivated his friendship. In other quarters in Damascus he met known pro-Arab notables, and talked of the future.

How this slight figure, with its brick-red, clean-shaven face, and noticeably blue eyes, managed to obscure his real identity under his merchant's guise can only be attributed to the ease with which he took on the manner and speech of his temporary roles. He had not only been at pains to master the various dialects but he knew tribal customs and tribal history. He knew Syrian politics, and he relied on his reading of men's characters to guide his bearing. He was usually a thought ahead of most men's minds, and it was this mental superiority which must have sustained him in the ordeal of an eighteen-day trek through a country occupied by the enemy and infested with spies.

His work at Damascus finished, he journeyed on through El Leja, the Hauran and the Belka, at each centre talking with the paramount chiefs of the Bishr, Wuld Ali, and other tribes. With each he made his plans for their co-operation when the revolt spread to their borders. He bargained for supplies. He bought camels in advance. He gave gifts and promised more, and left behind him plans which, if they matured, would sweep the Turks from Syria and northern Arabia and see the Arab flag flying as a symbol of conquest from Mecca to Aleppo.

Near Homs he blew in the side-arch of one of the bridges and disappeared into the desert in the dust of its fall. He upset the railway and its communications at various points between Amman and Katrani, and between Kalaat el Dabaa and Khan Zebib succeeded in laying a mine and blowing up a train single-handed.

Before starting on his journey from Wadi Sirhan, he had thought of Kasr el Azrak as his main base of future operations, and he paid particular attention to the old Arab keep when he called there on his return trip. He was there for less than a day, but found it all that he desired, noting its hard, yellow mud flats as possible landing grounds, its lagoon of fresh water, the old fort (an old Roman keep which had been completely rebuilt by the Arabs) and the grove of palm trees which had grown, withered and grown again since the hunting days of the Ghassanide kings.

He even visited Ma'an and remarked on the thick concrete-roofed shelters south of the station.

With the Bishr and the Beni Khalid he had arranged—when the word for action arrived—for attacks on the railway between Aleppo and Ras Baalbek, in daylight, all calculated to make the passage of trains difficult. He marked the Orontes bridge at Hama and another at Reston—unguarded when he inspected them—for demolition, attacks which would make the through passage of trains from Aleppo to Rayak impossible for at least two months. Five hundred men were to be used, and the operations were to be timed for the first half of September.

Between Ras Baalbek and Damascus, raids on the railway were to be undertaken by small parties of the Metawala and other attached Arabs, operating from the east. These were timed for the end of August.

He asked the Howeitat, Sherarat and Rualla to arrange for raids, in daylight, on the line between Deraa and Ma'an, to take place from the end of August onwards. The contingents, not less than 1,500 strong, could use Bair, Azrak and El Jefer as their bases.

The El Leja Arabs were to make plans to attack the railway under cover of darkness between Kiswe and Khirbet el Ghazale, but these were not to be undertaken until September.

One last and difficult operation was to devolve on a flying column composed of Howeitat, Sherarat and Hawama, moving from Azrak, which was to attack one or some or the bridges in the Yarmak valley between Deraa and Tiberius. Any one bridge wrecked or damaged would disorganise the line for at least six weeks.

All these plans depended on the successful occupation of Akaba, but once this was accomplished the effect of swift and sudden blows at the railway at such widely divergent points would make it possible for a force of something like 8,000 Arabs and Druse to make a general attack on Deraa and the three lines running north, south and east of it, from the Hauran. The men were not campaigners like regular soldiers, but they would be good enough to occupy the area and the bridges, and to hold them, with resultant risings in the hills between the Jordan and the Hejaz railway and in the hills among the Nazareth-Damascus routes—all of which would simplify the operations of the Egyptian forces and considerably shorten the campaign against Turkey.

In no case was any one operation to be undertaken until secret and authoritative word was received from Lawrence himself, as he had to secure the co-operation of the British forces. Large-scale operations by the latter had to be synchronised with those of the Arabs. If the British could only undertake minor operations, Arab action such as was planned would lead only to their own destruction, particularly of the Druse element.

On the other hand, whole-hearted co-operation between British and Arab forces would see Turkey out of the war. She would be forced out of Syria, Arabia and Palestine, and compelled to come to terms.

Lawrence's enforced " dreaming " at Wejh had evolved this plan. The first half of the journey to the Wadi Sirhan had been completed. The Turks had heard of a hostile concentration " somewhere in the desert," but knew little of its purpose. Lawrence had made his dash to the north under the spur of delaying and disheartening inaction, and then had inspired willing tribes, converted doubtful ones, talked with the enemy, and planned with them for the " destruction " of the British and Arab forces. It was reported that he had even dined with the military staff at Turkish headquarters. (He may have done more, but this is as much as could be built up on the reports received from the intelligence agents in the area.)

The plans were so far-reaching in their importance that their execution could not have been entrusted to others. They were so much out of the reach of set military strategy, and depended ultimately on what Lawrence could effect under the power of his own influence. He had to journey, plan, talk and even act single-handed, trusting to no-one but himself, divulging parts of the plan only to those who could move just when and where asked.[1]

On June 18 he slipped back into the camp at the head

[1] As will be seen from the progress of the operations, some of Lawrence's plans had to be postponed, even abandoned, through circumstances beyond his control, but the harvest of his propaganda was reaped in the last months of the campaign.

of the Wadi Sirhan, to find Auda and his men restive and
puzzled in the mystery of his absence.

To their questioning he had one answer, so astounding in
its simplicity that they actually failed to scoff.

" I have been to Ras Baalbek," he said.

" IMPROVE THY INTENTIONS, AND THOU MAY'ST SLEEP FEARLESSLY, EVEN IN THE DESERT "

MEANWHILE, in the field where words were weapons, the vague shadow of the Sykes-Picot agreement loomed up again. No one of the Egyptian command, and certainly no one in the Arab Bureau, knew in detail how far the agreement stultified the promises that had been made to the Arabs.

Sir Mark Sykes (from London), M. Picot, Colonel Beachman (from Basra) and George Lloyd (from Cairo) joined Admiral Wemyss' flagship and came via Wejh, where they took Feisal and Newcombe aboard, to Jeddah on May 19, 1917. Their concentration was wasted. Sykes made long speeches to the Sherif of Mecca through a Greek interpreter, in an attempt to explain to Hussein what Britain and France intended by the Sykes-Picot agreement.

Despite the care taken in meeting Hussein, once there Sykes for some reason appeared to be too pressed for time to hear the Sherif's views, or to make the situation clear to him.

Hussein summed up by saying that he appreciated all Sykes had said, but did not understand it. He had the British Government's (McMahon's) letters in his pocket, and they were good enough for him.[1]

Lawrence was now ready for the Akaba adventure, and he got his party together—five hundred carefully selected men, all hard riders and skilled desert fighters. They moved out to Bair in the third week in June, to meet their first obstacle, one which hinted of shrewd Turkish guessing. The wells there had been blown up and the water poisoned by dead camels, and the Arabs stayed there a fortnight while the damage was temporarily repaired. Lawrence used the interval to prepare the road ahead, bartering for the friendship of the tribes along the route, but the Turks were again one stage

---

[1] The diplomatic history of 1915 and 1916 was not disclosed to those British officers working with the Arabs, who had based their promises on the McMahon letters. They felt, therefore, that if and when these promises were broken, their " faces would be black." Lawrence knew nothing of the Sykes-Picot terms until July 1917, and then only heard vague details about it.

ahead, for when Lawrence and his men reached the next water, at El Jefer, the enemy had been there before them, the wells having been blocked by explosions.

In this part of the desert water was absolute life, and hours of desperate digging salvaged enough water for two-thirds of the force. While the Turks, a few miles away at Ma'an, thought they had taken effective steps to hinder the Arabs, Lawrence countered by striking swiftly at the railway. He swooped on Ghadir el Haj a few miles south of Ma'an, blew up the station and ten bridges either side, and at the moment when the Turks were preparing to send out cavalry to meet this menace, Sheikh Zaal and a hundred men attacked the line near Amman, well to the north of Ma'an. Bewildered, the Turks did not know which way to turn, and while they wasted time running up and down the line Lawrence slipped his force through to the hills overlooking Aba el Lissan. This guarded the Negb el Shtar, a steep pass with dangerously awkward hairpin bends leading to Guweira and the road to Akaba.

As he looked down on the wells he found the usual guard troop had been swelled to a Turkish battalion about nine hundred strong, who had been chasing the phantom Arab force, only to find heaps of their dead marking the route the Bedouin had taken.

Lawrence sent out men to cut the telegraph lines along the railway, filled the surrounding hill-tops with snipers, and fetched the Turks from their beds at dawn with a reveille of bullets. He kept his men moving round the hills all day, convincing the Turks they were hemmed in by superior forces. Ground and rock became so hot that it took the skin off the snipers' arms and legs, hands stuck to rifles, camels and men were lamed by the burning flints, and death and wounds took an alarming toll of his already too small force.

Desperate, Auda abu Tayi jibed at Lawrence, lost his temper, collected fifty of his horsemen, and went charging down the hill into the Turkish camp. The move was as unexpected to Lawrence as it was to the Turks, but the Arabs took it as a signal, and the hills around erupted camel-men, horsemen and infantry. At the springs the Turks, still strong with machine-guns and rifles, hesitated and, in that, signed their own death warrant. They scattered, and what had been a strong, compact, fighting unit, disintegrated into small knots of men who were quickly and viciously massacred by the yelling tribesmen.

Auda, crazed with fighting, laughed and shouted as he pointed to bullet holes in his pistol holster and sword scabbard, to his shattered field glasses, to bullet burns in his clothes, stained with blood, not a spot of which was his own ! " See what the old man can do ! " he had said when he began his mad charge, and now the way to Akaba was more or less open.

One post at Kethira, in the Wadi Itm, was Lawrence's last serious problem. It lay on top of a shelving cliff, commanding all approaches up and down the Wadi, and the hundred Turks there might be overwhelmed, but only at the cost of as many valuable lives.

Lawrence's ability to adapt odd knowledge to advantage was proved once more. The Arabs viewed the position with dismay. They were now short of rations, both food and water, and the wounded, maddened by heat and thirst, added to a general atmosphere of depression. Even as they talked of the danger of attack, Lawrence told them he would take the post that night—at the third hour.

The Arabs looked up at a cold sky, with a high riding moon, and listened politely, but doubtfully, while Lawrence— heartened by the knowledge of an eclipse due at the time— told them that the light of the moon would be blotted out at that hour, and that then they would rush the post.

When the first shadow touched the moon the astonished Arabs in the valley watched open-mouthed. The Turks above had also seen it, and while they, poor superstitious souls, fired their rifles at the shadow and rattled away with every tin can and pot they could find in an effort to frighten the evil away, Lawrence's Arabs crept up the cliff-side and took the lonely post in one mad rush.

This set the seal on Lawrence's leadership, and cautiously yet confidently they moved down the wadi to the last slopes leading to Akaba. There the Turks, all their strong defences facing the sea, guarded the strategic port whose possession was so important—and fell to an attack from the rear by an exultant Lawrence who had made a five-hundred mile detour with this one object in view.

The position of Lawrence and his men when they arrived at Akaba was miserable. They had no food, and hundreds of prisoners. The Arabs' riding camels were killed at the rate of two a day to feed them, while everybody caught what fish they could and tried to cook green dates.

The men were exhausted : so were the camels. Some of them had journeyed about one thousand miles in two months, and were in a fairly hopeless condition. The heroic five hundred mile flank attack would be absolutely wasted, and both victor and vanquished collapse and die together, if supplies of food could not be rushed to the port.

The quickest route to obtain help was over one hundred and fifty miles of hazardous country across Sinai, to the coast opposite Suez. A written message sent by Arabs, even if delivered at Suez, would be received with such disbelief that Lawrence could foresee disastrous delay while Suez and Headquarters exchanged opinions. He was faced with leaving a cantankerous, hate-filled crowd of Arabs in charge of Turks who were kin to those who had pillaged and murdered. Without a strong hand to curb passions, they had enough justification and needed but little encouragement to kill the prisoners and extend the lease on their own lives.

Equally, if help were not forthcoming, all would probably die.

A British armed tug—the *Slieve Foy* it afterwards turned out to be—had actually appeared off the port at dawn the same morning, but frantic signals went unheeded, either in ignorance or in a quite natural suspicion of a trap, and after firing a few shots into the hills the tug steamed away.

The party moved off in the early afternoon of July 6. They planned to reach El Shatt (near Suez, but on the opposite bank) in fifty hours, with a minimum of halts, and the already tired men—eight belonging to the desert and the other a conqueror only of its dangerous whims—plodded on at a pace which steadily became more wearying and more mechanical.

The only wells on the route, at Themed, were reached after a hard trek of forty miles, half of which was a one-in-three climb into and over the Wadi el Masri. They were then faced with at least another hundred miles, in which finding water would be a chancy thing of odd rain pools. The flatter mud plains were dancing in waves of heat during the day, and the party made their way through mirage after mirage until ruined Nekhl was reached.

They halted for an hour at sunset, and after a reluctant restart, rode on again through a night of moonlit brilliance until early dawn, when there was a welcome arrival at an abandoned melon patch. This was the last halt, and at three in the afternoon, forty-nine hours after leaving Akaba, Lawrence dismounted in the disorder of abandoned El Shatt.

That he did get across to Suez was due more to the forceful and somewhat impolite intervention of a friendly military telephone operator, and on July 13 the *Dufferin* was unloading a cargo of foodstuffs at Akaba, which not only saved lives but was remembered by Turk and Arab alike for years afterwards.

While Lawrence was away in the north, Joyce had been to Bir Derwish to report on Ali's force. He found the trained army and artillery in good order, and there was an obvious improvement in their handling of the guns—a relief to men who were never really sure that their own guns would not blow them to pieces. " Their general attitude," wrote Joyce, " and their discipline appeared far better than when I was with them at Rabegh, and they were much more friendly and less suspicious towards myself."

" HE WHO EATS ALONE, COUGHS ALONE "

On July 10 Cairo reported to London that " Captain Lawrence had arrived by land to-day from Akaba. Arabs in possession of Turkish posts between Tafileh, Ma'an, and Akaba. Arab force of 400 defeated Turkish, whose losses 700 killed and 600 prisoners . . . position very favourable to Sherif. Lawrence damaged railway at many points. . . . His performance necessitated extraordinary degree courage, coolness and persistence. . . ."

Meanwhile Lawrence had called on Clayton, to the latter's intense astonishment, and told him the news. At Suez he had made some notes of his more important journey and plans, and a few days later these were the subject of a conference in Cairo, which discussed the possibilities of Lawrence's scheme for risings in the hinterland, Syria and Palestine.

Lawrence recapitulated the plans he had made, and asked for the full co-operation of the Egyptian Expeditionary Force. Having heard that Allenby had now taken over command he planned rather to catch him in a first enthusiasm for what others had considered as a " mere side-line." An essential step was the immediate transference of Feisal's base from Wejh to Akaba, and it was agreed that Wilson should negotiate with Feisal to ascertain his views as to when and how this transfer should be effected, all in consultation with Lawrence. The latter was to proceed to Wejh, interview Feisal, go on to Jeddah to see the King, and then return to Cairo with all possible speed.

In order to keep the Mesopotamian command in touch with the new proposals, they were informed from London that :

" Captain Lawrence had just completed a very adventurous and successful journey over the whole of Syria . . . As a result he had submitted concrete proposals against the whole of the Turkish lines of communication from Aleppo to Ma'an and between points east of the line. Base supply to be Akaba. Provided Allenby agrees there is no objection to his proceeding with the above scheme at his discretion."

Allenby informed London that he intended to permit Lawrence to proceed with the scheme " working under my orders. This arrangement is essential in my opinion. I shall in any case keep in close touch with Wingate in regard to Lawrence's operations. Advantages offered by Arab co-operation on lines suggested by Captain Lawrence are in my opinion of such importance that no effort should be spared to reap full benefit from them. Successfully carried out, such a movement in conjunction with offensive operations in Palestine may cause the collapse of the Turkish campaign in the Hejaz and Syria and produce far-reaching results, both political as well as military."

Akaba's supply problems had been settled during these negotiations, but it was necessary to ensure that the Arabs there—who were mostly foreign to the area—should not evacuate the place and go home. They were very little use as a defensive force, and the navy were asked to give moral and material support to the suggested base by holding a warship there, or at least a monitor, until Feisal had effected his removal from Wejh.

The capture of Akaba, and Lawrence's wide-flung net of strategy, caught up other schemes. One was the formation of an Arab Legion recruited in the main from volunteers from the Arab and Syrian prisoners of war in the Indian and Mesopotamian camps, and its training supervised by British and French advisory officers.

The most distinguished of these volunteers was Ja'afer Pasha,[1] a Baghdadi officer who had been in high favour with Enver Pasha. He had fought well against the British, but was captured towards the end of the Senussi operations, and imprisoned in the Citadel in Cairo. He made one attempt to escape, using the conventional method of knotted blankets, but injured his ankle in dropping from a wall, and that put an end to his brief freedom.

Then he read in an Arabic newspaper about the Sherifian revolt. He was openly incensed at the reports of widespread executions and torture by the Turks of men who had been his friends, and he promptly volunteered for service with the Sherif.

[1] He remained faithful to the Sherifian cause, was twice Prime Minister of Iraq (1923 and 1926–28) and made many friends during his three terms of service in England as Iraq's Minister. He was assassinated in the coup d'etat of October 1936, when an anti-British faction seized the government.

Feisal had been angling for him for some time, and made him Commander-in-Chief of the regulars. Ja'afer himself had selected Nuri Said[1] (another ex-Turkish officer from Basrah, who had been with the Sherifians since the early days of the revolt) as his Chief of Staff. Lawrence already knew of their work, and worth, and had a high opinion of their ability.

Balfour had issued the instructions for the formation of the Legion " on a co-operative Anglo-French basis," but the beginning of the experiment was not a happy one. The volunteers were not correctly informed as to the intentions regarding their training and employment, and even before landing there were the beginnings of a mutiny on board one steamer, an excited mob proclaiming that they had only volunteered to serve the Sherif, demanding to be put in an Arabian port, and saying that they would refuse altogether to land in Egypt.

The oath taken by the officer prisoners was, " I swear by God and on this holy Koran and on my military honour to serve the government of the King of the Arabs, King Hussein ibn Aly, with fidelity and loyalty. I promise that after being set free I will not undertake any action contrary to the interests of Great Britain and her allies. By God, in God and for God."

For the men there was a variant, the oath ending, " I take God to witness that I shall not betray the Government of the King of the Arabs at any time or as long as I live."

The joint efforts of Wilson and Lawrence in securing a transfer of the sphere of operations quickly bore fruit, and on July 28 Hussein issued the following command :

" I beg to inform you that I have appointed my son His Highness the Emir Feisal to be my military representative in the north, and he will be supreme commander of all my troops operating from Akaba and northwards. The Emir Feisal will have a free hand but he will work with the British General commander in chief in all military matters which will facilitate co-operation with my army and that of Great Britain.

(Sgd.) HUSSEIN, SHERIF AND EMIR OF
MECCA AND KING OF THE
ARAB COUNTRIES."

[1] Nuri became Prime Minister of Iraq in 1932, and was afterwards prominent in his attempts to act as mediator between the Arabs and the British administration during the troubles in Palestine.

Clayton himself arranged for Lawrence " to serve with the Bedouin troops and to advise them and as far as possible direct their operations. Colonel Joyce to advise and control the training of Arab troops under Ja'afer Pasha."

Joyce had proved invaluable in the operations in Southern Arabia, and his regular-trained militarism was, fortunately, not so stiff in its work with the Arabs. His experience in the Egyptian Army had given him an insight into the native mind which he used judiciously, and he always commanded a respectful attention from the Bedouin chiefs.

"SINGING WITHOUT REMUNERATION IS LIKE A DEAD BODY WHICH LACKS PERFUME"

THE suggested move to Akaba found the French active. Headquarters were as dubious as ever. They pointed out to London that the French were determined to get a footing somehow.[1] The experts of the Arab Bureau, and Lawrence in particular were emphatically against it, and suggested that French machinations should be stopped at once before they developed into something larger. The French colonial administration was not a desirable growth in this part of the world.

London could not take this line : their hands were tied, and their movements hampered by the weight of the 1916 agreements. As a compromise, Bremond was informed that there was no objection to a party of French native soldiers proceeding inland from Akaba, once they made it their base, but Allenby wanted him to understand quite clearly that they and any other French contingents assigned to such duties must come under the command of Joyce, or whoever happened to be the Sherif's representative at the time. If Bremond did not like this, then any French troops landing at Akaba would have to remain there.

Once again the pattern and tactics of the Arab movement had to change. The Bedouin of the early days, when each man had his camel, his little bag of flour and his rifle, had to disappear.

The army now stood on the threshold of Syria, and they formed part of Allenby's army. Akaba was on his extreme right, and the Arab army formed his right wing. Lawrence's plans were now Allenby's plans, instead of being his own choice ventures.

Matters were also moving politically. The occupation of Akaba had raised the place to a position of considerable

---

[1] M. Picot had received secret instructions from Paris in April " to organise the occupied territories, assuring to France in all relations with the inhabitants a status equal to that which will be occupied by Great Britain . . . Wherever an occupation takes place, owing to the action of one contingent or another, you will have to see that the national flags of both governments are immediately hoisted." (Secret Treaties, *Izvestia*, November 1917.)

importance, affording as it did an alternative means of contact with the eastern Syrian tribes to the routes through the British sphere south of Gaza, and through the Arab sphere from the Hejaz. It also created a base for further operations against the railway, and for political activity among the local tribes.

Nasr had remained there, holding a series of receptions of local sheikhs. Feisal himself, long and patiently expected, had at last made his appearance with Ja'afer Pasha, on August 23. Auda had come in to pay his respects, and there were indications that Feisal's presence would have a widespread influence on the attitude of certain Sinai tribal sections who had hitherto shown coolness to the British.

Less than forty of the original six hundred of Akaba's population remained, and they were absolutely destitute. The town itself was a mass of ruins, but much had been done to prepare the place for future occupation. A jetty for landing supplies had been built with combined help from British and French engineers.

The arrival of the Arab army at Akaba was not without its trials. Ja'afer Pasha's section was full of trouble. The Meccan troops refused to obey the orders of the Syrian non-commissioned officers, but the disturbance was soon quelled by Ja'afer and others, plus the persuasive powers of machine guns.

One of Lawrence's first cares had been the preparation of a suitable landing ground as near to Akaba as possible, to be used by the Royal Flying Corps for bombing operations against the northern section of the Hejaz railway. The flight had been withdrawn from its operations in the interior, directed from Wejh, refitted there, and had been waiting to hear from Lawrence before flying north to the new base. He had managed to get a temporary ground cleared at Kuntilla, and a store of petrol dumped, and on August 26, two B.E.12's (piloted by Stent and Fenwick) and two B.E.2Es (Batting and Siddons) arrived. Two extras were carried, and the six of them spent a gruelling forty-eight hours loading and refilling the machines with petrol and bombs.

On the 28th all four machines left Kuntilla for Ma'an, but the 2Es missed their way. Batting returned with his bombs, but Siddons carried on to a station south of Ma'an and dropped ten bombs there. The B.E.12s found their way all right, and dropped 32 bombs on Ma'an, only two of which appeared to be ineffective. There was only one machine on the ground at Ma'an, and the British aircraft circled for twenty minutes in the hope that it would leave the ground. It did not look as if the Turks meant to fly it, as all they did was to keep the engine running and taxi the machine in all directions.

The next day Batting's machine refused to move, so the other three went to Fuweilah and Aba el Lissan, dropping 42 bombs with effect on the Turks camped there. One direct hit was observed on a field battery. The Turks were not silent, and kept up a continuous machine-gun and shrapnel fire. All the British machines were hit, but after they returned to Kuntilla, the B.E.12s did the same trip in the afternoon and dropped a further 32 bombs.

As Stent described it afterwards, the operations were really remarkable. The bombs had to be carried a distance of about one thousand yards to the machines, in a terrific heat. To ensure accuracy, the machines held their fire until they were only 1,500 feet above their objectives, and all the flights were hazardous because of their length, uncertainty and the intense fire which damaged all of them in the first attack.

Lawrence's efforts to make the temporary landing ground had their difficulties. During the days in which he and a few Bedouin from Akaba scratched away at the ground, clearing boulders and all other impediments from the flat, Bedouin from both sides of the old Turco-Egyptian border were coming into Akaba to salute Feisal, but they eyed the " infidel " British with suspicion. Old prejudices were still uppermost.

During August a machine gun section of the Indian Army and the British armoured car units were sent from Wejh to Egypt to be overhauled and refitted. The Egyptian artillery unit was recalled to Wejh, leaving a detachment of Egyptian machine-gunners and a company of the Egyptian camel corps, under Major Davenport, to undertake a few minor raids against the railway in the south to keep the Turks on the move.

"THOUGH THE BOW BE CROOKED THE ARROW REACHES ITS MARK"

THE value of Akaba to the Sherifians, and its menace to the Turks, resulted in the latter beginning regular bombing raids, the first, on September 12, accounting for seven Arabs killed and three wounded. Fortunately, even in the short time at his disposal, Joyce had achieved marvels with the regular Arab army, and the discipline he had instilled into their ranks prevented dangerous panic.

The men were not quite good enough for him—he had the standard of Egyptian soldiers to work to, and the Sherifian was nothing like the same material—and he felt that if the situation did develop seriously it might be necessary to detach a battalion of the Imperial Camel Corps from the Gaza front, to proceed to Kuntilla. Operating from there, they could form a very strong threat to the Turks' communications.

Clayton agreed with Joyce's estimate of Sherifian worth, but he knew, and appreciated fully, Lawrence's objections to the " intrusion " of a British expedition. There was still too much danger of collisions between British troops and the all too suspicious Arabs, and two or three days later Headquarters agreed that it would be " inexpedient " to send any British troops to Akaba, other than the small units of technical experts already attached.

For a time it was all administration and supplies, but a report from Jeddah brightened the Arab Bureau atmosphere for a few moments. Prisoners had sworn that supplies were being brought into Medina from Syria in " a huge aeroplane as big as a train, also carrying guns." Estimates in size varied, and only one prisoner could be found who could swear to having seen it, and he described it as a " huge cigar."

The Bureau knew of the activities during the summer of a Zeppelin over northern and eastern Africa, but the suggested appearance of an airship in Arabia, fantastically improbable, warranted further enquiries. However, nothing more was heard of it.

In September, the General Staff called for a special report on the situation. They had little faith in what the Arabs would do, but contrarily wanted to know what they were doing. It was emphasised to them that " if it is intended to undertake a serious offensive with a view to the dividing and destruction of the Turkish Army in Palestine, we are then justified in raising the Arab tribes in the north. If not, we cannot urge them into a position where they will be bound to suffer reprisals, and such co-operation would then have to be confined to the Ma'an area only."

The Akaba base on September 23 advised Cairo that " having successfully wrecked a train at Kilo 587, Lawrence returned to-day. Two engines destroyed, about 80 prisoners, and 70 killed, amongst killed two German officers."

On September 7 Lawrence had taken the Lewis and Stokes instructors with a raiding party to Guweira, from which place he proposed to join up with Auda Abu Tayi to attack the line near Mudawara. " Lewis " (Yells, of the Australian Light Horse), and " Stokes " (Brooke, of the 25th Royal Welch Fusiliers), as he called the instructors, had captured his interest, and he joined his English-speaking companions for odd hours during the evenings. Now and again some impish thought set his eyes puckering as the chatter flew about, and that most expressive mouth of his twitched into smiles deeply appreciative of some remark or other.

The company travelled lightly—a bag of flour weighing about fifty pounds, a little rice, and enough water to carry each of them between wells, which were about three days apart. During the day there was little said, because of the drowsy heat. Now and again an owl was seen, sitting on a telegraph wire, while once they saw gazelle, dimly moving objects in the shimmering air.

Mudawara was the first contact, when, with Lawrence in the lead, they crawled up to a straggle of empty trenches in front of the station. Lawrence came and went like a shadow, a sort of disembodied whisper. Nerves were on edge for the shout that never came, but Lawrence moved them back. He would not attack, he said, so they slept, and then went off to spoil the line on another bend.

Watching Lawrence prepare his mine was an experience. He did the job himself. Six hours it took him, and when he had finished he went over the ground on which he had been working and smoothed and shaped it into the surrounding ripples of sand.

There were several alarms the next day before they met with any success. Lawrence had arranged with one of his Arabs to work the exploder on his signal, and he sat on a sandhill to the north. He seemed as much exposed as a camel on a sandhill, but even when the puff and clatter of a train could be heard from behind the sand-dunes and the others fidgeted and fussed with their rifles and automatics, he did not move.

Like the beginning of an old-time Poole's Panorama, an engine came into sight round the bend. There were twelve wagons and they passed slowly over the embankment. The Bedouin were all lying behind their bushes, the Lewis gunners were under one arch, and the firing party under theirs, jumping up and down as the train rumbled over their heads.

Looks were switched between Lawrence and the exploder like spectators at a tennis tournament. He looked a harmless enough Arab, and the officers in the train amused themselves by firing at him with their revolvers. As soon as the engine was over the mine, he jumped up and waved his cloak, the watching Arab sent the plunger down, and instantly there was a shattering roar, a huge cloud of smoke and dust, a clanking of iron and the crash of woodwork and the whirring noise of fragments of steel.

Till the smoke cleared there was a dead silence, and then the Lewis guns which had come out to right and left of the edges of their abutments raked the troops as they leapt out of the derailed trucks. The Bedouin opened a rapid fire, and then Lawrence moved. Running a little, and then walking, he made for his companions. Brooke was just finding his range, and as Lawrence scrambled up, his face crinkled with excitement, then Stokes sent a second shell which dropped into a pop-pop of firing on the embankment and turned it into a crash and chorus of screams and shouts.

It was a mess, and the surviving Turks scrambled out and staggered away from the line in their effort to get away from disaster. As they broke for the open, Lawrence touched Yells on the shoulder and pointed. The others followed his lead, and shot at the Turks as they ran.

Then Lawrence ran down the line to inspect the damage. Little excuse was needed to turn from the sickening splash of bodies in the ruin of the train. Lawrence had hitched his hands to his middle and was lifting his robes as he picked his way in and out of the tangle of bodies and wreckage, examining one or two officers.

It was a scene of hysteria, triumph on the part of the Bedouin, and terror on the part of the survivors. Men and women scrummed round at Lawrence's feet, but they were hustled off and rounded up into a party of ninety odd. From the bend signs were heard of the returning Turks, so ammunition and rubbish were piled hurriedly together and exploded. The party then split up, each taking a few prisoners and all hurried back to Rum.

" IN PROPORTION TO THE LENGTH OF THY GARMENT STRETCH OUT THY LEGS "

On September 21 Joyce reported that "the morale of the Hejaz irregulars had been subjected to a very severe test. About 3,000 Turks attacked them in the Wadi Musa from three sides at once, with an aeroplane helping to make things distinctly uncomfortable . . . in this engagement the Arabs had about 40 killed and wounded . . . and altogether proved that they might make good material in the hands of energetic officers."

While Lawrence was still up-country, Commander Snagge, of the Humber, stationed at Akaba, sent a rather disturbing report to Cairo :

" Owing to the non-arrival of food " (he wrote) " there is a serious state ashore with regard to horses, mules and camels. They have had no food for four days, and an attempt is being made to get them to eat rice, but they are all looking very poor.

" Feisal appears to be depressed about everything. He complains bitterly of the withdrawal of naval support, and that promises have not been kept with regard to money. He says he undertook the Akaba operations against the advice of his brothers and against his father, and that if he failed there would be nothing left for him but to commit suicide. In view of the rains coming on, he feels that he has been let down by the British and the French."

" Lawrence has been busy," I recorded in my own notes at this time. "Between the 1st and the 9th he got out to kilo 489, mined a train, and reported twenty-six dead and about seventy wounded.

" Then came a request for Lawrence from Headquarters. An aeroplane took him up from Suez on the 11th, and on the 12th he was at El Kelab (Allenby's headquarters), the next day at Ismailia, and on the 15th he was back at Akaba all ready for his next move.

" Here at the base I have been kept busy with report after report, and telegram after telegram. Hussein and his sons are not easy correspondents, and I have wondered at the patience of both Joyce and Lawrence. Actually one seems to be as good a diplomat as the other. They make a good team.

"Joyce stalks in and out of the camp and up the hill to the Sherifian headquarters. Then he comes back. " Care to do some more ? " he says, and proceeds to tie up the loose ends. He is carrying practically all the weight of communications now.

"Lawrence wanders in and out, almost vaguely. I sit tight and try to visualise the future. I try to form a better judgment of the man, but everything seems so nebulous. The more obvious comparisons are the physical. It is laughable to see him standing by the side of Joyce. They have been talking of Allenby's plans and of Dawnay and Bols. Gaza and Beersheba come into talk, Dawnay evidently being the one with a settled campaign about the latter.

"Lawrence's contempt for the regular army has gone ahead of him, and in his very lack of notice of anybody it is easy to colour one's opinion from the palette of rumour. I think he sees something in Joyce though, for it is rare that anything is done without he consults him.

"I hear, perhaps imagine, a derisory tone as Lawrence turns over this and that aspect of Headquarter's suggestions. ' Slowness ' ' faulty tactics '—these I remember. Lawrence's voice is a little higher. It is strange to hear anything like a shout from him. ' Deraa '—he stabs at the map—' that's the point,' he says to Joyce, quickly, ' and even now we could whip up about twelve thousand men and surprise it.'

"I cannot hear Joyce's reply, but I know what it is for he had a note on his pad in his marquee. ' Deraa—where are the supplies coming from ? ' That seems to be something Lawrence leaves in the background sometimes. He is so used to his six week's trek on forty-five pounds of flour.

"I gain the impression from the talk that Lawrence is for ever doubting the ability of Egyptian Headquarters to act quickly and decisively. There is that obvious annoyance with what he terms the " cumbrous ' methods of military procedure, which always exasperates him.

"He has broken a little from the reserve which I began to imagine was impenetrable. He has never been unfriendly ; rather he has been detached. He always seems that, but there is a greeting now and then, with a few harmless platitudes about the weather, etc. Perhaps the journey in September made a difference."

During the last three months about thirty raids had been made on the long stretch of line between Bowat in the south and Ghadir el Haj in the north. Some interruption of the line had, indeed, taken place about every second day.

Lack of fuel was holding up trains, some having to stay for hours in stations while more wood fuel was brought down. The upshot of it all was that the Sherifian forces and the Turks were settled down in the south to a long tug-of-war.

The hour had not yet struck for bringing in the Arabs of the Syrian desert, the trans-Jordan lands, and Syria proper, but considerable progress had been made in the preparations for their co-operation. At least the stage was set.

Wingate wired to London on October 2nd : " Our Hejaz operations are going on fairly satisfactorily, as you will have seen in the various telegrams, and Lawrence has again shewn great gallantry and initiative in wrecking Turkish trains and inflicting a number of casualties on the enemy. . . ."

Allenby noted it, and wired his " best congratulations " to Lawrence, but the latter was away up north again and before the congratulations found him another two-line report reached the Arab Bureau telling them that he had ' torpedoed ' a train at kilo 500.

Joyce went out to Shobek on October 12, but the only actual result of the raid was that thirteen gendarmes, who composed the garrison, came over to Maulud, the Arab commander, and were sworn into the Sherifian service. The Turks were reinforced from Ras el Hadid by a company of infantry with two mountain guns, and Maulud only got out of Shobek with difficulty. The thirteen gendarmerie again changed their politics and returned to the Turks !

" The raid, though in some respects regrettable, may have had a good effect," wrote Joyce. " It has demonstrated to the Sherifs that the ' tip and run ' operations to which they have been accustomed in the Hejaz will not suffice in Syria. . . . The raid also demonstrated more than ever the necessity of a trained Arab Legion to occupy and defend points captured by the Bedouin. The Arabs in Syria are used to regular troops, and Bedouin allies alone are not sufficient to overcome the fear of Turkish reprisals."

An outbreak of cholera added to the difficulties of Akaba.

There were twenty-five cases and twenty deaths between October 14 and 24, all among the Bedouin and Sherifian soldiery, with the exception of an Egyptian telephone operator. The medical authorities found preventive measures difficult, owing to the dirt and indiscipline of the Arabs, and the number of open wells generally shared by men and animals alike.

Zeid's contingent from Wejh arrived at this awkward time, numbering about fifteen hundred, together with a mixed crowd of about 400 men of the Arab legion, and strenuous efforts were made to keep them away from the infected regions, fortunately with success.

An outbreak of fire also added to the excitements of the month. Clouds of smoke curling up from a marquee near the temporary pier brought the men out with a rush. Goslett was quickly there, and called on the British details. They rushed in one end of the marquee and out the other, staggering through with box after box of stores, and stacking them well away from the flames.

When it was all done, and the smouldering remains stamped out or smothered with sand, Goslett came up with his grimy men, standing by the dump where the rescued goods had been piled, and pointed to the contents—ammunition, bombs, dynamite !

"HE WAS ONCE ANVIL BUT IS NOW HAMMER"

CAPTAIN GEORGE LLOYD paid a visit to Akaba, and he took an opportunity of accompanying Lawrence on one of his raids. The party included Peake (Egyptian Camel Corps), Wood (Engineers), the Indian Machine-gun Corps detachment, and two Vickers and two Hotchkiss. Lawrence had his Syrian servant, and Lloyd his yeoman, Thorne.

They reached the well at the foot of the Wadi Itm about nine p.m. on October 24, when Lawrence and Lloyd joined the hamla there, with the Indians and the gunners in the centre and Wood a little behind.

Basalt and granite rock, jagged and menacing, towered up on either side, with the moon casting fantastic shadows on the bobbing forms of the caravan. At midnight they halted, to find Wood and Thorne missing.

Lawrence and Lloyd rode back about a quarter of a mile to the one place where they might have missed the path, cast about a bit for them, and finally slept at the head of the junction to the pass till dawn. But when they awoke there was still no sign of the missing pair, a situation which found Lawrence resigned and Lloyd distinctly angry. However, they rode back another mile, and four hours later rejoined the others, having failed to find either of the missing men.

There was nothing to do but to ride on, and Lawrence and Lloyd were soon lost in argument about the Arab movement. They were both agreed as to the necessity of tying it down to its military purpose, and to its original aim and objective. Lawrence was in high spirits, talking in terms of success of his northern adventure. Lloyd said he would try to raise Kerak on his own if it came off, but then "what was to be done vis-a-vis the French in certain northern contingencies?"

The answer was lost in a clatter as the camels literally scrambled their way to the top of the first plateau, with the scent of wormwood filling the air. As they sat down to a meal of rice, they could see ahead the great rocky avenue leading to Rum—an avenue of sandstone cliffs rising in a perpendicular splendour of riotous colour to about the height of a thousand feet. Two miles separated the flanking walls, and the little group, dwarfed into pigmy-like insignificance, drifted on in a softness of sound which was lost before it reached the towering walls.

There was a flicker of flame in the distance, a few words with encamped Bedouin, the offer of a freshly-killed sheep, and its refusal for lack of time to eat. Then came faint shouts from the well ahead which resolved into a bad-tempered and obviously nervous Wood. He had turned aside in face of threatening Arabs, lost his way, and had been at the well but an hour.

Lawrence and Lloyd were rather surprised. All had been riding for twenty out of the last twenty-four hours, and were very tired, so that in comparison the Engineer's behaviour was no happy sight in the face of the Arabs and the Indians.

Thorne said little, he being a private, but he was in no such state as his superior. Lloyd forced Wood to drink some whisky—he refused to eat—and then went on to one side to talk over with Lawrence the advisability of sending him back. In the end they decided to wait until dawn, when his nerves might have quietened down. If he was no better, Lloyd would go on with Lawrence, although the latter quite frankly said he wanted an engineer with him, or no-one, to help with the mines.

Lloyd himself reported to Headquarters on this part of the journey : " The camels had to go a long way up the cliff to water and this made an early start impossible. Lawrence and I went off to see Sheikh Hashem, who is a sort of O.C. Rum and lives in a rock near the well. He is about as typical of a proper Sherif as Edgar Speyer is of a medieval baronet. I imagine, however, that he has only got acting rank. . . .

" I had a conspicuous success in making Lawrence eat a real European breakfast, tea, bully beef and biscuits. He is only too glad to behave like a Christian—gastronomically at all events—if he is taken the right way.

" I borrowed some writing paper from Sherif Hashem—the colour of Seville oranges with gold edges—very taking. Hashem explained it was loot from the last train, and was German. It should have been used by Ibn Rashid. (How lucky that the Germans have not the same amount of political imagination as they have economic. We should have exported grey Silurian notepaper.)

" Lawrence and I visited Wood and found him restored, and Lawrence talked to him like a father ; he was, however, keen to go on, and we hoped for the best. It decides me, however, to go on to Jefer with Lawrence in case he breaks down again, but this may mean that I shan't be back in time for Mudawara, but in Arabia it is very difficult to be late for anything. . . .

" We left at 1 p.m. and rode down the great avenue. Lawrence and I made great plans for a peace tour in Arabia after the war. We would defy Victorian sentiment and have a retinue of slaves and would have one camel to carry books only . . . and we would talk desert politics all day.

" Lawrence went on to tell me of his family and early upbringing, of his Oxford days, of Carchemish and of Hogarth. He talks very well. Wood . . . refused all company or conversation all day and rode a quarter of a mile behind us."

Even when the party reached Wadi Hafir, a valley nearly as beautiful as Rum, with the same scent of wormwood intriguing the nostrils as sleep spread its blanket over them, Wood slept apart, a dark smudge on the landscape.

The next morning, after saddling up at dawn, they reached the top of the Negb el Shtar after a climb in which they were lucky in losing only one camel. It was Lloyd's first trip up the hair-pin bends of the Negb, and he stopped many times to enjoy each new view until the summit was reached, where he halted to take as many photographs as time and materials would permit.

Continuing the journey, they made their way to the railway. " We had no guide with us," Lloyd reported, " and Lawrence who had professed to know the way was in reality completely ignorant of it. At sunset we decided we were too near the line to go further safely before it was completely dark, and we halted and ate large quantities of Maconachie. Lawrence took kindly to it. About an hour after sunset Lawrence and I rode ahead to reconnoitre and put out a couple of connecting files between ourselves and the hamla. About this time a white camel in the hamla of obvious pro-Turkish proclivities began bellowing, and we discussed putting it to death. As we could neither shoot it nor hang it, and we disliked cutting its throat as this would have simply meant interminable delay while the

Arabs ate it, we decided to go on and make the best of it.

"Some two hours later we found ourselves within a few hundred yards of Ghadir el Haj Station, which suddenly appeared behind a hillock. We beat a hasty retreat in time to stop the hamla and made a detour. At this period we lost our way, Lawrence for some reason or other being convinced that if we marched faithfully with our eyes fixed firmly on Orion we should find the railway again.

"An hour's pursuit of Orion shook Lawrence's faith, and I insisted on a compass, and at midnight we struck the railway. We got the hamla across and let it march on about a quarter of a mile while Lawrence ran some four hundred yards down the line to find a milestone and see exactly where we were. Meanwhile I occupied myself in attempting to get to the top of a telegraph pole and cut the wires, but fell from the top. On Lawrence's return we hoisted in combined effort Thorne, who cut them successfully with some very blunt nippers."

Lawrence was only too pleased to get the party over the line unperceived, for there were too many Turks near for comfort. Thorne and another scouted ahead and reported all clear to Captain Lloyd before they turned in for the night.

The next day opened with a scare. Two or three of the reconnoitring Arabs put up a rabbit and fired at it—and missed—at the same time that some Abu Tayi horsemen rounded a hillock. Fortunately, both rabbit and men were missed in the exchange of shots, and Lawrence urged his camel forward to smooth things out. The Abu Tayi led the party to El Jefer, where Auda was encamped. Both the British and the Arab chiefs were glad to meet, and then Lloyd discussed with Lawrence, whether he or Wood should go north.

Lawrence did not mince matters. He liked Lloyd and yet the addition of even one man to his party who was not an expert would only add to his own risk. "He would like me best to go home to England," reported Captain Lloyd "for he felt that there was a risk that all his work would be ruined in Whitehall and he thought I could save this."

The risky and more trying part of the journey was before them—the rush to the bridge at Tell el Shehab, a large bridge in the Yarmak valley, a vital point on the Turkish railway in their front from Jerusalem to their Damascus base, so for the rest of the evening Lawrence and Lloyd talked times and dates.

By morning Lawrence had decided that he could not get to the bridge before November 5—at which Lloyd laughed (" I said I thought it traditionally suspicious," wrote Lloyd " and decided to do it that night if in any way possible ! ")

Then the camp went into a scare. Large clouds of dust in the plains between us and Ma'an seemed to indicate the approach of Turkish patrols. The Arabs struck their tents and drove in their camels. Lawrence and Lloyd stationed the machine guns, mounting them with a very commanding sweep which would give the approaching enemy a warm time. Everything was packed, ready for action, and for half an hour they merged as well as they could into the surrounding landscape. But nothing happened, and they breathed freely again.

Lawrence and Lloyd were still talking of the future— aeroplanes, the Imperial Camel Corps, armoured cars, attacking Ma'an—and then, with the scare definitely over, Lloyd departed for Akaba. He and Thorne had obviously enjoyed the diversion, and the latter had proved himself, to the Arab's ungrudging praise, a really fine camel rider. They started on their return journey on the afternoon of October 29, while Lawrence and the rest started for Bair. Rain had fallen heavily, and the plain was far too slippery for the camels to make any real progress. The Irbid hills were full of woodcutters, and the route full of hazards. They pushed ahead, but were only able to do thirty to thirty-five miles a day, instead of the fifty Lawrence had planned.

The Indians were riding automatically, tired out, and as the Abu Tayi refused to join the raid, Lawrence was forced to rely on about thirty last-minute volunteers from the Serahin at Azrak. Now the mutter of guns which had reached their ears, rather unbelievably, two days before came rolling up more clearly on each errant puff of wind, and encouraged the stragglers. Lawrence was ahead, shouting in the ear of one of the chiefs, who was deaf, and soon Azrak was far behind.

Abd el Kader, a Druse who had been one of the party as far as Azrak, and who was over-lord of the villages near the bridge, had deserted when within fifty miles of the objective. He had galloped off in the dark with his servants, and as

Lawrence heard afterwards, disclosed the whole Yarmak scheme to the Turks. The Druse had, however, acted both Turk and Arab too well in Arabia, and the Turks had lost faith in him and his stories, luckily for Lawrence. So they arrested him and sent him to Damascus.

The line was in sight, and the camels' heads were blanketed, except where the owner knew his beast and could gentle it down to silence. All through the day of November 6 nerves were tried to the limit. They were behind in their time-table, the Indians were tired and moody, the Vickers, the ammunition, and the explosives had to be watched with one eye, and an uncertain crowd of Serahin with the other.

When night came Lawrence picked six Indians and mounted them on the six best camels. Then followed Wood and the one Vickers gun, and about forty Serahin, some carrying the hastily assembled thirty-pound parcels of blasting gelignite. There were eighty miles to do, out to the bridge and back, before sunset and dawn.

Lawrence was decidedly anxious. He wondered how far Abd el Kader had spread his news. So far as it was possible for a man to be in all places at once, Lawrence did it. He was at the head of the party, then in the centre, then at the rear, and so on, backwards and forwards, cajoling, encouraging, urging. In the end he had to take up the rear to stop stragglers.

It was growing darker. Rain-clouds had blotted out the light, and then came a soft, sliding descent into a darker, more towering mass—the bank of the line. Lawrence and Wood quickly marshalled the final party together. They were in the lead with two or three scouts and fifteen Serahin with the bags of explosive, with the Vickers as some sort of rear-guard, indeterminate and nervous.

They scrambled up the bank, in single file, and then along to the black shadow of the bridge. Wood and the Vickers were posted as cover to Lawrence, and then the latter disappeared in the gloom ahead. There was one sentry on the bridge, marching slowly up and down in front of a brazier fire. From the valley surged and whispered the rushing waters of the river.

For a second the sentry's figure was the only one visible. Then a faint, moving blob was seen close to the shadowy shape of the girders—Lawrence. Straining eyes followed the cautiously moving figure, in a silence in which the blood pounding in the listeners' ears drowned the sound of the swirling waters—a silence split by a shout from the sentry and a shot from his rifle.

The moon was through a rift in the clouds, picking out the Indians climbing down the hill-side.

Shots, shouts and volleying came from the now thoroughly alarmed guard, and the Serahin carrying the explosive dumped it down the steep bank, and fled. Up and down the line the clamour grew, while Lawrence and the rest scrambled hastily for their camels and bolted helter-skelter after the retreating Serahin.

The line was alive. Each guard-house took up the alarm and added to the general row. Awakened villages spluttered with lights, and the night echoed to the shrieks of scared women and disturbed dogs, a chorus of queer, maddening sounds that lingered in the ears until the fleeing huddle of camels had run themselves to a standstill.

Dawn, and the sound of Allenby's guns, brought home to Lawrence the galling evidence of failure.

When his party halted, Lawrence went round estimating rations. The Bedouin were so ashamed and yet so mad at their desertion that they wanted to dash straight back and fight—anywhere and against any enemy, but fight it must be ! They wanted to blow up a train, and responding to their mood Lawrence sat them down in a circle, drenched by a steady drizzle, munching a last meal which would but hold already tired bodies to a desperate endeavour and no more.

Lawrence had decided that Wood and the Indians should be guided back to Azrak, especially as the engineer was showing signs of chest trouble which further privations would only aggravate. He then took Sherif Ali, with ten men, fifty of the Sukhr and Serahin, and the Vickers. They had all eaten, and then they set out on the trip without food and water.

Minifir was the object, but the first attack failed owing to a faulty exploder. Lawrence, the plunger having gone wrong, had been kneeling patiently by the side of it until the train which had come up from the south had passed. He was in no way hidden from the Turks, yet the train went on. It was fortunate, for if he had been seen he would have had a long and extremely dangerous run to cover.

When the last truck had disappeared, he got up, detached

the exploder, brought it back, carefully examined its inside and put it right, without a word. His only outburst came when he went back to the wires—a sarcastic rebuke to tribesmen who wanted to know why "nothing had happened."

The next day his mine caught a troop train right under the engine, but when the dust had settled the surviving Turks proved too many for Lawrence's handful of Bedouin, and they were lucky to get away.

However, the campaign on the line was having some effect, as evidenced by the following comment by Liman von Sanders, the German commander in chief :

"The situation east of the Jordan was not without misgivings, since the organisation of the insurgent Arabs was steadily becoming more extensive and stronger, British officers, machine guns, field guns, aeroplanes and armoured cars were attached to them, and since the capture of Akaba the sea route was open for any kind of effective British assistance. The Hejaz railroad again and again was interrupted by the Arabian troops of Sherif Feisal, to whom British pioneers with explosives were attached, and the weak Turkish forces along the line, running for the most part through the desert, were unable to prevent interruptions."

At the beginning of November, the Arab Bureau had lost Newcombe. He had left Jeida and Wejh at the end of July, for sick leave in Egypt. When convalescent, he asked Allenby's permission to use his knowledge of the Bedouin and the country around Beersheba, which he had mapped in 1914.

This permission granted, he took a body of some fifth Imperial Camel Corps and machine-guns (with eight Ababdeh guides from the Sudan) east of Beersheba, to sit astride the Hebron-Beersheba road and hold up the Turks when returning from Beersheba. The party were on the Hebron road on the night of October 31—November 1, captured some prisoners, and repulsed a Turkish attack. But the Turks, defeated at Beersheba, did not fall back as far as was anticipated, and Newcombe's little crowd found itself isolated twenty-five miles behind the Turkish lines. The latter, alarmed at the presence of this force, detached a whole brigade from Sheria, put in a slow, encircling movement, and after inflicting some losses on Newcombe's already reduced party, forced him to surrender.[1]

[1] This reduced the Turkish forces defending the Gaza-Beersheba line, so the effort was not wasted at this critical moment.

In the south, the Arabs had succeeded in bringing down the last Turkish aeroplane remaining at Medina, and Abdullah and Ali smashed up an important sector of the line between Abu Naam and Bowat. This drove the Turks once more into serious plans for evacuating the Hejaz—excluding Medina this time—and Sherifian activity was accelerated to prevent their execution. It was, at that time, highly undesirable that the Turks should move thousands of their men to the north, as they would prove too great an embarrassment to Allenby's meagre forces.

One attempt was made on Bowat itself on November 11. Ali's artillery bombarded the place and exploded an ammunition store, setting a fort on fire. But the Arabs neither took nor held the station, though they captured the fort and wiped out its garrison—of three.

The Arab dispatch writers used a style which our most picturesque reporters might envy. " The fighting was worth seeing," wrote one. " The armed locomotives were escaping with the coaches of the train like a serpent beaten on the head."[1]

Lieutenant Kernag, the French officer who commanded the artillery in the engagement, was openly derisive of the utter lack of co-ordination in the Arab command, and of discipline among their officers. The infantry resolutely refused to advance beyond the screen of their artillery, with the result that throughout the greater part of the fighting the guns were actually engaged in front of their own infantry, and in the final retirement the artillery were the last to withdraw.

Hogarth had no illusions about the problem of Medina, or the Hejaz generally. " Our advance in Palestine," he advised London, " has put the Turks in a quandary about their Hejaz forces which, all told, have a ration strength of about 23,000. These are in danger of being cut off and lost to an army which wants without delay every trained man it can get. The peculiar politico-religious value of Medina to the Ottoman empire caused all the earlier counsels of prudence to be rejected by the Higher Command, and these

---

[1] So, too, the official epistolary style. " And now, O excellent," wrote Sherif Hussein, " would you allow me to ask whether the dispatch of two or four aeroplanes would make any appreciable difference to Great Britain's total of aeroplanes, which are like the locusts in number ? "

H

troops, originally drawn from the best in Turkey, have been left till the last minute. . . .

" Notoriously, the powers that be in Turkey are convinced that general peace is not far distant. They believe it will be concluded, at the best on *status quo ante bellum* terms : at worst, *uti posseditis*. On this conviction they are disposed to gamble. Therefore, seeing the immense importance of still holding the Medina card in their hand at the Peace Conference, they will not regard military reasons alone or primarily in regard to the Hejaz."

The Hejaz now had an operations' staff, formed with a view to control, from Cairo, of all military operations in Arabia. It had a dual relation, to Allenby on the one hand and to Wingate, as G.O.C. the Hejaz, on the other. For this reason it was decided that Cairo should exercise a general supervision of all events, being responsible to Allenby for all operations north of the line Akaba-Tebuk inclusive, and to Wingate for operations carried on south of that line.[1]

So far as Allenby's advance was concerned, preliminary conversations had been taking place with regard to " procedure " in connection with the capture of Jerusalem, which was expected in the near future. All the Christian nations were bickering as to precedence in representation, or to equality in the historic ceremony which was to mark the restoration of the Holy City to Christian hands.

Balfour (then British Foreign Secretary), with an eye to future possibilities, set the seal to many years of quiet, persistent Jewish propaganda when, on November 2, 1917, he wrote the following letter :

Dear Lord Rothschild : .

I have much pleasure in conveying to you, on behalf of His Majesty's Government, the following declaration of sympathy with the Jewish Zionist aspirations, which has been submitted to and approved of by the Cabinet :

[1] Nov.–Dec. 1917 : " The Hejaz Operations Staff was formed in Cairo, and throughout was responsible for the general supervision of operations and administration in both spheres. It must not be supposed, however, that the guerrilla warfare of the Hejaz was or could have been controlled from Cairo in the same sense that British campaigns were controlled from Whitehall. That was prohibited not only by the slowness of communications, but by the nature of the fighting and of the men who were her allies. The British officers in Arabia had a general programme before them : if they could not encourage the Arabs to carry it out they endeavoured to accomplish part of it or take some action as substitute. Frequently there was not time or opportunity to consult Cairo : then they were thrown entirely on their own initiative." (Official War Report.")

His Majesty's Government view with favour the establishment in Palestine of a national home for the Jewish people, and will use their best endeavours to facilitate the achievement of this object, it being clearly understood that nothing shall be done which in any way prejudices the civil and religious rights of existing non-Jewish communities in Palestine, or the rights and political status enjoyed by the Jews in any other country.

At the time of this declaration, the Arabs totalled approximately 90 per cent. of the population.

While the idea of a national home for the Jews had been " in the air " for many years,[1] definite negotiations with regard to its establishment in Palestine began in February 1917 between Dr. Chaim Weizmann, Sir Mark Sykes, Balfour, and Lord Rothschild, all with the approval of the United States Government.

In April, the British War Department had circulated a statement on the war aims of the near east which included the following scheme for Palestine " for Jewish resettlement in accordance with Jewish national aspirations " ;

(1) Basis of settlement—recognition of Palestine as Jewish national home.

(2) Status of Jewish population in Palestine generally : the Jewish population, present and future, throughout Palestine, is to possess full national, political and civic rights.

(3) Emigration into Palestine : the suzerain government to grant full and free rights of emigration into Palestine of Jews in all countries.

The Balfour declaration transposed it to a national home in Palestine. The Russian Bolshevik Government (in 1924) disclosed that in March 1917 Sir Edward Grey had cabled to the British ambassador in St. Petersburg " that the agreement would be much more attractive to most Jews if the scheme should foreshadow authorising the Jews, when their colonists

---

[1] " In leading Jewish circles a great war was clearly foreseen and preparations were made to turn it to the advantage of Jewry.

" As long ago as 1903 Nordau, the then Zionist leader, was explaining to the Jews the reasons which caused his predecessor, Herzl, to reject Mr. Chamberlain's offer of Uganda as a national home. ' Rungs of a ladder leading upward—the English Uganda proposal, a future world war, the peace conference, when with the help of England a free and Jewish Palestine will be created.' "—J. de Haas, " The Great Betrayal."

in Palestine become strong enough to compete with the Arab population, to take into their hands the administration of the inner affairs of that region (except Jerusalem and the Holy places)."[1]

Mr. Lloyd George and Mr. Winston Churchill had quite opposite views about the intention behind the Balfour declaration, but they gave their evidence in differing circumstances, the first before the Palestine Royal Commission of 1937,[2] and the other in a State Paper in 1922,[3] when he was busy attempting to placate Arab opinion.

It was not a happy moment for such a declaration. A polite, seemingly insignificant request from Hussein, contained all the possibilities of trouble. With his eye to the main chance, and following a turn of his ever-revolving mind, he had asked, not suggested, that a guard from his troops should be placed over the Mosque of Omar in Jerusalem.[4]

Wingate thought otherwise, and advised London that the handing over of the Mosque to the Sherif might induce people to think that Britain had fixed on him as the Caliph of Islam, an act which was entirely opposed to the declared policy of non-interference. Politically, also, it might give rise to certain aspirations which were clearly excluded from the Sykes-Picot agreement. (The Sherifians were, even yet, still

[1] " The Zionist leaders (Mr. Lloyd George informed us) gave us a definite promise that, if the Allies committed themselves to giving facilities for the establishment of a national home for the Jews in Palestine, they would do their best to rally Jewish sentiment and support throughout the world to the Allied cause. They kept their word."—Palestine Royal Commission report, July 1937.

[2] " We have been permitted to examine the records which bear upon the question and it is clear to us that the words ' the establishment in Palestine of a National Home ' were the outcome of compromise between those Ministers who contemplated the ultimate establishment of a Jewish state and those who did not. . . . Mr. Lloyd George informed us that ' the idea was, and this was the interpretation put upon it at that time, that a Jewish state was not to be set up immediately by the Peace Treaty without reference to the wishes of the majority of the inhabitants. On the other hand, it was contemplated that when the time arrived for according representative institutions in Palestine, if the Jews had meanwhile responded to the opportunity afforded to them by the idea of a national home and had become a definite majority of the inhabitants, then Palestine would thus become a Jewish commonwealth."—Palestine Royal Commission.

[3] " When it is asked what is meant by the development of the Jewish national home in Palestine, it may be answered that it is not the imposition of a Jewish nationality upon the inhabitants of Palestine as a whole, but the further development of the existing Jewish community, with the assistance of Jews in other parts of the world, in order that it may become a centre in which the Jewish people as a whole may take, on the grounds of religion and race, an interest and a pride." —Statement on " British Policy in Palestine," June 1922.

[4] This is the mosque said to have been built by Omar in the seventh century. It is supposed to hold the rock from which Mahomet ascended to Paradise.

in ignorance of the precise terms of the Anglo-French division of Arabia.)

So far as the French were concerned, the British authorities had to proceed with circumspection. The French wanted both diplomatic and military representation, in any official entry to Jerusalem. They attached great importance to this, but Britain's first reaction was to order Allenby to refuse entrance to any French diplomatic representative. This suited both Wingate and Allenby, who considered that matters in Palestine should be kept on an exclusively military basis. They had arranged that French and Italian troops should take part in the official entry, and they felt that M. Picot, who was under special instructions from the French Government to attend the ceremony, should be " dissuaded " from doing so until after the official entry had taken place.

M. Picot, hearing of this in Cairo, registered a protest to Wingate, pointing out that the British action would be strongly resented in France. Over a year ago, he said—a disturbing and surprising piece of information for Wingate—it was agreed between the British and French governments that pending a final settlement of peace terms, any conquered portions of Palestine should be jointly administered by the British and French, exclusive of Italian or other interests.

Cairo also knew nothing of this, and told London so, but the latter in turn shifted the responsibility to the shoulders of Wingate, arguing that as the French and Italian military contingents would take part in the entry, they could see no objection to M. Picot joining Allenby and entering Jerusalem with him—a complete *volte face*.

This was not the end of Cairo's troubles. Jemal Pasha had found some very good cards to play, and he could not have selected a better time, a time when the Sherifians were feeling betrayed.

The Russian upheaval which resulted in the new Bolshevik Government also saw the deliberate disclosure of the world's imperialistic secrets. They were a shock to an already distracted Europe, and a veritable bombshell to the near-East. Russian newspapers published the hitherto closely guarded terms of the Sykes-Picot agreement of May, 1916, and, armed with this, Jemal Pasha made one more determined bid for Sherifian favour. Speaking at a municipal banquet in Beirut, he took up his old role of a pro-Arab Turk, and towards the end of his speech detailed at some length his correspondence with leading Arab notables since the opening of the war, particularly with Sherif Hussein and his sons.

He admitted that his overtures had never been met, but, he said, " I now possess new cards in the revelations made by the Russian Foreign Office regarding secret treaties, and I intend to play them."

Jemal had written to Hussein, telling him quite plainly what the latter had, and had not, to expect from the Allies. He had great hopes that the Sherif would repent at the eleventh hour, and return " to the bosom of Mother Turkey," deserting the anti-Islamic Britons. This letter did not reach the British authorities, but two others, dated November 13, reached Feisal and Ja'afer Pasha.

To Feisal, Jemal pointed out that the Young Turks had entered the war " to stay the degradation of Islam, to live in majesty and independence, or to perish with honour," and continued : " You really think you can establish an Arab Government, but if, as is known now, Palestine is to be international, Syria French, Irak and Mesopotamia British, how can such an Arab Government be ? " The spectacle of the British in Palestine should be enough, he emphasised to Feisal. It was not too late for an amnesty and negotiations in the best interests of Islam, if he would come to Damascus under safe conduct.

The effect of these disclosures was nearly disastrous. Feisal passed his letter on to his father, and Ja'afer Pasha also sent his on to the old Sherif. In due time they reached Wingate and Allenby, but both had already heard from Lawrence and Joyce of the danger which was threatening not only Arab but British plans.

Lawrence's fears had come home to roost with a vengeance. One opportunity had been lost when Sykes had been in too much of a hurry in his call on Hussein earlier in the year, and now the latter had every cause to lay charges of treachery and betrayal against his British allies. The British authorities he said, had known of these treaties when they sent their Mark Sykes down to see him. Why did he talk so glibly then of the necessity of coming to some arrangement with the French when he knew that an agreement had already been made in which the Arabs had not been consulted ? Was not the agreement counter to all that he was fighting for ?

Joyce once again proved his worth. He met the hysterical talk of resignation from the Sherifian officers with careful diplomacy, in which he succeeded in so discounting the Russian disclosures that sufficient time was secured to enable Lawrence and himself to control the exchange of vituperation between Hussein and his sons. The black tone of treason was shaded down to the indefinite grey of specious diplomacy.

Hussein was told, in short, that Jemal had distorted the facts.[1] Feisal forgave his father, who in turn graciously withdrew all his charges. At any rate, that is how the cables read, and their skilful manipulation actually convinced father and sons that they had themselves arrived at so worthy and honourable an understanding.

Peace was restored, Allenby assured that the Arabs were as firm allies as ever, and the way left clear for the great entry into Jerusalem. The Holy City was ready for the new crusaders.

Britain gave imperious orders. " No communication is to be made from Egypt to any foreign government or press of our occupation of Jerusalem, in order that the news may first be made public in the House of Commons."

French pressure persisted. M. Pichon, Foreign Minister, had made an obviously inspired demand for what he termed French political rights in Palestine—views which the French Prime Minister did not entirely share, as he said, but of which he was bound to take note.

In London it was felt that the French were overstepping the mark. Their military contribution to the Palestine campaign was extremely small, and Britain did not feel inclined to interfere with the present purely military government of the occupied territory. It seemed obvious that, with a very jealous eye to the future, France wanted an allied commission in Palestine at once. The Holy places were her chief concern, and it was evident that her clerics felt that a predominating French influence would establish, once and for all time, France's lead in Christendom.

---

[1] The following is the actual text of the reply handed to Hussein :

" Bolsheviks found in Petrograd Foreign Office records of conversations and provisional understandings (not formal treaty) between Britain, France and Russia made early in war to prevent difficulties between the Powers in prosecuting the war with Turkey. Jemal either from ignorance or malice has distorted its original purpose, has omitted its stipulations regarding consent of native populations and safeguarding their interest and has ignored fact that subsequent outbreak and success of Arab revolt and withdrawal of Russia had for a long time past created a wholly different situation."

It was a claim which not only failed by reason of history's verdict, but it also failed if only because of France's meagre contribution to the near eastern campaign.

"CORRESPONDENCE IS HALF A PRESENCE"

JERUSALEM was surrendered on December 9 and on the 10th the British Parliament made its historic announcement to Britain and to the world : " General Allenby," it was stated " reports that on the 8th he attacked the enemy positions south and west of Jerusalem . . . The Holy City being thus isolated was surrendered by the Mayor on December 9 (cheers) . . . General Allenby proposed to enter the city officially on December 11, accompanied by the commanders of the French and Italian contingents and the head of the French political mission."

Bonar Law announced that the capture had been delayed in some degree in consequence of the great care which had been taken to avoid damage to the sacred places in and around the city.

The next day the Prime Minister (Lloyd George) amplified the news. " The following statement has been received by me to-day," he said, " from General Sir. H. Allenby :

'Jerusalem, 2 p.m., 11th December, 1917. I entered this city officially at noon to-day with a few of my staff, the commanders of the French and Italian detachments and the military attachés of France, Italy and the United States. The procession was on foot. At the Jaffa Gate I was received by guards representing England, Scotland, Ireland, Wales, Australia, New Zealand, France, India and Italy."[1]

While the Staff moves were going on, Lawrence's party had reached Azrak from their abortive attack on the Tell el Shehab bridge.

" We actually got back to Azrak on November 12," I noted in my diary. " It was raining and it was cold. Very bad for most of us, as we had little or no protection from such weather. The camels made rotten going of it, slipping

[1] " In connection with General Allenby's entry into Jerusalem, Major T. E. Lawrence took part in the ceremonial entry, being attached to the staff." (Official War History.)

121

and sliding all over the place. On the 14th, Wood, with one or two men went back to the base. We hung about for the next two days, trying to keep warm. Lawrence has said little, to us at any rate. He has been engaged in interminable talks with Bedouin chiefs, who come in at odd times.

"On the 16th he disappeared. The last few days have been a terrific strain on him. He seemed displeased. Moodily he viewed the storms of sleet and snow that beat about us among the ruins of the keep, and his increasing nervous tension hinted at further action. He placed the Indians and myself in the care of Ali and went off himself with one Arab. He left word for me to make my way to Akaba as best I could. He would see me there. I soon had an escort, and off we went, but it wasn't easy. Eight days by devious routes it took us to Akaba, where I reported to Joyce. Lawrence had already been in, left a note and gone off by air to Kelab to see Allenby.

"Marshall dropped in, and while I typed they talked. Apparently Lawrence had received 'orders' to go to Headquarters, but they were worried about his health. He'd had some sort of shock, for something had happened to change him. He ate more sparingly than ever, and rarely in company. Where he might mark a day with two or three words of greeting, the minimum was reduced to absolute silence. Of his gentleness, none was left. His humour turned to bitterness, and in his fighting from this time onward he spared neither himself nor his fellows nor his enemy."

(The puzzle was solved for us years later when we read in the " Seven Pillars of Wisdom " of his arrest and torture in Deraa. It was then easy to understand the Lawrence of the last year of his campaigning.

But we were without that tale of horror, and merely knew that we were dealing with a changed man.)

"A French Algerian detachment with machine-gunners," my notes went on, " mountain guns, and six auto rifles—a total of 56 men and thirty mules—has arrived on the *St. Brieux*, having been placed at Feisal's disposal by the French authorities. It complicates matters.

"I have had a few reports to do. One concerned a talk Lawrence had had with Feisal, significant for the latter's reference to Ibn Saud.[1] He said it was inevitable that the Wahabi leader would eventually impose his rule over the whole of Arabia.[2] This would mean a new doctrine, which might or might not favour Britain."

" It is bad weather for operations," ran another of my personal notes, " but small parties of Arabs are keeping up their raids on the line. On the 12th a train was wrecked between Al Akhbar and El Muezzam, after the party had waited five days for one to come along. The Arabs captured £24,000 in gold, and some high Turkish officers were killed, including Suleiman Pasha ibn Rifada.

" Wilson has been evacuated to Egypt from the south. He is down with dysentery. A bad loss to Wingate. Bassett has taken over.

" Things are at a standstill, and we are actually wondering whether we can make ourselves think of Christmas. Some of our spare time is spent firing explosive bullets into the sea, for with good luck you can explode one underneath a fair-sized fish and then plunge in and grab the corpse.

" Actually Christmas Day. Commander Snagge as senior officer has given a party to all the British here (about 120 of us all told) and Lawrence lands up in the middle of it. For once he smiles, but he soon moves away out of the circle, and with his departure goes Christmas. Sight of him was quite enough to put the celebrations in their place.

" I did not see Lawrence until next day, and then it was to be ordered up to Guweira, where the armoured cars and Talbots (the latter carry 10-pdr. guns) have made a more or less permanent forward base. L. was away first on a tender.

" December 28. Lawrence once more away to Akaba but

[1] Ibn Saud founded a brotherhood of preachers, the Akhwan, as an agricultural colony some twenty years ago. His idea was to attach a body of fighting men to his service, to put a stop to inter-tribal raids, and to bring a measure of prosperity to his country.
He offered the only inducement which has ever made an appeal to the Arabs—to point them the way to Paradise. His missionaries stressed that he who would live a religious life must live among the Akhwan. Of course, they had to give up raiding, but there was always the possibility of a holy war against unbelievers. This would bring them spoil, and, if they died on the field, they would be admitted at once to Paradise. It was no new religion. It was the revival of the fanaticism which had led the followers of Mahomet to victory centuries before.
Soon thousands of would-be farmers were digging in the sand for water. The land was irrigated. It prospered and brought forth fruit. The settlers soon learned to read and write. They had their promised wars—against Ibn Rashid and King Hussein—and being victorious in both accepted with acclamation Ibn Saud's prophecy that their lives were pleasing in the sight of Allah.

[2] Amazingly prophetic, seeing that Feisal made this remark in 1917.

123

he is coming back the next day for an attack on Tell el Shahm (north of Mudawara)."

A continuation of my own notes opened the year 1918. " What a puzzle Lawrence remains ? I've been with him now for a year, played soldiers with him, and taken his reports. He will go to any lengths and any journey to work out each phase of his operations. Since he altered his mind down in Wejh, all he planned he has stuck to, and more or less carried out.

" There is still very little suggestion from Headquarters that he will get concrete help. While recognising that any success on the part of the Arabs would be a continual embarrassment to the Turks, Headquarters inclined to the idea of allowing Lawrence to act so long as he did not ask for more men or guns.

" His plans admit no ' ifs.' He writes that he proposes to do so and so, and go there, and accomplish this or that, then return at such and such a time. Whatever he asks for has no plea in it. Rather there is the inference that he demands it : but—and this is always evident—he leaves the definite impression that if he doesn't get what he asks for, he will have a shot at his plan with what material he has to hand. It is always ' take it or leave it.'

" Arab co-operation has been a discredited weapon for some time. The home authorities, Egypt and India are in conflict about it, and what to most is a fantastic, even an impossible experiment, is left to the inspiration of one man and the help of a few advisers.

" The Sherifian soldiers seem to have little backbone though I doubt if I should have, with a heritage of five hundred years of terrorism and oppression.

" Occasionally there would be a flurry in the camp. Hussein and his sons would quarrel again, or the sons would quarrel among themselves. Feisal would storm at Ali ; in turn they would storm at Abdullah. Then the telephone line and cables would be full of long, effusive, politely-worded, but poisonous messages. A few hours of threats, resignatious, curses, oaths to Allah—and peace would reign again.

" I had an uncomfortable pillow for two or three days. A sack of gold—about £10,000 it was—doesn't shake up easily like a flock of feathers . . ."

Lawrence and Joyce left Guweira with the armoured cars

and a ten-pounder section on December 30, arriving about twelve miles west of Mudawara station by sundown.

The arrival of the cars on the line was undoubtedly a surprise for the Turks. Although they had been in the Hejaz nine months, this was the first occasion on which they had got within effective range.

Hogarth saw Hussein for the first time in January. He was in Jeddah from the 8th to the 14th, during which time he had ten interviews with the old King. H. St. John Philby[1] had come overland from Riyadh to Jeddah by a new route, accompanied by twenty-six finely mounted Bedouin of Ibn Saud's following, drawn from various tribes. He had accomplished a remarkable journey in very fast time—it was the first crossing of the peninsula since Captain Sadleir's journey from the Gulf to Medina and Yenbo in 1818—in order to have a conference with Hogarth, and between them they tried to smooth over the difficulties between Hussein and Ibn Saud (whose confidence St. John Philby had gained) and to secure a working arrangement between them in the interests of Arab unity.

Hogarth also had the more particular and difficult mission of informing the King about the Allies' intentions regarding Palestine. Britain had written to Hussein at the beginning of January to the effect that, as far as Palestine was concerned, they were determined that no people should be subjected to another, but that there must be a special regime, approved by the world, to deal with the Holy places in that country belonging severally to Islam, Jewry and Christendom. The Mosque of Omar was not to be subjected directly or indirectly to any non-Moslem authority. In conclusion, the King was informed that " insofar as was compatible with the freedom of the existing population, both economic and political, no obstacle should be put in the way of a return of the Jews to Palestine."

The King was as awkward as he could be over Ibn Saud. St. John Philby's unheralded appearance " out of the blue " had (not unnaturally) irritated his susceptibilities. What, he asked, would the people of the Holy Land think of an Englishman having come at his own pleasure to Taif and down to Jeddah ? Would not all say that the Hejaz was sold to the British ?

---

[1] At that time a civilian officer in the Political Department of India, attached to the Mesopotamian force.

He was in no conciliatory mood. He feared Ibn Saud as leader of a revivalist movement which was anti-Meccan and hated him as a formidable obstacle to his kingship of the Arabs. However, in the end he agreed to keep the peace on his side, and to maintain " correct relations."

On the major point of Hogarth's mission, he was more reasonable. He declared himself quite in sympathy with both international control in Palestine, and the encouragement of the Jews to settle there. He also volunteered the remark that the course of the war must inevitably modify in certain points his own agreement with the Allies. He asked only to be informed " frankly and fully " of such proposed modifications and the reason for them if they should arise. His belief in Britain's power and good faith was unbounded. She was " the great sea in which I the fish swim, and the larger the sea the fatter the fish ! "

He was, however, sceptical of Hogarth's interpretation of British policy. " You speak to me continually," he said, " of the British Government and British policy. But I see five governments where you see one, and the same number of policies ; your Foreign Office, your army, your navy, your Egyptian protectorate, your Indian Government. Each of these seems to me to have an Arab policy of its own. What are the Arabs to do now, and what are they to expect of you after the war ? "

The Grand Sherif brought up the subject of his title at every opportunity. Again and again he said, if Britain thought him unfit to be King he would bow to her judgment, but then he must quit the country and end his days " in the shadow of her peace in Egypt."

"A WELL IS NOT TO BE FILLED WITH DEW"

THE next important battle was for Jurf el Darawish station on January 12. The Beni Sakhr's five hundred men under Sherif Nasr had been reinforced by Nuri with one company of mounted infantry, four machine-guns and a small French contingent with Hotchkiss automatic rifles.

At dawn Nasr's one mountain gun and two machine guns opened fire on the Turks and took them completely by surprise, knocking out the Turkish guns with the first burst.

The Bedouin were so encouraged that they got on their camels and repeated the charge that won them the road to Akaba. Bullets have little immediate effect on a camel going at twenty miles an hour, and before the Turks could do anything the Arabs were over the trenches and in the station buildings.

The Turkish casualties were twenty killed and 150 prisoners. The Bedouin, as usual, went mad over the supplies in the station and left all the explosives behind in order to assist in the looting. It took five hours before the dynamite could be brought up, and the engines, trucks and station buildings were then blown up. A six-arch bridge north of the station should have been completely destroyed, but this was imperfectly carried out, and the bridge was repaired by the Turks twenty-four hours after the Arab troops had retired.

The total Arab casualties were two wounded.

An attack was made on Mudawara station ten days later, but the Beni Atiyeh did not behave at all well. They were not really out for a fight, and had refused even to leave Abu Suwana until Sherif Feisal had sent to Guweira and received money to pay them.

The Bedouin made attempts to storm the fortified hills overlooking the station, and without infantry co-operation all the assistance the British could offer with their guns and aeroplanes was in itself insufficient to completely silence enemy resistance.

The French contingent operating from the north-west had been delayed, but they came in at the end of the engagement, firing over a hundred rounds from their mountain guns. They would have ably supported an advance even at that late hour had the Bedouin attempted it.

Valuable support from the Royal Flying Corps was more or less thrown away, because on the morning of the 23rd all the Arabs returned to Abu Suwana, having run out of ammunition and water. An attack would probably have succeeded if the position had been rushed at dawn. Joyce had advised this, but the Arabs favoured the noisy, preliminary bombardment.

It was difficult to combine modern weapons with Bedouin tactics. They sat on the hills and watched the bombardment with great interest, and each shell fired or each bomb dropped was assisted on its way by fervent imprecations that it would fall on the heads of all the Turks and destroy them.

The next news of Lawrence came from Tafileh, dated January 26th, 1918. It was his report on the battle he had just fought, and won. Caught there in an unfavourable position, with inferior numbers and equipment, he used his more mobile forces in a series of decoy moves which in the end led the Turks to occupy the very positions which Lawrence had himself found so exposed and dangerous. Once the Turks were trapped, one final rush from all quarters broke the last shred of their resistance, and the surrounding villagers joined in the massacre.

Lawrence lost about eighty men, killed and wounded, a serious depletion of his trained fighters, but he had accounted for four times as many of the enemy, in addition to taking over two hundred prisoners.

In the south Ali's army had done practically nothing since October in the previous year, except throw forward its left wing towards the railway near Bowat and effect some minor demolitions. Some small enemy posts were also captured. The rest maintained a watching brief, with occasional interludes of absolutely futile artillery bombardments. Abdullah was a little more effective. He had moved his headquarters to within striking distance of the railway, and at some time or other during the past five months had managed a series of demolitions over something like one hundred miles of railway. If they did not really tax the enemy's supply of spare rails, they ran them out of bolts and nuts !

The winter rains had also amplified the work of the Arabs, and the interruptions of the northern section under Lawrence had reduced traffic in the south to such an extent that Medina had the utmost difficulty in securing supplies, and was more or less isolated.

Egypt's headquarters found time in January to pass on a gem of inter-departmental humour. The Hejaz campaign had been in progress for fifteen months, with the railway as its chief objective. The Roads and Railways Department at the War Office in London had at last noted the campaign, and, in secrecy and haste, wrote " demi-officially " to Cairo, to " draw attention to the fact that some of the bridges, etc., of the Hejaz Railway might now be within distance for bombing by aeroplane."

The information was passed on to the General Staff with a very brief note : " I think this might interest you. I suppose the D. of R. & R. thinks we are not perhaps aware of the fact that there *is* a Hejaz railway."

I

"THE MAN WHO IS LEAN, NOT FROM HUNGER, IS HARDER THAN BRASS"

LAWRENCE's next diversion was to arrange a raid on the Dead Sea. The Arab horse, under Sherif Abdulla el Faiz, with the help of the Arabs of Beersheba, crept through on the night of January 28 and charged up the east bank of the Dead Sea from its southern end. They came flying through the defiles between the hills and the lake, and before the Turkish patrols ahead could give any warning they passed over the route of the promontory called the Lissan and came gently through the bushes until they were within easy shot of El Mezraa harbour, where half the Turkish Dead Sea "Fleet" was moored.

The crews were on shore, breakfasting, and the Arabs in their swift charge destroyed them, sank one dhow and several launches, and got officer-prisoners and sailors away before the garrison on the bluffs above had realised that irregularities were being committed.

The fleet was, of course, only motor launches and dhows, but there were few sea forces which have been captured by cavalry, and the disgust of the very smart naval officers at their capture was too comical for words.

I have one note to January. "It has been a queer, cold month, with abrupt changes in temperature. We were holed up at Abu Lissan for four days by snow, and some deaths occurred among the Arabs and Sherifians through exposure. They hadn't enough blankets and tents to ward off the weather, although we'd warned headquarters enough times about these cold spells. To them Arabia *must* be a hot country. The text books say so."

Meanwhile, Egyptian headquarters had their worries. Cairo had had a report from Geneva, to the effect that the ex-Khedive of Egypt was using a fund of two million francs for carrying on anti-British propaganda in Egypt and Arabia, and many prominent Egyptians in Europe had voluntarily gone to Constantinople to assist in the work.

More serious still were the continued representations from the French regarding military co-operation in Palestine and Syria. This at last led to London sending France a gently, delicately worded refusal. It was pointed out that there was no possibility of using additional French troops in Palestine for some months to come. Allenby was getting a division transferred from Mesopotamia, and Indian troops were also on their way to assist in the reconstruction of his forces. It would only add to Allenby's difficulties it was pointed out, if troops were sent which could not be used at the front, and he did not want them. Later on he would be glad of reinforcements, provided they were of good fighting value.

Abdullah's camp had now heard of Jemal Pasha's disclosures of the secret treaties to the Sherif, and they created a considerable stir, because Abdullah was already in troubled circumstances. His army's spirit had been impaired by various causes—the winter cold, failure of supplies (which was not always attributable to breakdown of transport), enemy propaganda, and, most of all, by arrears of pay. It was to the Aneizah and to the French Algerian detachment that Abdullah chiefly owed his major successes, such as they were, of the past five months.

Intelligence reports now confirmed the reduction in the enemy's lines of communication at the southern end. In Medina the strength of the garrison had fallen below two thousand effectives, scurvy was rife, and their morale low. Mounted troops and aeroplanes were no longer available, and food was so short that all the civilians had been sent out of the city.

At the beginning of February Lawrence flew over to Headquarters at El Kelab to discuss a diversion against Amman, with the aid of British units. He told Dawnay that co-operation would be difficult, and the latter emphasised to his superiors that the action of the British troops must be " quite distinct and should be removed as far as possible from the area of operations by the Arabs."

Dawnay himself flew back with Lawrence to Abu el Lissan for a consultation with Joyce, and there the plan advanced, aided by the presence of £55,000 in gold.

" Three days later " (this is from my own notes) " we were at Abu el Lissan, where Kirkbride turned up, another fine specimen of manhood, over six feet high, good at Arabic.

Lawrence seemed to take a liking to him at once. (It's just struck me that practically all the men Lawrence has around him are on the six-foot mark. Of set design?)

" Lawrence went off on one of his jaunts alone, and I waited on with the others, to be joined later by Joyce and Marshall. They went over to Zeid's tents, and came back with serious looks. Later in the day Lawrence returned. It is the first time I've really sensed another Lawrence. It is the first time I've seen him hurry on foot. I can see from my tent into Joyce's, and there Lawrence is, actually storming up and down. He is making some sort of statement, and then stands in front of the burly Colonel, emphasising a point. Joyce and Marshall join in, and the Colonel speaks earnestly for a few moments. Lawrence leaves the tent and makes for Zeid's camp. I'm wondering.

" Joyce came over and instructed me to get a message away to Headquarters at once, asking for a machine to take Lawrence to Beersheba on the 21st, as he wished to get to Allenby.

" On the 22nd we heard that Allenby, Hogarth and Clayton had been in conference with Lawrence. From what I see of the cables he threatened to throw his hand in, as the Sherifians had squandered all the gold, and were not even inclined to say how. This gold was necessary to Lawrence for his latest " diversion." For two or three days messages crossed, and Lawrence is still away. From the dispatches, it is evident that he is being shunted back and forth between Beersheba, Jerusalem and Rafa.[1] On the 28th we hear that he has left Rafa for Cairo, and for the first time for a few days Joyce laughs.

" The camp has been without movement, not only because the weather holds us up, but also because the Sherifians were a little perturbed as to which way Lawrence was going to turn.

" On the 28th I went off to Akaba with a convoy. No car was available, and the journey down the Wadi in the face of a cold blast was the most unpleasant I had known for some time. Once in Akaba it was a little better, as the base had a few more comforts, but even then the torrential rains and more snow

[1] " We had occasional meteoric visits from Lawrence, when he came in Arab dress to confer with the Commander-in-Chief regarding Feisal's co-operation. An entry in my diary of February 22, 1918, tells of his arrival in camp after riding 100 miles on camel back from a station on the Hejaz railway to Beersheba in less than twenty-four hours, coming in at once by motor-car to G.H.Q., and returning almost as rapidly as he had come." (Sir Robert Windham Graves, in " Storm Centres of the Near East.")

drove us in once again and kept us in. For four days we read and gambled alternately, with rupees for counters, until on March 4th an aeroplane came in on the wind, with Lawrence.

" The whole camp was glad about it.

" But the next day we were just as puzzled as ever. The *Borulos* was in harbour, and Lawrence boarded her on the 6th for another trip to Cairo. This business of constant rushing about by 'plane alternating with slow sea transport seems without reason. The wires on the 8th mentioned a meeting between Dawnay and Lawrence in Cairo, and that Lawrence would be back in Akaba on the 15th. He did turn up, but left for Guweira on the 16th, was back in Akaba in less than twenty-four hours, away up the Wadi Itm again, and back with us for the third time within four days.

" Then he anchored for a while, looking a little more rested, and he was more inclined to talk with the others. But he mostly sought consolation in *Morte d'Arthur*.

" We have been joined by Major Young, an Indian Army officer skilled in Arabic. I have never seen so many contrasts. Lawrence, as enigmatic as ever, once a grave, soft-moving wraith, with a warm, endearing smile : now a bitter, hard-smiling man, given to queer suggestions of temper. Joyce, striding about with a great laugh for the occasion, and a brow-beating manner for trouble-makers. Marshall, the medico, always ready for a joke, very cool. Goslett, spruce, ever accompanied by a dog, irascible at times, generally politely sarcastic, but terribly efficient. Now came Young, dark, bearded, heavy in build, slight rolling walk, as slow in that as in his speech, but oh, so exact !

" Yet they make a machine, and it is gathering momentum. Before a screw was missing here, a part there, and most times there was no fuel, or what there was was rotten. Now the machine is assembled and despite a certain stiffness in the joints there is definite power."

Dawnay was taking an active interest in Sherifian affairs. His Oxford drawl began to permeate the councils of war, but his reasoning was typical of the gulf between the handling of Bedouin irregulars by the regular type of officer, and their treatment under the " rules " followed by Lawrence. Dawnay argued that the Arabs invariably looked to the British troops to achieve a speedy annihilation of the enemy " as if by magic," whilst declining to offer any assistance to that end.

However, with Allenby promising help, plans were put in hand for an offensive against Amman in about two months' time, the necessary camel transport being loaned from the British forces.

Dawnay's trained staff mind now set to work to make this particular operation a model of success. He prepared marching tables for the camel units, from information supplied by Lawrence, who was arranging for the guides. The latter also saw to it that the Arab tribes, through whose territory they would have to pass, were warned of their identity to secure safe conduct. Dawnay, thoroughly happy in his active participation in these forays, accompanied the mobile force which was using Guweira as its base. There were armoured cars and ten-pounders, the latter on Talbots, supported by Egyptians and regular and irregular Sherifians. Aiding and abetting were Peake (Egyptian Camel Corps), Hornby (demolitions), and Brodie (in charge of the ten-pounders).

The attack on Tell el Shahm station, successful in one respect, nearly wrecked the operations in the beginning. The Egyptians, as regular in their fighting habits as the British units, resented the haphazard fighting methods of the Bedouin. The latter, as usual, dropped out of the fighting at every opportunity of loot, and so strained did the situation become that there was danger of a pitched battle between the two parties. The British could do little in the matter, and just at the moment when one more jibe seemed likely to stampede the opposing factions, Lawrence came in from the direction of Ma'an. He sized the position up in a moment, had a short parley with the Bedouin, talked to the Egyptians and the affair was over.

From Tell el Shahm the column had a look at Mudawara, but found it garrisoned by five hundred well-armed troops, with two long-range Austrian guns, two mountain guns, and well fortified machine-gun emplacements to support them. The only advantage was that while the raiders could not attack, the Turks dare not leave, and they had to watch, raging and firing ineffectual volleys, while the armoured cars demolished a ten-arch culvert five miles down the line.

The next day they moved on to Wadi Rethm, and drove the enemy from Ramleh station to a fortified escarpment twelve hundred feet above the railway. The attack was noted for a remarkably cool piece of work. Under cover of a concentrated artillery and machine-gun barrage, an armoured car, in which Dawnay and Hornby were the principals, dashed forward, loaded with explosives, and a few seconds later the buildings went up in a smother of smoke and sound.

The station was destroyed and half a mile of line on either side. Once this was done, the cars and the tenders moved forward to attack the enemy's new position. Both units put in some very accurate shooting on the heights held by the Turks, but the slope stopped any direct attack, and the long-range battle ended automatically at dusk.

For five days the force adopted such hit and run methods over about thirty miles of the line, and returned to its base with a bag of three stations, five miles of line destroyed, twenty bridges and culverts blown up, and many miles of telegraph poles and wire rendered completely useless. The casualties were nil.

News came in later to Guweira that Lowe of the armoured cars had been hit in the stomach by a bullet during a quarrel over water rights at the Wadi Ithm well. There was an emergency operation at Akaba on the 14th, but by noon the next day he was dead. This was the first and only casualty to date among the British soldiers attached to the Hejaz forces.

"THE CAMEL THAT TRAVELS OFTEN TO MECCA WILL RETURN LAME AT LAST"

IT was during this month that Major Young came up ready to take his part in the operations between Jurf and Amman, with two guns. During a rest period he dictated his experiences to me,[1] and the concluding paragraphs are worth repetition.

" 'It is a most unfortunate thing,' said Emir Feisal to Major Young, ' but there has been a mistake about the day. To-day is really the first of the Arabic month, as last month had only twenty-nine days in it. But the Bedouin, on whose co-operation we are relying for the successful capture of Abu Jerdun, are convinced that there were thirty days in last month, and that to-day is, therefore, the 30th. I much regret that we shall not be able to attack Abu Jerdun until to-morrow, but please God you will certainly start off the next day.'

" It was no good protesting. I sat at Abu Lissal that day and drove off in the motor in the morning (the 12th). The attack on Abu Jerdun was brilliantly successful, and everybody was so pleased with himself that no one worried much about me or my guns. When Nuri and Zeid returned from the battle, which they did about noon, I went to talk to them for a while, and found to my disgust that neither of them had had my orders at all. In any case, they refused to send more than two guns, and even these could not start because the camels and saddles which Feisal had promised for the escort had not arrived.

" I was determined not to be defeated, so I got on my camel again and rode back to Abu Lissal the same afternoon, where I found Feisal in great delight at the successful operations of the day, and full of more voluble promises than ever about the camels and the saddles. He even went so far as to telephone to Akaba for twenty camels to be started off immediately for them to complete the required number.

" I felt bound to interpose at this point, and suggested to

[1] A full version appears in " The Independent Arab."

136

him that General Allenby was presumably waiting for his co-operation and that it would be difficult for me to explain to General Allenby that fourteen days delay had been caused owing to Sherif Feisal having been unable to produce twenty camels. He seemed surprised when I told him that General Allenby, in common with most people who had never actually seen the tribesmen, probably imagined that every Bedouin owned at least one hundred camels. I suggested that such a reason as the foregoing would sound very much the same as General Allenby explaining delay in his operations by saying that he was short of rifle ammunition.

" Feisal seemed very much struck with this argument, and immediately purchased twenty camels from my old friend Auda, who had got as far as Abu Lissal during these twenty days, in preparation I presumed for his final attack on Jurf. Things now seemed to be moving a little. The next difficulty was to provide saddles for the infantry escort of the regular army to ride upon. It struck me that I might be able to borrow one hundred from the Egyptian hamla which happened on that day to be at Abu Lissal, but as Colonel Joyce was due about the next day and we were bound to be delayed one day in any case owing to the mistake in the date, I thought I would wait and arrange with him first.

" To make quite sure of catching him, I went down to the foot of the Negb, where I met him, Wilson and Lawrence on their way up from Akaba. We soon arranged for the temporary loan of one hundred saddles from the hamla, and Feisal promised to send the twenty camels which he had just bought to load them up and take them to W'Heida the next morning.

" When we got up to Abu Lissal, we found Peake and Hornby, who had just come in from destroying the line at Batn el Ghadir. I suggested that their lot should come with me, and it was agreed. Next morning I saw the twenty camels start loaded with the one hundred saddles, which were to be distributed among the camels waiting for them at W'Heida. After them, Hornby and Peake started out, and after them also I started on a Ford car, delighted to think that this time, at least, I had left nothing behind. After passing Peake and Hornby, who gave us a cheer, we caught up with the twenty camels, which immediately took to flight and scattered to all parts of the compass, their loads falling off in all directions.

" The disorder was completed by Ja'afer Pasha also passing

through half an hour later in another car. When I got to W'Heida I had to arrange with Ja'afer Pasha to send out horsemen to collect the camels and saddles during the night. By about eleven o'clock they had succeeded in collecting fourteen camels and eighty saddles, which Ja'afer said would be enough. It was too late then to think of starting off with the company of infantry, and I was assured that they would march off first thing in the morning. I settled myself down in Ja'afer's tent, where I slept the night.

" I got up early in the morning, to see no sign of movement anywhere. When Ja'afer awoke about seven, I told him that the company had not started. After asking God to curse their fathers two or three times, he sent a messenger to hurry them. The messenger came back at about nine to say that the detachment had not yet received its pay. Ja'afer promised that they would be paid when they arrived at Fageia.

" At about ten another messenger came up to say that the eighty saddles were not enough, and Ja'afer made up the number from his own private saddles.

" A third messenger came up and reported that as the victorious Sherifian Army was on its way to join forces with General Allenby, it would be as well if each man were given a new pair of trousers ! Another hour was spent in issuing a new suit of clothes all round, and at twelve o'clock they actually started.

" Peake and Hornby had gone ahead to Udreh, where Nasr with the Bedouin and guns were waiting, so that after having a meal with Ja'afer I started off again at half-past one, feeling that once more my whole army was in front of me, and that with any luck we should start from Udreh the following day.

" I arrived at Fageia in the evening, to find the company had not yet arrived, and would not be able to get to Udreh the same night. I accordingly arranged with Nuri that they should be sent on the next morning to Doshe, where Nasr, with Peake and the guns and I should join them. I then climbed on to my camel again and rode on in the dark to Udreh to tell Nasr that all was now ready. He told me that he himself had ridden to Fageia that morning, and had confirmed the plan which I had made with Nuri for the simultaneous diversion north of Aneiza, when Nuri had promised him an escort of twenty-five cavalry, in addition to whatever men Nasr might have with him. When the guns were taken away he had written to Nuri saying that he was now dependent entirely on the twenty-five cavalry, and Nuri had replied ordering Nasr to provide his escort from his non-existent force of Bedouin.

" I am not sure whether I would have made any more effort, but my last ride from Fageia to Udreh on a hard saddle without any pad resulted in internal damage, which put camel riding out of the question for some time.

" I rode over to watch the attack on Abu Jerdun next day. After all the journeys, the rebuffs, the arguments, the delays, the quarrels between the Sherifs, the attack failed. Nuri, despite his book of rules, which he should by now have known by heart, omitted to cut the line during the night, and an armoured train arrived from Aneiza and drove the Arabs off ! "

"ALL MY GOODS ARE OF SILVER AND GOLD, SAYS THE BOASTER, EVEN MY COPPER KETTLES"

ALLENBY'S operations—to which Young had made passing reference—embraced the cutting of the Hejaz railway at Amman by demolishing the tunnel, breaking up the line and destroying the viaduct. Simultaneously, he wished to draw the Turkish troops away from Ma'an, so that Lawrence could have a free hand in his own operations.

Unfortunately, Allenby relied more on information from his own headquarters than from the Hejaz side, and landed himself in difficulty. Heavy rains made the tracks impassable for his artillery, and he felt that any attempt under such conditions to reach the viaduct and tunnel would cost him far more than he could afford.

A few of my notes supply background for this period.

" Impatience to be moving has been growing daily. Postponed plans have made it very difficult for the restless Bedouin to be kept together. Gold has been thrown about like coppers on Derby Day. Paper money is practically worthless here. In fact, if I had about a thousand pounds in gold now it would purchase five times its value in banknotes. As it is I have turned fifty sovereigns into £200 in notes. Notice the absence in moral values. There aren't any in this part of the world. It's a drawback to possess them.

" I have been working mainly with Joyce. Lawrence comes and goes. His last visit to Palestine and his consequent return to Abu el Lissan pulled the chiefs together. Headquarters were taking notice, guardedly of course, of this forlornest of forlorn hopes. 'It might help.' 'It might distract the attention of the Turks.' As I heard Lawrence remark, 'They're about two years late with that, but it shows they're catching up.'

" Slowly but surely the plan which Lawrence put forward so boldly in 1916 is—despite the authorities—shaping towards success, and it has now begun to be treated as a sideshow to the G.H.Q. scheme. Not that Lawrence worried, except that he was determined to do all he could with the least possible loss of life to his own side. Failure would bring disaster and torture. I attached little importance to this phase of the argument for some time. After all, this sort of thing doesn't come home until it is pushed under one's nose a good many times. And war, and anything to do with it, blunts one's perceptions.

" But there it is. Undoubtedly all Lawrence's previous plans were made with an eye to the absence of casualties. It might be the supreme art of the strategist. It might be a more obvious reason—we cannot afford to lose men, for our numbers are small enough as it is. Then again, loss of life and loss of skirmishes is a big deterrent to the courage of our Arabs. They'd sooner go home to their herds and their tents if they cannot win and loot. But from what I have seen of Lawrence and any sort of human agony, he hates anything which causes it, and hates more to be the cause of it himself. What he will do when he is angered is another proposition. He hates the Turks now.

" As yet, the only heedless risks he has taken have been with his own life. And I remember his bitter attack on his Bedouin guard when he found they had left behind one of their number wounded after the attack on Mudawara. He told them—quite needlessly, for they knew it too well—what the Turks did to captured prisoners. Then he went back and shot the man, because he was too badly hurt to be moved. There's not much argument with a man like that.

" The whole campaign could admit of no half measures. Success must be achieved with superior mobility—hit and run, hit and run. We are out-numbered at every exploit and we fight nearly all our engagements in enemy country, behind their lines. As the fighting tended to increase, we found we could not carry wounded men. It would merely have postponed death for them, and hastened it for us.

" So Lawrence welcomed the turn from haphazard encouragement of his guerrilla efforts to the acceptance of the Arabian revolt as a contribution to the allied cause. As he put it to Joyce, something had to be done to help the western front, and Allenby had instructions to plan some relief from the intolerable pressure in the main theatre of war.

" Lawrence's own relief at this turn of events communicated

itself to us all. The months of hard, seemingly endless demolitions and raids were meaning something. Through all the conflicting opinions of both friends and enemies, forced to soldiering when absolutely opposed to warfare and all its horrors, impelled by his " plan," he held to his dream of empire. One of his greatest difficulties had been overcome when he surmounted, with Joyce's help, the diplomatic *impasse* brought about by the disclosure of the Sykes-Picot agreement. Since that time he and Joyce had engineered peace again and again in the Sherifian camp, and cajoled what was actually unofficial support for the irregular levies, but now he had the seal of Headquarters' blessing.

" The joint plan was for the British to take Salt and smash up the railway south of Amman. The Arabs were to take Ma'an as a supporting stroke. This was no mere demolition campaign, Lawrence said. They had asked the Arabs for their help. According to plan, Lawrence moved up to the Atatir, joining with the Beni Sakhr near Themed, to wait for news of the British advance. He was quietly confident. He could prove to the Arabs what his own people could do.

" He very rarely raised his eyes from the ground as he walked around. From camp to camp he moved, followed by his band of gaily-dressed cut-throats, and when in the first week of April came the news that the British had taken Amman, there was a lift to his head rarely seen. He led a jubilant crowd across the Hejaz line to Themed. Then came trouble.

" An Arab came racing up. ' The English are falling back.' Our Bedouin muttered. Yet another came clattering up : ' They have fled from Salt ! '

" Lawrence sat motionless on his camel, staring at the messenger. ' Fool, it cannot be. There is no truth in it,' he said. Another galloped in with still more disquieting reports. Two days the English had attacked and failed. Jemal Pasha was in Salt hanging Arabs who were known to favour the English, and he was pursuing Allenby down the Jordan valley.

" Lawrence did not speak again. I looked at him, wondering what was in his mind. He never needed proof of what he termed the ' ignorant ' and ' stupid ' plans of the regulars. The words were too often on his tongue and in his reports to be under-valued. Yet he had nearly boasted of what would be done this time with the aid of 'our British allies'; and at the very outset of a clear-cut plan, with the Arabs bursting with enthusiasm, it was his own countrymen who had let him down."

Actually the Twentieth Corps had been instructed to make a demonstration against the enemy for two days from April 18, concentrating on their position at Shunet Nimrin with a view to stimulating the idea that further operations against Amman were contemplated. It was intended to inflict severe losses on the enemy, territorial conquest being secondary, and if the Turks retired on Es Salt they were to be followed up to the town, but the town was not to be entered.

Allenby could not afford to hold the bridge-head, and the Turkish habit of ill-treating the inhabitants of districts where British troops had been tolerated was so cruel and disgusting a business that a temporary military success was more harmful to his interests than otherwise.

The Twentieth Corps made their demonstration, but were immediately halted. (Lawrence, knowing the Bedouin and their motives, had repeatedly advised Headquarters that help offered by Bedouin tribes should be treated with reserve, but Allenby was persuaded to meet a deputation of Arabs from the Beni Sakhr, and with them he agreed to operations round Es Salt. The main Turkish position was at Shunet Nimrin, where they had some five thousand rifles, and once this was destroyed Es Salt was to be captured and held till the Arabs could come up and relieve the British.)

Allenby brought his plans forward from the middle of May to the end of April, based on the Beni Sakhr offer, but the latter did not turn up.

Ignorant of this development, the 4th Australian Light Brigade, carrying out its orders, crossed the Jordan to protect the rear of the troops moving on Es Salt, and were caught by the 3rd Turkish Cavalry division and part of their 24th Division, who drove them back with considerable loss in men, and the added loss of nine guns. The Turks in turn crossed the river and threatened the one remaining line of supply, a threat which would remain until the 60th Division advanced.

The defection of the Beni Sakhr led to a hurried call to the 60th, who attacked the Shunet Nimrin position from the west, while the 5th and 2nd Mounted Brigades advanced from near Es Salt to attack the enemy in the rear. This left the Australians in an awkward position. They were already harassed by the attentions of the enemy, who were attacking them not only with two battalions detrained from Amman, but with troops from the force which had crossed the river and additional cavalry units from the north.

There was nothing for Allenby to do but to order a retreat, and this was effected with slight losses. It was unfortunate that Lawrence knew only of the British plans, and of course his own, and had not been told of the Beni Sakhr move, which had been made with a local eye on looting; it had no connection with Sherifian aspirations. However, failure though it was, it made the Turks extremely nervous of further operations east of the Jordan, and undoubtedly increased their watchfulness.

"WHERE THE BEE SUCKS HONEY, THE SPIDER SUCKS POISON"

FOR some months now Allenby would have to reorganise his divisions, and he was faced with the fact that the failure at Es Salt would give the Turks the food harvest which he himself hoped to win. For at least three months he would have to be content with a watching brief, while the Arabs in the east kept the Turks on the *qui vive* with sporadic raids.

Feisal's army now was estimated at about 18,000 men, apart from a few hundreds of trained troops. It included 5,500 Beni Sakhr, 3,000 Howeitat, 1,200 Ageyl, 2,300 Beni Atiyeh, 700 Serahin and 600 Druse. There were some 3,500 of the Tafileh and Kerak Arabs, and about 1,500 from other small tribes. With Abdullah there were about 2,000 Ateiba, 3,000 Juheinah, 2,500 Aneizah and 300 to 500 each of the Harb, Hoteim and Moahib.

The actual numbers in the field, however, were about half these forces, for they mostly took turn and turn about to go home and look after their flocks. The eighteen thousand represented potential strength.

The tribal situation in the north was less promising. After much shilly-shallying, Nuri Shala'an made it quite clear that he did not mean to help anyone but himself, and he and his son were actively promoting enemy trade through Jauf. The Rualla policy was practically that of all the great Aneizah people in the Syrian desert. All were standing outside the revolt, and carrying on favouring both sides as of old. The Druse of the Hauran were ready to come out as soon as they had adequate support, but the Beni Sakhr and other tribal Arabs lying north had, naturally, been discouraged by the British withdrawal from Es Salt, and Feisal's failure to hold Kerak, where pro-Turk chiefs were now supreme.

The chief success had been scored south of Ma'an, and one of the important aims of the Sherifian operations attained. The whole of the line between Ma'an and Mudawara—a

145

K

distance of sixty miles—had been in Arab hands since the middle of April, and systematically kept out of action.

So far as the southern Arab forces were concerned, hitherto neutral or covertly hostile tribes were changing their attitude, and were now openly promising allegiance to the Sherif. What Abdullah had done in the way of destruction on the line had been helped by the weather, whole lengths of rail and embankment having been swept away by the floods.

As regards Medina, the last incoming train had arrived the second week in April. The garrison's position was serious. The daily ration was a small portion of bread and dates, and except for help from tribes running the Sherifian blockade, the garrison could look for no further supplies until the next date harvest, five months ahead.

This was really a period of inaction, and probably justifies the interposition of a few notes written at that time.

" I needed a rest. I had been wearing badly lately, and when Lawrence went on down to Akaba for a trip to meet Allenby I was dumped into the base for a month. This developed into two, various irritating complications setting in before I was once more fit to take up my unorthodox yet comfortable camel seat. Lawrence dropped in once or twice, just talked of " fitness " and " we shall be moving in August." There was a hint of impatience but it was born of progress.

" I stayed in Akaba helping in the now compact base headquarters. We had collected a young army of troops, what with supplies, other service details, and additions to the Air Force.

" Sergeant Perry, Army Veterinary Corps, is worth noting. A real out-and-out regular, with a funny halting, snuffling way of talking, he performed miracles with the animals, particularly the mules and camels. For hundreds of years sick camels had soon become dead ones. But Perry studied their ailments, treated them, saved many beasts which ordinarily would have had a knife across their throats, and generally became an object of veneration to the Bedouin. This " inglisi " who could take time to stuff this camel with pills, dress that one with ointment, and cut and carve the other to curtail a destroying growth—he was worth watching, and many a herder miles away from the base learned of his fame, and marvelled.

" It was a relief to argue and quarrel with one's own kith

about the war, and all that was happening, and retail all the worst jokes one could remember. We were fairly well disillusioned, and, discounting communiques and very old newspaper reports, looked merely to an indeterminate future of more sand, more fever—and no return home.

" Lawrence is not always with us for protection. Egyptian Arabic, however well one may swear in it, is no insurance against attack. Sheer forcefulness and a drawn gun were much better arguments. There was never time for niceties.

" I began to get a clearer picture of Lawrence. Everything centred on him. There was no question of hero worship. He piqued me time and again with his aloofness. Not once has there been a real break through his reserve. One thing, he treats officers and men alike.

" He has an insight into native character, some special sympathy. One of our troubles is to keep out of our contacts with the natives that so obvious feeling of superiority. Lawrence viewed things differently.

" At times it has seemed as though he has sought protection by an affectation of cynicism. I could never determine whether his satire, his brilliant flicks of conversation, were uttered for the sake of their effect, or were the opinions of a genius. One thing, he is sincere in his hates. He abhors all Turks, German officers, and has as strong an antipathy to France.

" The last months have turned Arabia upside-down. The desert has been invaded. Aeroplanes have filled the air, and motor cars have worn a way through the country. But the desert itself remains aloof.

" I suppose that brings me back full circle to my unanswered query—why will Lawrence keep himself away from his fellows ?

" May, 1918.

" The first fortnight in May was a record of aeroplane journeys for Lawrence between Headquarters at Kelab and Cairo, and Kelab, Abu el Lissan and Akaba. It was a flurry of planning. There was more activity in the armoured cars, and a reconnaissance round Jurf. Lawrence was developing more into a driving force than a leader. Wherever he lighted he left a plan and something to be done. He went to Egypt and to Palestine, and immediately there was some other development. Obviously the northern Hejaz operations had some importance, and, imperturbable through it all, Joyce smoothed the workings of the machine with his organiser's mind.

" We heard that Lawrence had been awarded the *Croix de Guerre* on May 18.

" Advance Headquarters at Abu el Lissan were never too secure. Agents, both spurious and genuine, were always in and out. There were air raids, some by bomb and others by leaflet. The latter constantly advised the Arabs to leave the Sherifians and return to the 'true cause.' The camp was always on edge, and neither night nor day was peaceful."

Joyce eyed with great suspicion a small party which came in from the direction of Ma'an under a white flag on May 3. The officer in charge carried a letter from Jemal Pasha, dated from Es Salt and addressed to Feisal, and the latter handed it over to Joyce as soon as he had read it.

" At the present time (wrote Jemal) the Ottoman Government, the mightiest representative of Islam, has obtained superiority over the greatest enemies of the Mohammedan religion. I am persuaded I am honouring the Prophet's name by inviting his most excellent and noble grandson to participate in the protection and advance of Islam by ensuring the superiority of the Turkish army, when a safe and happy life will be obtained for all true believers.

" I have the honour to state that I shall be pleased to converse with your Excellency in four days' time at Your Excellency's place of residence."

There was a significant postscript : " I feel sure we shall be able to fulfil the wishes of all Arabs."

Joyce recommended Feisal to send the party back to Ma'an without reply, and this he did.

As light relief, a copy of a long letter, addressed to the King of England from the Yemen, had been passed on to Joyce. It was a remarkable effort, full of professions of good faith to Britain, but its opening phrases were startling :

" To the benevolent King, the Magnificent Monarch, the great Sovereign, the honourable Emperor of the Christian Nations, the kindest King over the followers of Jesus, He who was submerged in baptismal water, He who drags the tail of respectfulness and veneration, He whose veneration is dreaded by the inhabitants of the land and sea, He whose

148

administration is longed for by cities and kingdoms, the brave Lion, the magnanimous Lion, the King of the English, the pure gold."

Hussein entered the lists again. He wrote to Wilson on May 15 a letter in which he expressed more forcibly than usual his personal view that Ibn Saud was " not playing an honest game," but was using the protection he secured under Britain's treaty to go counter to British interests in Arabia.

" You have already been informed (the King wrote) of the oppression and encroachment against the tribes who have been firmly bound to the Emirs of Mecca from ancient time to the present day, in a way clearly pointing to his (Ibn Saud's) intention to override their local rights. Yes, such encroachments and intentions, nay greater than these, should not be attended in view of the present situation and what may result from it. (Ironical).

" But our object now in informing you of this is the effect on men's minds, inasmuch as he is known and famous through his alliance with Great Britain, and his rise to-day and his determination to commit such acts, and anything leading to discord, firmly establish and point to the fact that he is following the path of Ibn Rashid in helping the policy of the Turks. His intent to help them against us, while he is an ally of Great Britain, who is managing our affairs—that is the important point which will produce anxieties of all kinds in the minds of all peoples of the country and will affect the course of ordered political life of the country, which continues and God willing will continue."

The King, however, concluded his letter with an assurance that the force he had sent to Khurma would avoid encroachment on Saudi territory, and at a subsequent interview which Wilson had with him at Jeddah for the express purpose of impressing him with the necessity for keeping on terms with Ibn Saud, the King placed himself unreservedly at Wilson's discretion, putting his two hands to his forehead in the attitude of submission.

"YESTERDAY'S SPARK MAY BE TO-MORROW'S FIRE"

The Hejaz operations had grown up. There were now (May, 1918) eight British officers attached "for special service," and of these Joyce and Maynard were with the Arab army, and Lawrence and Young with the Bedouin.

The British units consisted of the Armoured Cars (officered by Gilman, Dowsett, Wade, Grisenthwaite and Greenhill); the 10-pounder section (Brodie and Pascoe); "X" flight of the Royal Flying Corps (Furness-Williams in command over Siddons, Makins, Junor, Divers, Latham and Oldfield); a detachment of the Camel Transport Corps and one of the Egyptian Camel Corps (under Bimbashi Peake).

Akaba had a Base Commandant (then Major Scott of the Inniskillings) with Royal Engineer, Army Service Corps, Ordnance and Medical details. Goslett was the Supply Officer, and when Marshall was away Ramsay acted as Medical Officer.

In the south Wilson was the Senior British Advisory officer and Pilgrimage Officer, and Major Bassett his assistant. Captains Clayton and Goldie were on special service with the Arabs.

AKABA

With the Arabs, 15 guns, ranging from a 5-in. howitzer to 15-pounders, and 20 machine guns.

Egyptian Army : eight officers, 270 men.

French : four guns, four mitrailleuses, 10 fusils mitrailleuses ; five officers, 204 men.

British : Two 10-pounder guns (mounted on Talbots) ; eight machine guns (Light Armoured Cars) ; six Hotchkiss (on Ford tenders and attached to the L.A.C.) ; 38 officers, 228 men. Four armoured cars, two Nieuport planes, 2 B.E.2E.s and six Martynsides.

Indian Machine Gun Company : four machine guns, one native officer and 22 men.

SHERIF ABDULLAH

His Headquarters were near Abu Naam, and he had the following :

Two each of 5-in. howitzers, 2.95 mountain guns, 77-mm. guns (both of which were useless and were just for show) and 75-mm. quick-firer field guns ; nine machine guns, (three useless).

There were 450 infantrymen, and attached were 3 British officers and 76 men of the Egyptian Army, with four machine-guns ; two officers and 87 men of the French army, with 12 fusil-mitrailleuses.

SHERIF ALI

He was in the neighbourhood of Medina, and seemed to be better off.   He had :

Four 5-in. howitzers, two 75-mm. quick-firer field guns ; six Turkish mountain guns (old) ; two 10-pounder mountain guns of Indian mountain pattern, of little use ; one Turkish 75-mm. mountain gun, also useless ; 12 maxims and four German machine guns.

2,500 men (including Camel Corps, infantry and engineers).

The French unit attached to him consisted of four officers and 72 men, armed with 11 fusil mitrailleuses and two mitrailleuses.   They also had six mountain guns, but these were old and practically useless.

WEJH

110 Arab regulars with two Turkish 75-mm. mountain guns, supported by the Egyptian Army with three British officers, 579 other ranks, one 5-in. howitzer, two 15-pounder field guns, nine maxims and two German machine guns.

JEDDAH

Garrisoned by about 100 mixed Arab, Egyptian, French and British details, backed by the possession of two 15-pounder field guns.

YENBO

A mixed force of 60, with no guns.

MECCA

Arabs : 225 officers and men, looking after eight old Turkish 75-mm. guns without ammunition.   There were also 16 Egyptian Army instructors, and 12 French Moslem soldiers with 16 fusil mitrailleuses.

A telegram from Feisal to Allenby during the month explained and emphasised a weakness in his position :

" In the event of fresh Turkish offensive operations I do not consider that the Arab Army in its present condition can successfully deal with them. In that case I foresee considerable danger of Arabs being compelled by the enemy to retire from the positions captured by them in the recent fighting, and communications with Ma'an reopened in consequence. It is vitally necessary that our army should be reinforced and I trust General Allenby will assist us and send all volunteers from Egypt and Palestine as quickly as possible. I also ask that no effort should be spared to enlist volunteers from prisoner-of-war camps in India and Mesopotamia. I have great fears that a check to our army at this time would preclude our taking the offensive later on, and I feel I must report this if I am to fulfil my duty to you."

Allenby sent him a reassuring reply, realising " to the full the added strain that is imposed upon your army at the present time by the special effort which enemy is making to recover in part at least the losses he sustained at your hands, but remembering the great achievements of your gallant troops I await with confidence the sure overthrow of his designs and the final victory of your arms which the Arabs' steadfast valour must inevitably ensure."[1]

London, realising Allenby's difficulties, remembered the French detachment camp in Palestine, and suggested that he should use it as a reinforcement. Allenby was still averse to using the French troops, not because of their nationality but because they were insufficiently trained and equipped. Steps were then taken to reorganise the unit so that it could be fit to take over a sector of the line about the middle of August, by which time Allenby hoped to be ready for his new offensive.

In the southern Hejaz there had been a succession of minor engagements, under Ali on the one hand, and Davenport on the other. Valuable camel convoys were taken, about £10,000

---

[1] " On the other hand the English are carrying out their plans with grim tenacity in Palestine, and are cutting the Turkish communications with Arabia by cutting the Hejaz railway east of the Jordan. If this succeeds then Arabia will probably be lost to the Turks. The fighting in Palestine is therefore of great political importance." (The German Vorwaerts, May 10, 1918.)

in gold captured, bridge and line destroyed, and hundreds of Turks killed and wounded.

Davenport's operations were not without their difficulties, but this time it was the Sherifians who failed, and not the Arabs as was Garland's complaint in the attack on Wejh. The Baghdadi " officers at once began delaying the guns . . . and were in a great state of fear. They had placed them behind a high hill which they could not possibly clear. . . . They gave many excuses for not coming away from the mountain. . . . Ibn Thawab then went down with a lot of Bedu and forced the guns to come into the ' fire ' position. The Bedu had drawn their knives and were making suggestive gestures across their throats, implying that that was how they intended to treat the Baghdadis if they did not come into action." Eventually they began firing, but whatever success was achieved was due to the Bedouin rushing three strong Turkish posts after dark.

As for the railway itself, this year's rains had caused the Turks a lot of trouble. As Hogarth noted : " In the rainy seasons the Turk has to perform enormous labour to keep the railway running. The embankment becomes so sodden that, before now, railway service has had to stop for three months at a time. This year there were exceptional rains, and at the bridges the flood flowed over the top. In the valley the ballast was often entirely washed away from under, bending the rails. The Turk used to pick the line up, re-lay the bed and straighten the rails ; raiding parties would then blow the line up for him, and the Turk would re-lay it again ; then would come a sandstorm and cover the line feet deep for miles ; The Turk would come out and remove the sand ; and so *ad infinitum.*"

HUSSEIN was harping again about his kingship, and at the beginning of June (1918) he talked it over with Wilson. The title of " King of Hejaz " meant nothing to him. What was wrong with " King of the Arabs ? " The British Agent gently pointed out that such recognition was impossible. Other great Arab chiefs did not recognise it : why should the British Government do more than they ? The King then talked for about three hours on the history of his negotiations with the British, and Wilson this time took notes, for comparison with what were the apparent facts.

Soon after the outbreak of war, Hussein told him, Sir Henry McMahon sent a messenger asking what the Arabs would do in the event of Turkey entering on the side of Germany. Hussein said his reply was according to the Law, " Do not make war, and only make ' Jehad ' if approved by the Ulema of the country concerned." Six weeks later a messenger came with a letter from the High Commissioner, informing him of the declaration of war by Turkey, and of the promise by the Allied powers not to hurt the Holy places of Islam. To this he replied that he would not take action against the Allies.

Some time later Hussein sent a messenger to McMahon telling him that Great Britain had nothing to fear from the Arabs. The British reply to this was a promise to renew the Caliphate, to assist the Arabs in every possible way, and to guarantee their independence after the war.

Here the King interrupted his review to point out that he considered the agreement between himself and Britain meant the unity of Arabia under one government, which could be his or that of any other Arab chief. What use was there in anything he had done if this were not so ?

Wilson reminded him that the declared British policy was to welcome Arab union and an Arab nation, but it could only come from the Arabs themselves. Britain had never agreed, he said, that the Arab people should be united under one head. Then followed involved argument as to the " one head," and in the end Hussein said that McMahon's letter included much that meant the acceptance of the principle of a single nation. " A nation must have a head," was his point. Wilson countered with Britain's persistent refusal to recognise such an overlord, whereupon the King changed his tactics.

" Well, suppose no agreement had been made, and that we are now talking about it for the first time. In those circumstances I would say I will not do this until all the country from Aleppo to the Persian frontier and on to Aden is independent and under one Government."

He did add that the High Commissioner had written that Mosul could not be included in the independent area, but opposed this with the information that Sir Mark Sykes had told him when he visited him in Jeddah in 1917 that the Arabs could have Mosul.

This was not helpful to Wilson, and Hussein left the British Agent even more puzzled by his concluding remarks. He remained loyal to Britain, said Hussein, but even if he had a written decision from the British Government, he would prefer to rely on Sir Henry McMahon's letters as Britain's word of honour !

Having dropped so heavy a hint, Hussein waited a fortnight, but—tied as they were with their other commitments—the British authorities could say little, and that little was very discouraging to the ambitious Sherif. He gave vocal proof of his disappointment at their attitude, and in the end took refuge in talk of abdication. " I request you to inform me as to what place you think I and my family should reside in," he wrote in one impassioned and very involved letter.

Then the Jews moved into the field of negotiation. Dr. Weizmann, the leader of the Zionist Mission[1] left Suez on June 1, accompanied by Major Ormsby-Gore, for a flying visit to Feisal. Palestine was the subject, and while Weizmann was more or less privy to the Franco-British opinion on the matter, he had instructions to find out what the Arabs thought about that country and its future.

Joyce took him north to Guweira, and acted as interpreter, because Ormsby-Gore had to stop behind owing to illness,

[1] The Mission arrived in Palestine early in the year and had been formed to assist in relief work in the occupied territory, and to do liaison work between the Military and the Jews.

and Lawrence—who should have been, and wanted to be, present—was away on operations.

The meeting was more or less a fencing match, with Weizmann making the more definite moves. Feisal would not make any political declaration as to the Arabs' intentions in Palestine, saying that that was his father's business.

The Jewish leader, apparently amicably inclined, told Feisal that the Jews did not propose to set up their own government, but merely wished to work, under British protection, for the colonisation and development of Palestine.

Feisal emphasised the danger which the enemy could enlarge from any inference that he, Feisal, might agree to non-Arabs ruling a land which was understood to be Arab territory, but personally he saw no reason why Dr. Weizmann's plans should not in some sense be realised.

There was no practical result from the meeting : it was all preliminary to a bargaining match. The trouble was that Joyce had to listen and interpret, knowing well enough that the Arabs would not get Palestine, treaty or no treaty.

An attack on Jurf by the Arabs was timed for June 9. On that day five 'planes bombed the defences there, but the Arab army did not get into position in time, and could not follow up the attack. Next day three 'planes again bombed the station, and Sherifian and French guns co-operated, but again no attack followed, the regulars and Bedouin not working together. In the end, the engagement fizzled out into a futile long-range bombardment.

Turkish posts between Jurf and Anazeh were rushed on the 12th by some Rualla, with the help of two companies of regulars with two French guns.

A week later four Turkish 'planes bombed Nuri Shala'an's camp at Azrak, inflicting severe casualties among men and animals. As a result the camp was moved, but the more important development was that Nuri's Sherifian tendencies notably stiffened—a welcome change in his suspicious neutrality.

The Howeitat's loyalty to Feisal remained constant, but their successes in the field had resulted in so much profit that it was more difficult than ever to persuade them to enter the firing line. Their attitude was something in the nature of a strike—more fighting if they could have more pay !

As for Auda, he had become inflated with self-provided proof that his " descent " from the Prophet gave him equality with other Sherifs. He was flirting with the idea of some grandiloquent title, and was using Turkish prisoner labour in the building of a great mud-brick castle at El Jefer. For its roofing he was collecting telegraph poles from the railway.

Lawrence was mainly concerned with preparing the tribes for the operations in the autumn, and with the then difficult problem of keeping Feisal's spirits out of a rut of pessimism, which had been caused by lack of action, and lack of money.

In Akaba and Abu el Lissan, the beginning of June marked a period of transport calculations. Lawrence was backwards and forwards between Palestine, Egypt and the Hejaz, for talks with Wingate and Dawnay. There was a diversion to Alexandria, where he saw General Bols, of Intelligence ; then back to Cairo, and from there to Kelab again.

If there were any restraint in the unorthodox methods of Lawrence, it came from Joyce, but even when there were disagreements, and Lawrence won his point, Joyce would then throw all his weight into the project. His patience and loyalty were as colossal as his size.

London was asked if Young could be appointed as special service officer to assist Lawrence in conducting the Bedouin operations. " The value of these irregular troops," cabled Allenby, " depends entirely, it should be borne in mind, on the leadership of British officers, and in view of the fact that Lawrence has to proceed on special missions from time to time, and may at any moment fall ill, the provision of an understudy for the purpose of securing continuous control becomes essential." Approval was granted, and Young immediately and voluntarily took in hand the organisation of the force's transport.

Then came a hitch. As part of the plan it was, in Lawrence's opinion, essential that Abdullah and Zeid should shift the majority of their forces to Akaba. Allenby agreed, and Lawrence went down to Jeddah to secure Hussein's consent to the move. When Lawrence did get down to Jeddah it was only to hear that the old King had gone into sanctuary at Mecca. He was " not at home."

Lawrence did not waste time. He talked with all he could and on his return sent in a note regarding information he had received as to Ibn Saud's activities in central Arabia.

The circumstances pointed to the possibility of a major clash between the Sherifians and Ibn Saud in the near future.

Both were attempting—in some cases with success—to collect taxes from tribes on a disputable border, but Ibn Saud had scored over his rival by imprisoning the Sherifian collector. Hussein was arranging with Abdullah for a force to be sent to release his representative, but Abdullah was acting on his own initiative and more or less declaring war on Ibn Saud. This at a time when Arabian unity was an essential contained all the elements of disaster.

Lawrence's information was quickly followed by a counter-report from St. John Philby, now firmly established in Ibn Saud's favour. He cabled to Cairo that the Wahabi chief was in possession of letters written by Abdullah on July 13 to certain sheikhs of the Ateibah. In his letters (which evidently did not impress the recipients, who passed them on to Ibn Saud) Abdullah said, first, that the Sherif and Ibn Rashid had made peace, and that God was supporting him against the rebellious Ibn Saud; secondly, that he was in command of a punitive force concentrated with a view to attacking Khurma. He requested the Ateibah to join him.

The action of Abdullah, in thus running contrary to the King's policy, perforce aroused the Arab Bureau to swift action. The King was informed at once, and strongly urged to write to Abdullah that his honour was pledged to refrain from aggression against Ibn Saud.

Meanwhile, the calls of the western theatre, which was using up thousands of men daily in mass assaults, had led to a demand on Allenby for two divisions to be sent from his forces to France. He protested immediately. His line, he said, was the shortest and best he could hold in anything like security, and unless he could blow up the Jordan bridge-heads —an operation in itself costly and problematical—there was no shorter line to which he could withdraw. In any case, if this were done, it would make it impossible for him to keep in touch with Feisal's troops, whose co-operation was absolutely essential.

With two divisions taken away, Allenby felt he would not be able to give any assistance to Feisal, either directly or indirectly, by exerting pressure on the enemy on his northern front. In addition, the enemy would, on learning of his weakness, soon return to the attack, and in all probability they would have sufficient strength to regain all the ground they had lost in the north.

A set-back of this nature would have repercussions beyond calculation. Its serious effect on the political situation in the east, and particularly in the Arab movement, would be immensely greater than mere military defeat, and it would end up in Hussein being driven into the arms of the Turks.

Critical as was the situation in France, the position in Palestine and Arabia, put so forcibly to the ever-distant London, led to orders for one division only to be transferred, and Allenby re-shuffled his line to meet the deficiency.

London, with its usual unthinking disregard for consequences, also selected this moment to reduce Feisal's grant, and the latter was quick to protest. Allenby had found it possible to send more material, and had also accelerated the supply of Sherifian volunteers, but at the time that Feisal's financial requirements were increased, the home authorities knocked £25,000 off his monthly subsidy. What Allenby did not know, and still less London, was that Egypt was nearly without gold. Incredible though it appeared, four thousand pounds only could be found. The gold was anywhere but in the hands of the Egyptian authorities, and a consignment expected from Australia was late.

In an effort to loan from Peter to pay Paul, discreet inquiries were made as to whether Jeddah, or even Akaba, could supply £25,000 in gold for immediate transportation to the north, and while these were going on, Allenby temporised. The Sherifian troops, and their Arab irregulars, were getting restive. Some had been without pay for weeks and even months, and at this time, when unified action was an absolute essential, the signs most evident were those of disintegration.

Wilson sent a most pessimistic report to Wingate. The local military moves against the Turks, he said, were not progressing well. The southern Arab army needed reorganisation, and if Hussein would only help, matters would improve. His loyalty was not weakening, but he was nervous, tired and more than usually difficult to deal with. The world war was not worrying him, for he was preoccupied with Ibn Saud, with whom he had been exchanging letters which, to say the least, were very acrid in tone. The old points of variance—frontiers, use of water, taxes—were as evident as ever, but what was troubling the old King now was what he regarded as Ibn Saud's opposition to his personal ascendancy and to his schemes for the unification of Arabia.

Knowing the British agreements with the other allies, Wilson said he could not in any way reassure the King, or even say that he was right and Ibn Saud wrong. Perhaps if he could give Hussein a more definite statement of the British policy as regards the future of the Arabian peninsula, all Arab parties could be persuaded to put aside local disputes until the Turks had been defeated.

Wilson himself was very concerned about the gold supply, for there were elements of danger if the Arabs suspended operations through the non-payment of their subsidies.

The Egyptian authorities did not wait for instructions from London. They circularised every bank, converted all local resources, and by the beginning of August had " scrounged " —to give it its widest meaning of effort—sufficient gold and silver to meet the August subsidy of £200,000 as well as an advance to Feisal of £75,000.

Allenby told London what had been done, and added " The maintenance of the Arab operations is of vital importance to my operations, and this can only be done if subsidies are paid regularly. No risk must be run therefore of a repetition of the present critical situation in regard to gold."

"A BARBER LEARNS TO SHAVE ON THE ORPHAN'S FACE"

THE Imperial Camel Corps were now the main subject on the Hejaz wires, and on July 11 Lawrence was in conference with Allenby and the head of " Q "—Bartholomew. Two days later he was in Cairo with Dawnay, and orders speedily followed for Buxton to take command of the I.C.C. companies and march to Akaba for special operations. These were intended to increase Turkish speculation as to Allenby's intentions, and to secure some period of delay while the enemy made up its mind what to do.

Ten days were spent in discussing the best use to which the Camel Corps could be put, Lawrence, Dawnay and Bols meeting day after day. The men marched out from El Kubri on July 24—14 officers, 314 men, 411 camels, and 6 Lewis guns. They travelled via the Mitla pass and Nekhl, and arrived at Akaba on the 30th. Marshall, with a section of Field Ambulance consisting of 30 cacolets and men of an Egyptian Camel company, together with a special demolition column manned by Lawrence's bodyguard, joined them there.

Lawrence had a talk with the men on the morning after their arrival. It was, he said, a quiet talk for their own welfare, to warn them of the rigours and dangers of fighting in the desert. The camels would have to be their first consideration. The surface sand baked hard, and was studded with small flints. These would become almost red-hot in the fierce sun and play havoc with the camel's feet. They would have to dismount, the camels would be irritable and weary, and they would have to be hand fed. The Camel Corps were the first white troops to be brought to Arabia as an actual fighting unit. The Arabs themselves, blood enemies, had been won over only at the cost of desperate diplomacy, and the British would have to see that nothing was done to destroy the Arabs' faith in the cause. They should not fraternise too freely and, if, when the fighting was on, the Arabs started looting, it would be well to leave them at it. It was their life, and to interfere would start trouble.

It was all done so nicely, and quietly, yet before the rather astounded company had accustomed themselves to the seeming insignificance of Lawrence, and to the fact that they had really seen the mystery man of their war, he had turned and left them.

Camels were watered, fantasses filled, rations drawn, saddlery and kit overhauled, unfit camels exchanged and all preparations completed by the morning of the 2nd. In the afternoon the column left Akaba and proceeded inland. On the morning of the 4th they reached Rum, the first ration dump, but the watering of the camels was a slow affair—and a quarrelsome one—as the water, which in some cases just percolated through the rocks, was not in sufficient quantity to water many at a time.

By the 6th, the column was 16 miles from Mudawara, and after a reconnaissance by Buxton, Marshall and Brodie, the former, with the aid of an air-photograph, arranged his attack. About an hour before sundown on the 7th, raiding parties were in position west of the station's redoubts, about a mile away, and settled down there until one in the morning, when the main attacking parties were due to be in position between the southern redoubt and the station, ready for the attack at 3.45.

It was very cold. The ground was stony and not ideal for sleep. At 3.45 all were on edge. By 3.50 nothing had happened, and five minutes later all was still silent. Dawn was rapidly approaching, and with it the danger of discovery. Suddenly a bomb exploded in the southern redoubt. The attack was on. The station fell quickly, then the southern post. Queerly enough, there was still no sound from the middle redoubt, when, silhouetted against the eerie light of the hastening dawn a long file of men were seen clambering up the steep sides of the earthworks. Aeroplanes now came up, and amidst the fall of their bombs, some very accurate shooting from the guns, and sharp bursts of machine-gun and rifle fire from the east and west, one Turkish gun kept up a hopeless struggle untl sheer numbers smothered it. By seven o'clock the capture of Mudawara was complete.

The British lost one officer and three men killed, and ten wounded. The Turkish killed numbered one officer and 20 men, there were 34 wounded and 150 prisoners. From morning until evening the camel cacolets and the Talbot cars—the latter denuded of their guns—were busy evacuating the wounded. The rest of the force was busy filling the wells with rails and rubbish, and they were finally blown in.

At last, in the fading evening light, the final demolition took place—that of the immense water tower. It went up in a puff of smoke and fell like a pack of cards, and only a deserted, waterless and useless station remained. Camels were mounted, " walk march " given, and the column marched northward into the night.

Three days later the I.C.C. arrived at El Jefer, where they were met by Lawrence, Joyce and Dawnay, and immediate arrangements made for an attack on the viaduct at Kissir, approximately 145 miles north. They left El Jefer on the 14th, and next day were at Bair. Here the discovery of pilfering in the rations led to about fifty men and one hundred camels being sent back to Akaba, to give the force a chance to finish the raid. Lawrence and Joyce went ahead to Azrak to discuss its possibilities as a base. Rolls and Sanderson drove them out on a ride they never forgot, coaxing the armoured cars over ever-changing surfaces, vexed by tyre troubles, pleased with the screaming whirr of sixty-mile an hour spurts over mud-flats, angered by frenzied digging in soft sand patches, at long last clattering back to Bair with the last set of tyres in strips.

Lawrence switched from camel to car again, and Joyce went back to Abu el Lissan with their joint report on Azrak's use as a forward base.

The Camel Corps moved off on the night of the 15th for the last of their raids, and by midnight of the 20th, by forced marches of about forty miles a day, were about twelve miles from the Kissir bridge and within sight of the railway. Unfortunately, two enemy planes spotted them, and the country ahead turned out to be full of native encampments, among which Turkish mule-mounted infantry were busy assessing grain taxes. It was disastrous, for the Bedouin were suspicious of the strange British troops, and frightened of the Turks, so the column had to turn east in a hurried, evasive march to Azrak.

Here the gun-cotton and demolition stores were buried, in hopeful anticipation of the operations planned by Lawrence for the coming month. The Camel Corps tidied themselves, resumed more orderly formation, and by easy marches returned from the freedom of their brief desert campaign to the restraining influence of Beersheba and its commandments.[1]

They had covered nearly a thousand miles in forty-four days, fourteen of which had been spent in watering, and six for rests and rations—a remarkable achievement for such a unit in a strange and unfriendly land.

With Allenby's plans reaching something like maturity, the Commander-in-Chief, knowing the scope of Lawrence's arrangements in northern Syria, found it advisable to send a cautionary letter to Feisal, in which occurred the following significant paragraph :

" There is one point which I find it necessary to make quite clear to your Highness in order to avoid any misunder-standing in the future. It is that in the event of your extending your military operations far in advance of the right flank of my force, you must not reckon upon the support and co-operation of my army, as you will enter districts which are outside the sphere of my operations, and to which my force will be unable to penetrate at present. I thought at once to inform you of this in order that your Highness might be under no misapprehension when formu-lating your plans."

Liman von Sanders, in his memoirs, wrote that in the second half of August 1918 he was " informed by Djemal Pasha," commander of the Fourth Army, that Sherif Feisal was willing to take over the front of the Fourth Army with his troops, providing he received guarantees from the Turkish Government that an Arabian state would be formed, that according to the statements of Feisal a great British attack was in preparation in the coast district, and that in this case the troops of the Fourth Army would become available to reinforce the front between the sea and the Jordan. I instructed Djemal Pasha to open negotiations to that effect. In the same way I requested Enver to give the desired guarantees.

" Neither from Enver nor Djemal did I ever receive information or a reply concerning this matter. I an unable therefore to judge the sincerity or the scope of Feisal's offer. From the report of my Turkish chief I gained the impression

---

[1] A communique published on August 14, 1918, dealing with the raid on Mudawara, was noted in the " Official History of the War " as " the first public announcement by the War Office that British troops were acting with the Arab forces."

that the Turks distrusted the offer, and considered it merely a trick to put our Jordan positions in the hands of the Arabs, while the British main attack took place on the coast sector, or between the sea and the Jordan."

In the south, Wingate began to be further troubled about the growing importance of Ibn Saud, especially when he heard of the arms and ammunition he had received recently, through the backing of the Indian authorities. Military and political interest switched for a time to the situation in the Nejd. The controversy between Hussein and Ibn Saud over Khurma, which had first given rise to anxiety in June, created a very critical atmosphere. This quarrel, essentially religious at bottom, now found active expression. Hussein's punitive expedition against Khalid had failed, and he had sent a fresh force to Khurma early in August. Its dispatch led to immediate and violent protests from Ibn Saud, but little reliable information could be gleaned as to the operations.

Wingate sent a reproachful cable to England, asking if the despatch of further arms and ammunition to the Saudi could not be delayed " pending assurances from him that he will withdraw his support from the anti-Sherifian elements in Khurma."

This threat from the desert was heard but vaguely by Lawrence, like the mutter of a distant storm, but he felt assured that Ibn Saud would be held in check while he made his last plans for the final overthrow of the Turks in Arabia.

Either politically or diplomatically inspired, Allenby thought it wise to inform London of the development of the Sherifian Army into an " efficient fighting force, with improved discipline." Properly clothed and equipped, he said, it should now be capable of keeping the field during prolonged operations. He considered the time had arrived for recognising that the status of the force now approximated to the other regular forces in the field.

An official comment from British Headquarters indicated their considered opinion of the Sherifian co-operation.

" A few figures will suffice to show the value of the Arab operations in the E.E.F. after the call had come to it to send to France most of its best troops.

" The ration strength of the Hejaz Expeditionary Force (Turkish) in the Medina area and that of the 2nd Composite

Force with headquarters at Tebuk, was about 13,000, some of the battalions being good troops. These forces would have been invaluable to Liman von Sanders either at the moment of Allenby's greatest embarrassment, or that of the final offensive. The Turks' German advisers, and the most enlightened Turkish officers, had again and again urged the evacuation of Medina, but the authorities in Constantinople wavered. Strategically, the city was worthless at this moment, but politically and from the religious point of view it had yet a value in its traditions and dignity. Baghdad, Mecca, Jerusalem were gone ; it was hard to abandon Medina, a spot where Mohammed proclaimed his new religion, the capital of the first Khalifa. It is possible, however, that the enemy would actually have done so (for it is known that he had made preparations for a retreat) if his communications had not been severed by the operations of April.

" There was only a trifling amount of rolling stock at Mudawara, so that the whole evacuation would have had to be carried out by march route at least as far as Ma'an. In the Ma'an area, north of the bridge over the railway, there were over 4,000 men. Another 6,000 from the whole area between Tafileh and Ma'an were evacuated as prisoners of war to Egypt up to the end of August, 1918. Deaths from sickness accounted for many more. The casualties in killed and wounded, according to Arab claims, amount to 5,500. Even if this last figure is heavily reduced, the fact remains that prior to the final offensive with its many thousands of prisoners, the Arab campaign killed, wounded, captured or isolated well over 25,000 troops. Like the Spanish guerrillas of the Peninsular war, the Arabs gave the British invaluable help while wholly dependent upon them for opportunities." [1]

[1] " Official History of the War."

"THE PROVISION FOR TO-MORROW BELONGS TO TO-MORROW"

I MUST use my own notes on the last phase of the campaign as "scaffolding," and I do not apologise for the very personal element that intrudes. Their youthful foolishness shout to high heaven, but someone *must* do the shouting.

"*August* 26.

"Lawrence and Marshall have come in from Azrak. They bring news of Lieutenant Rowan's tragic death killed by the accidental discharge of an Arab's rifle. He is buried in the quiet of Mejaber, by the side of the pools there.

"Abu el Lissan is alive. Young, Dawnay, and Joyce catch Lawrence's infectious keenness, but they rarely get him to smile. He is unquestionably a bitter man.

"Out of the tangle of talk between Lawrence, Joyce, Stirling and Young, with a glimpse now and then of maps, I get an idea that we are doing something worth while. If our luck, my luck, still stands, one day I might sit in some odd corner and attempt to decipher my notes. Not that they will be worth much. We're just a handful of daft loons running up and down sandhills, playing with dynamite.

"Young had one job now, and one job only. Lawrence and he, together with Feisal and Joyce, had talked over the transport plans for the establishment of a raiding force at Azrak some time in October, prepared to co-operate with Allenby. The detailed scheme which Young drew up for submission to G.H.Q. was a good a plan as has ever been devised. This was no eighty-mile-a-day dash by Lawrence's irregulars. It was the move of a regular force, working with two thousand transport camels. The Bedouin "to-morrow, or perhaps the next day, God willing," would not do. Young had to drive into unwilling minds a fixed programme, first that the supplies had to be at a given point at a given time, and second that the units using them would themselves have to strike on a given day at a given point and time.

"Two things nearly wrecked his careful scheming—the

loan of the Imperial Camel Corps for Mudawara, and Allenby's sudden advancing of his own operations into September.

"Where before Young had a month to get his supplies to Azrak, and his replenishment convoys on the move, he now had eighteen days to get two convoys of 600 camels each from Akaba to Azrak. There were five different kinds of rations, none of which could be mixed, for religious as well as edible reasons—water for men and animals, explosives, petrol, forage, tents, even canvas hangers.

"Convoy No. 1 started on August 26, and was nearly scattered all over the desert by an enemy air-raid. After some hectic hours, it re-formed and went crawling away on its first stage to Abu el Lissan, up the tricky Negb el Shtar with its four-in-one zigzag paths. Convoy No. 2 left two days later, and then Young followed it up, caught it and passed it on his Ford, to find more trouble at the forward camp at Abu el Lissan.

"Old Hussein had struck dismay into the camp. Intrigue and jealousy had fanned his own annoyance at the growing importance of Feisal and Ja'afer Pasha, and he published in the Qibla (his official gazette) what amounted to a disclaimer of the latter's rank and work :

"'Whereas the title of Commander-in-Chief applied to Sheikh Ja'afer, one of the chiefs of the army in the northern Hejaz camp, is current in certain circles, both in conversation and in private letters, and whereas this is inconsistent with the truth, and the Arab Government has not conferred this title on anyone or defined the ranks of the commanders, as other governments do, and whereas the said Sheikh Ja'afer is undertaking the supervision of a section of that army and no more, now therefore the above explanation is imperative.'

"This absolutely paralysed activities. Ja'afer and scores of his officers came into camp ready to resign, and their men were openly mutinous. Feisal refused their resignations, but telegraphed his own to his father. All military operations were suspended. The artillery actually mutinied and turned their guns on the officers' tents, only to find that their temper had already been suspect and the breech-blocks thoughtfully removed over-night.

"The wires between Abu el Lissan, Akaba and Mecca flicked messages to and from Sherif Hussein and his sons which increased in their tempo of rage as each exchange was read and absorbed. This *impasse*, when we had a hard and fast timetable to work to, tried the tempers of everyone.

"But Lawrence was not standing for this last, stupid obstacle. He roped in Allenby and Egypt to help to settle the difficulty. " Must " was his demand, not " try." I only sat and wilted under an accumulating pile of translated vituperation. Lawrence and Joyce looked at some of the messages, and altered them both in code and translation. Three or four days this goes on, Lawrence moving in and out with a quiet fixity of purpose. The messages from Mecca are descending the scale into more malleable phrases, and one last effort, still further ironed out by Lawrence, brings Feisal round to resume his leadership and placates Ja'afer and his officers.

"September 1918.

" Somehow or other Lawrence balanced the scales of this and that opinion, with Joyce hovering largely and comfortingly in the background, and despite the quarrels we got our columns started for Azrak on the right day. Lawrence had a talk with Stirling and Young, and these two officers, rising to the occasion, cajoled and bluffed and swore, until at last, when we were nearly two days behind, the whole of the force was on its way.

" That done, Lawrence moves on. The Rolls tender, with Green at the wheel, starts off, Lawrence sitting by his side, crushed against Winterton (just borrowed from headquarters), while I am hunched up in the back with Nasr.

" Feisal watches the men and camels moving away, from the eminence of his new green Vauxhall—an orderly, picked fighting force which had literally been licked into shape by the master hands of such men as Joyce, Stirling and Young. Rolls was driving the other car, and both were getting all they could out of their machines. Forty miles an hour over surfaces varying from hard-baked mud to treacherous sand, and then along stretches covered with wire mesh, then twisting turns between odd-sized rocks, avoiding the knife-like edges of lava with inches to spare—that was driving.

"September 6.

" The campaign has actually begun ! We have our force of 450 camel corps of the Arab regulars, Arab Vickers and Hotchkiss gunners ; a French mountain battery of q.f. guns ;

three British armoured cars and tenders ; a section of Camel Ghurkhas, a company of Egyptian Camel Corps, and two aeroplanes. Lawrence's private bodyguard added to these make up a total of something like one thousand picked men, and we are concentrating at Azrak.

" The problem of supplies is a serious one, but so certain is Lawrence of success that he has made no provision whatever for our return. We have to win, or there will be no return, unless it is as prisoners. From what we know of it the Turks have promised all Lawrence's men something very special, dead or alive. However, much as he is sure of triumph, we small fry are disposed to wonder what will happen to us.

" But it is the move Lawrence has been waiting for, and now that he is moving at last we have confidence in the fact that he will not have left any loop-holes. Actually, the one thing we are really doubtful about is the success of the British arms on the other side of the Jordan. If they fail, heaven help us.

" *September* 8.

" We are at Azrak. Lawrence is definitely impatient. He wants to stride over all limits. Even now with success at hand, he remains just on the circle of comradeship, but not inside. There is a pardonable amount of nervousness in our own movements. We turn each corner searching for the never-appearing enemy. We scan the dancing horizons and see an army in each cloud of dust, a trap in each glint of metal.

" Lawrence walks in circles, or sits apart, drawn into self-communion. You feel he is saying with all his personality ' I am right, and you cannot alter it.' I am very little nearer a reasonable measurement of his character, except that I feel an unreasoning loyalty that has grown with each variation of the campaign. It is only a loyalty which differs in degree from that shown by all grades, and it demands an unquestioning acceptance of his final orders. This, we feel, is his last throw. He over-rides disbelief by his very silence, while the Arabs swear by him.

" *September* 10.

" Murphy and Junor, with their aeroplane, from Akaba. They say Feisal will be with us to-morrow.

" *September* 11.

" Joyce, Stirling and Young come in. The excitement grows. ' Where's Feisal ? ' ' Marshall is bringing him in.'

The arrivals fill Azrak with a company its ruins have never held before. A plane brings some sort of message from Palestine. Joyce, Stirling, Young, Peake and Scott-Higgins are in conference. Lawrence just isn't there.

"A GOOD LIAR IS BETTER THAN AN HONEST FOOL WHEN LIFE IS AT STAKE"

" LAWRENCE has tired of the noise and our company. Even with Feisal here, the chiefs of the local tribes, the Frenchmen and all the hotch-potch of our campaigners, he has left a rather bewildered Joyce to arrange some action which he himself was to engineer, and disappeared. He has gone off on his own, and it isn't easy to convince ourselves—and the Arabs—that he is merely resting. We never know what action is linked up with these movements.

" We are making a flying attack on the railway to the north, west and south of Deraa. This is being preceded with typical methods. ' Secret instructions ' for the collection of barley dumps for the British and for ourselves have been sent out, dumps which are supposedly for use in connection with a combined attack on Salt and Amman on the 18th of the month. ' Instructions ' have also been sent for the Beni Sakhr to gather at Ziza. Palestine helps in a confirmation of this plan, and as the orders have been sent out by most doubtful agents—which means they will be sold to the Turks at the earliest possible moment—the latter will now keep their eyes on the Jordan and east of it to the detriment of their Palestine commitments. Their lines in the Hejaz can only be kept by an expensive use of men, and the length of the defences creates conditions peculiarly vulnerable to a force of our character and mobility.

" *September* 13.

" To-day we have reached the country of the Druse. Fortunately for our future, one of our Bristol fighters spotted a German near Um el Jemal. It was a two-seater, and had been in sight long enough to have gathered an idea of our dispositions and probable intentions. Its knowledge was of little avail, for before it could turn and run it went down in flames from about two thousand feet. This was Murphy's bird, but his own wings were very much clipped in the action, with the result that our air-force is now reduced to one machine.

172

" To give colour to our fictitious operations, it is still necessary for us to demolish the line between Amman and Deraa. Actually, it is an essential part of the operations, as it will prevent reinforcements coming up from the south to Deraa. It marks a crucial point in the moves. If Lawrence shifts his force from Deraa to Amman he will not do Palestine any good, and as for our force, we shall be smashed like a nut between crackers. But in putting his force between Palestine and Deraa he makes the Turks reinforce the latter from the former, an extremely useful aid to Allenby. Of course it concentrates the Turks' attentions on us, an attention that can be too pressing, but we are making allowances for that.

" After all, we are built for speed of movement, and can go up and down the line at will, on the same old game of hit and run. The Turks' garrisons on the line must stay. Their long line of posts and the necessity for a fairly regular and safe communication by rail—all this keeps them well occupied from Damascus down to Ma'an, and any movements near the line keep them strung up in a tension very damaging to their morale.

" *September* 14.

" Peake, with one of the reconnaissance parties, has returned from the line near Azrak. They came across a party of hostile Arabs who simply could not accept the existence of so mixed a force as being anything but objects of suspicion—two armoured cars, Ghurkhas, Egyptians, and two strange beings, one with a light beard and the other with a dark one. If the Turkish lines were attacked, the Arabs would fight on behalf of the enemy. If they didn't attack the line, then the tribesmen—who numbered some two thousand—were our friends, but nothing else. These Arabs had their camels on both sides of the line, and in close proximity to the Turks. Here they were grazing their camels, trading with the Turks, and allowed many concessions. In return for them they acted as guard. There was nothing for the party to do but to turn back and report to Lawrence.

" *September* 16.

" As we are going up the line we see our first big crowd of bombers, on their way from Ramleh to Deraa. We *are* growing up ! The actual blowing up of the line was left to the armoured cars, and before a post of the Turks knew anything about the presence of a hostile force, we had taken them open-mouthed.

"Lawrence went over to the bridge. This was no active service : it was an archæological survey. He took his time about it, studied its architecture, commented on the flattering inscription to Abd el Hamid, and said that the whole thing was "very pleasant." One hundred and fifty pounds of gun-cotton altered the inscription considerably.

"*September* 17.

"We are near Tell Arar, and Lawrence has been planting some of his ' tulips.' The Egyptians did six hundred pairs of rails in this fashion, and well pleased with ourselves we climbed to the top of Tell Arar, to see Deraa four miles off. We were not looking because we must, but because we wanted to see the country ahead. But we were too impetuous, too inquisitive. There were nine enemy aeroplanes on the aerodrome outside Deraa station, and before we could get away from the sky-line and out of sight they had spotted us.

"They got into the air very quickly, and were soon round us like a swarm of angry bees. They bombed and machine-gunned us as we scattered for the shelter of the hills, and had accounted for at least fifty before our air-force of one (the B.E.12) sailed up and into the fight. The armoured cars took to the sides of the valley quickly, but fragments of bombs were finding their way through the observation slits, to the discomfort of the drivers and much to their annoyance, but without any more serious result.

"The B.E.12 was a much slower machine than any of the enemy, but in their anxiety to dispose of the intruder, the whole of the enemy planes turned from us to chase him. With one eye on the manoeuvres of our solitary defender, we scampered back again to view our casualties. Those who could not walk we dragged to the shade of the rocks and gave them very rough attention, leaving a little water by their side while we arranged for camel litters to take them back to the nearest village. The worst cases we finished—we had no hospital equipment, and could not carry casualties. Those with mere flesh wounds were patched up, and they carried on.

"It was no time for sentiment. Junor had disappeared with the others on his tail. We had to collect our effectives and prepare for the enemy's return, which was inevitable. Part of the crowd were sent into Mezerib to cut the line there and create a diversion. Shortly after their departure, there were shouts and cries, and to our astonishment we saw Junor returning, with three unwelcome attendants. He managed to avoid them, putting his bus through a series of amazing evolutions that threatened to burst its ancient frame at any moment. He then circled us and dropped a message to say he was getting out of petrol. We were firing ineffectual bursts at the attackers, who were very much out of range, and then Junor landed on bad ground. His run ended in an abrupt somersault, and as we ran through a burst of bullets we saw him scramble out from underneath his bus and crawl to one side. As he did so, a direct hit from a bomb dismantled it, but even as the shower from the explosion was still raining round, Junor was back in the wreckage, pulling and tugging at his Lewis gun, swearing at such a rate that it was nothing but unintelligible gibberish. Young and the others ran up and helped him free it, and Junor ran across the open to a Ford tender which was fussing about in the shadow of the gorge, mounted his gun on the back-board, and, with Kirkbride spent the rest of the time peppering the Turks with tracer bullets.

" For some reason this was the end of the enemy's bombing activities for that day, and we devoted the rest of our efforts to Mezerib. Joyce and Stirling were behind, high up on a ridge, with the difficult job of seeing that our rearguard was unhampered.

" *September* 18.
" We intended to attack Tell el Shehab, and had got within three hundred yards of the Turks' positions when we saw that reinforcements had arrived with guns. A German colonel was in command, and taking it all round they were much too formidable a mark for us. Our lives were more dependent on discretion than valour, and we retreated quickly. What was more to the point, we did it without attracting attention.

" *September* 19.
" This finds us at Remthe, a post well defended by artillery and a strong guard. The resistance has been stubborn but the post has gone, and the big bridge to the north of Nasib left to our mercy. It was one of the finest we had seen in the

campaign, standing on three very good seven-metre arches, and was the 79th bridge demolished by Lawrence.

" Kirkbride and his Scotch servant have come in, both dirty, bearded and utterly disreputable, but cheerful.

" *September* 20.

" We got up very early this morning, and our departure was hastened. A field gun, mounted on a train, found us out and speeded us on our way, landing several rounds on the rearguard. We then made for Umtaiye, where Lawrence had seen an enemy aeroplane, and he went out with the armoured cars to give it an official welcome. When we got within sight of the 'drome the force had grown to three, but this did not deter us. The approach, however, was very difficult, and before we could get within effective distance they were warned. We hadn't got a shot in when they were round us, and we were the attacked. Fighting in an armoured car is all very well, but it makes a very good target for aeroplanes, and it was only good luck on our part and bad marksmanship on theirs that enabled us to escape without serious damage.

" However, we managed to dispose of one of the machines by putting a few hundred bullets into it—it ventured much too low and too near—but the other two haunted us all day. When their bombs were exhausted they hung around swooping down and pelting us with machine-gun fire, and at the end of the day we found ourselves without many of our best fighters. Harassed as we were, we had to scatter, but the cars managed to escape further attention and persuaded the repair party, busy on the bridge, back to Mafrak at top speed.

" *September* 21.

" An Australian pilot landed at Um Serab with dispatches from Allenby. Young, after much bullying, had succeeded in getting some ground cleared for a temporary aerodrome. Lawrence was very much concerned about the difficulties of his men. The German bombs and machine gunning had struck a heavy blow at the nerves of the Arabs, who were still inclined to scatter in panic at the enemy's planes. They did not trouble the small force of regulars who were the core of the operations, but the irregulars who were maintaining a guerrilla campaign on the flanks and rearguards of the enemy units, and who were also keeping the country ahead for the advance of the Sherifians.

" Lawrence went back with the pilot to appeal to Allenby for British 'planes to engage the Germans, and three Bristol fighters from an Australian squadron, in the hands of Ross Smith, Peters and Headlam, with Mustard, Traill and Lilly as observers, flew over to the Arab encampment before seven in the morning.

" One enemy machine was attacked, forced down and burnt by Smith and Mustard as soon as they arrived. Later the same two attacked three Germans single-handed, forced two down on the desert, and drove the third to the aerodrome at Deraa. Peters and Traill shot down another, killing both pilot and observer.

" It was very quick work, nearly too quick to be believed, and in that hour we saw the end of the enemy's aerial offensive. It meant a lot to our small force. We could not afford to lose twenty to thirty men daily, as we had been doing, and their continuous reconnaissance tended to discount all our chances of surprise.

" Lawrence came over to Young, Kirkbride and the pilots, discussed Allenby's advance, and then said : ' but we're in the way of the Fourth Turkish Army.' His remark had a sinister hint—' we're in the way ! ' The same day Lawrence went back to Azrak and returned with a Handley Page. When the machine was in close view, and landed so easily, it astonished us, but it was a miracle to the natives. It was the ' father of all devil birds,' and they amused themselves for a while dashing about on horseback under its outstretched wings.

"AT THE NARROW PASSAGE THERE IS
NO BROTHER AND NO FRIEND"

" September 22.

" South of Um Serab the armoured cars went into action at 8 a.m. for an attack on the right flank. They proceeded against a three-arch bridge, and in face of much opposition the two cars fought their way to within five hundred yards of the bridge, which was strongly held by the enemy with two machine-guns in position behind several railway trucks on the south side. The cars had to retire behind a small hill, their tyres having been shot away. They took a quarter of an hour to change—absolutely marvellous work—and then were back at the attack. The crews got out and bombed their way to the bridge, fired the charges and got away with the dust still falling round them.

" September 25.

" Between Nasib and Mafrak the first stragglers began to come up from the south and immediately Lawrence spread his men on the hills on either side. They began to snipe at the hurrying Turks, some of whom dropped behind the rocks and attempted to reply to this new attack. The others, with one desire only—escape—increased the pace of their retreat and struggled north. Occasionally a band of the Arab horsemen would swing out from behind a bend in the valley, swoop down with shrill cries on the fleeing enemy, dash in, kill and turn about for the hills.

" The narrow gorge began to fill up, and in the end the desperate Turks could stand the pace no longer. In an attempt to save their lives they abandoned all the transport and the cannon. The bustle of the retreat became a headlong flight. Sniped at from the hills, raided on all sides by the fierce rushes of the Arab tribesmen, frightened that if they did not hurry north the pursuing British would get them, they scurried forward. The road along which the Turks were retreating was a wadi, an old river bed, dried up for centuries and used only for camel caravans. Precipitous crags and rocks rose sheer on either side, with edges that tore arms and legs when any attempt was made to find a footing.

"The Turks were driven to what remained of the narrow, winding track of the valley. They could not scatter. There were horses, men, camels, transport, guns—a hopeless, fear-stricken mass. As they straggled pell-mell north, death struck from all sides. Bullets from unseen marksmen dropped them in the path of unheeding, crushing feet. The stragglers at the sides fell to the swords and daggers of the raiding horsemen, and some to the stones and bludgeons of revengeful villagers.

"Others were knocked under foot by the scattering rush of scared animals. Then destruction dropped on them from the skies. All the aeroplanes had to do was to follow the winding line of the retreating force and drop their bombs. In the end even the airmen got tired, and left the valley to its shambles.

"For miles the road was strewn with clothing and arms. Miserable and thin ponies, mules, donkeys and cattle were all over the place, dead or dying from wounds and exhaustion. At one place two machine-guns pointed crazily to the heavens on the top of a heap of dead and wounded.

"Nothing could be done for the latter. We had to push on. Many of the prisoners surrendered without fight. Cavalry, ridiculously mounted on tiny starved ponies, infantry—Turkish, German and Austrian—camels, donkeys, all clamouring for water which could only be got slowly from a well.

"We took a few German prisoners who gave themselves up at the bridge. Poor devils, they had tried to escape, and the Arab villagers had looted them of everything. They left them with only a pair of drawers and a vest, no footwear. They were in a bad way—some with ghastly mutilations, when they got to us."

"A MOUTH THAT PRAYS, A HAND THAT KILLS"

" Lawrence called his crowd in and held a council of war. He is now arranging for his force to be placed between Damascus and Deraa. By this move he hopes to deal with the retreating Fourth Army, and, strength and opportunity being available, hold the remnants of the enemy who might get into the district from Semakh and Irbid. Allenby asked Lawrence to communicate the following to Feisal :

" (1) There is no objection to your Highness entering Damascus as soon as you consider you can do so with safety. (2) I am sending troops to Damascus, and I hope they will arrive there in four or five days from now.

" I trust your Highness's forces will be able to co-operate but you should not relax your pressure in the Deraa district as it is of vital importance to cut off the Turks retiring from Ma'an, Amman, and Es Salt."

" *September* 26

" We moved with such rapidity, and secrecy, that the Turks between Ghazale and Ezra have surrendered more through astonishment than anything else. The enemy are rattled. They do not know whether our force is nine hundred or nine thousand. The Germans have destroyed their remaining aeroplanes (five I think) and orders have been issued for the evacuation of Deraa.

" Despite our successes, our position is a precarious one. We have been seriously depleted by casualties, and are likely to be overwhelmed at any time by any large wave of retreating Turks. The hills around are seething with movement, and we have to move along each valley with extreme caution. Any bend might bring us face to face with the enemy, and we cannot afford, neither can we stand, a fixed engagement.

" Rations are limited, tempers frayed, and we see danger in every movement in the hills. One can never be too certain of the tribesmen through whose country we are passing."

" At dawn we arrived at Sheikh Saad, to see two Austro-Turk machine gun companies on the way to Kuneitra to oppose the British. Our luck still held. They were the surprised party, and before they could get into action were forced to surrender. They had fifteen machine guns with them, as well as rifles and ammunition, but the sight of the encircling enemies must have demoralised them. One pathetic figure had retained sufficient of his property to be able to wave something white and shout, ' I am a major ; we surrender.'

" It was touch and go then. A mistake, and delay, and the first burst from them, and they could have wiped us all out.

" Tired out, desperate and weary, we have been more or less on the move for fourteen days and nights, fighting, very rarely retreating, making flying dashes across and up and down the line, living on our ever decreasing store of rations, nerves on edge with the uncertainty of our position.

" We do not know whether Allenby has succeeded. Our force is now less than nine hundred, and to add to the tension a plane dropped a message telling us that we are in the way of two retreating Turkish columns—one six thousand strong and the other two thousand. The first is a hopeless proposition and we are leaving it alone. The latter is a different matter, and we are going out to Tafas to meet it, as it is about our size. We are arranging at the same time for the outskirts of the larger column to be attacked and worried by the Hauran peasants. This may whittle it down to a proposition within our power.

" We met an infantry battalion on the way, and for the good of our future had the best of the encounter, but this little action delayed our progress, and the Turks went through Tafas ahead of us. But while we were delayed, we halted in sullen, vengeful rage. The Turks had, even in retreat, got hold of all the women they could and raped them, generally killing them afterwards. Their death was never pleasant. We counted the bodies of about fifty women and infants lying mutilated in the dusty paths, killed with lances and rifles.

" Death by now is so common ; yet, however blinded by blood and weary with fighting, how strange and awful to see a little child a victim. We Europeans regarded the scene with stony, ominous silence. Some of the Arabs shrieked and gibbered with rage, but all were full of that daft insane desire to *feel* the enemy in one's fingers. For a moment it seemed as if the Bedouin would break from the column and lose their lives in a hopeless attack on the retreating Turks, but we held them together, and just stared and stared at the enemy's handiwork.

" Then a maniacal yell from Talal turned us. The villages here belonged to him. They were his people, children of his tribe, women of his men. He was trembling. We all respected him and knew him to be one of the finest, and yet the craftiest of fighters. But this was too much for him.

" He yelled again, wrapped his face in his kafieh and headed his horse for the enemy. They were still in sight, and you could see them turn as they heard the beat of the frenzied gallop. Machine guns and rifles were turned on the mad rider, but his speed was so great that it was not until he was among their lances that he and his mare actually collapsed, riddled with bullets.

" Lawrence quickly aroused us from the daze that seemed to fog our movements. ' No prisoners,' he ordered, curtly, quietly. And so we split the enemy into three sections. One with Jemal Pasha got away, thanks to a wonderful fight put up by his machine gunners and also to the speed of his cars. The other two sections were wiped out.

" In and out the valleys, up the hills, into corners, we chased them. Some fought and died like cornered rats, fighting to the last and carrying an enemy with them to the peace of death. Others suffered the end even as they raised their hands in surrender. ' No prisoners.' Some fled from the avenging death, along the valley, up hill, anywhere—but found it from behind, either by knife or bullet. No prisoners !

" One crowd escaped the slaughter. Our reserves, fresh and not knowing the terrible sights of the previous hours, had caught and rounded them up, and they stood in a huddled mass as we gathered together again, spent of all effort. We were too weary to kill any more and anyway there was no one standing up to fight. Then came a cry from a corner, a shouting, and the men round the prisoners began to crowd and mill about. One of ours had been found pinned to the ground with two mortal thrusts from saw-bayonets. There had been the outrages, the little children, Talal—other memories of sitting on hills watching, impotent, the Turks throwing our wounded into burning railway trucks—and then this.

" Lawrence rapped out an order. We turned our Hotchkiss and Lewis guns on that company of prisoners—250 there were,

Turks, Germans and Austrians. Better that way than have the Arabs run amok among them. In two or three minutes they were a huddle of dead, tumbled down like nine-pins. We only stopped firing when the heap was silent and motionless. Reason does not rule when the brain is tortured with horror; and death is death, whether it comes to one or a hundred.

" Exhaustion has slowed us down, but the Rualla horse, comparatively fresh, has attacked the trenches at Deraa and blotted out the enemy, riding over the positions and taking them at a gallop. They brought in over five hundred prisoners, guns, etc., but no stores. We cannot get food, all having been destroyed by the retreating forces, and we are half starved.

" The condition of the wounded was terrible, lying in hollows, or in rows on the level stretches, with dull blotches of brown where the sand had sucked greedily at life. That dull moist brown also caked faces and bodies as the wind scattered it or our feet and those of scampering animals splayed it around as we rushed helter-skelter in our business of killing.

" Shouts for water, groans for water, and signs that had no meaning—all these we had to ignore. Some of the wounded were beyond hope, so we shot again as we passed them to give them liberty from this tortuous bond, whether Turk or Arab. Then on again, in the service of freedom ! (Writ sarcastic !).

" Lawrence and Nasr have been in to Deraa, the former to clash with General Barrow, who objected to the lawlessness of Bedouin war as compared with his own brand. Young has left us to join the British.

" We picked up from messengers more copies of British army wires, which Lawrence and the others crowded round to read. Here's one :

" ' 28.9.18. Chaytor to Desert Corps : Beni Sakhr tribe in large numbers south of Ziza threatened to attack surrendered Turks. Have been told that Turks will be protected by force if necessary. Please send someone who knows Beni Sakhr tribal chiefs urgently to prevent trouble.' "

" Lawrence sent an envoy right away.

" Another message was tapped from the Germans :

" ' Armed bands of Arabs arriving in Damascus. Population flooded with British leaflets.'

" The afternoon and night passed in uneasy speculation. Have we won ? Where are the rest of the enemy ? What are

their numbers ? Do they know where we are ? The suspense
is terrible, to be so near success, and yet in so much danger,
likely to be wiped out any time by an overwhelming horde of a
fleeing enemy.

" An aeroplane dropped the following for Lawrence :

" ' 28.9.18. Advance Desert Corps to General Headquarters : Route march will be so timed as to arrive within
striking distance Damascus 0500 (5 a.m.). Every pre-
caution to be taken to prevent troops entering town.' "

" *September* 30

" We had had time to think of the Turkish column from
Deraa. It had left there six thousand strong, but the tribesmen
by skirmish, attack, sniping, ambush, reduced them to something like three thousand by the time they reached Mesmiye.
At Kiswe they collided with General Gregory's brigade, and
this cost them another thousand. That reduced them to
within the limit approachable by our depleted numbers, and
we set about the final action. Nasr and Nuri Shala'an joined
forces, with their slaves, and, knowing that the British were due
to arrive at any time, threw themselves into the woods to delay
the column's progress.

" Stirling and Lawrence turned back in the Blue Mist Rolls
tender, at full speed, to get the horse artillery pushed forward
by the leading cavalry division. They got to the Kiswe road
just before dawn, but were pulled up by a Bengal Lancers'
patrol, taken prisoner, and prodded forward at the lance-point,
despite great protests and very good English oaths, until at last
an English officer was reached, to whom the situation was
explained.

" This awkward difficulty over, Gregory opened on the
enemy with his horse artillery. By dark they were fleeing from
all manner of death. We were on one side, the bloodthirsty
Nuri Shala'an and Nasr on the other and all around were little
groups of villagers, taking toll. Through the hills and over the
passes to Mania they fled—there to run into traps prepared by
the Wuld Ali and the Abu Tayi.

" Copies of the latest wires from the British stirred Lawrence
to swift movement :

" ' 1955 (7.55 p.m.), 30.9.18 : Advance Desert Corps to
Headquarters : Australian Division west and north Damascus not entering account machine guns in orchards, gardens,

etc. . . . . Will surround Damascus to-morrow and demand surrender.'

" ' Headquarters to Advance Desert Corps, 2055 (8.55 p.m.), 30.9.18 : Fourth Turks army retreating into Damascus and attempting to leave by train and road. Australian division is astride Amara and Barada roads. To-morrow troops will surround town cutting off all avenues escape and to obtain surrender Turkish army by bringing all descriptions fire to bear on its troops taking care avoid all holy places and property. If possible no troops enter town. Australian division will maintain present position.'

" Another tapped wire from German headquarters said :

" ' 30.9.18. Damascus full of Feisal's agents. Sherif's flag flown from many houses.' "

" *October* 1.

" DAMASCUS ! Seven o'clock in the morning. We saw and cheered a party of Australians on the bridge over the Abana They looked tired.

" Our Arab horse got into the town last evening, to hear that there had been a bitter fight between Turks and Germans over transport. We had wondered why there were so many German corpses lying about.

" Lawrence rode in with Stirling, Nuri and Nasr and went straight to the Town Hall. Ammunition dumps were going up, and all the streets jammed with wildly excited inhabitants, most of whom were making our arrival dangerous by firing salutes which sometimes went straight up in the air, but others whistled unpleasantly close to the ear. As a contrast, through some streets we were smothered by scented flower petals and even scent poured recklessly out of bottles by joy-crazed women.

" We heard that the Arabs' independence was proclaimed about two o'clock yesterday, while Jemal Pasha and other Turkish and German commanders were still in the city.[1] The

[1] " ' Between 6.30 and 7 a.m., October 1, Major Olden (second in command of the 10th A.L.H.), galloped up to the Serai, and he and Temperley, taking their revolvers and followed by a few troopers, entered the buildings and demanded to see the Civil Governor. . . .

" ' When the clamour caused by the appearance of the Australians had ceased, Emir Said advanced. (Early in the afternoon he had advised Djemal Pasha to leave the city, hoisted the green flag of the Hejaz over the Serai, and proclaimed Hussein King of the Arabs). Olden, unaware of the situation, told him that Damascus was surrounded by many thousands of Chauval's troops and resistance was impossible. . . .

" ' Emir Said said : ' In the name of the civil population of Damascus I welcome the British Army." Olden left immediately and rode straight through the city for Homs.' " (" Australian Official History.")

people straightway refused to sell provisions to the enemy, even for gold.

"Feisal and Lawrence quietly removed the flag and the bronze wreath laid by the Kaiser on Saladin's tomb in 1898."

Here the personal narrative must end.

More official wires handed to Lawrence later completed the story of the entry to Damascus :

"1.10.18. Advance Desert Corps to Headquarters 0515 (5.15 a.m.). Fourth Cavalry Division marched 0300 (3 a.m.) in touch with Sherifian troops and blocking all roads to south and south-west. Thus it is hoped to obtain surrender of Turkish army in Damascus."

"0600 (6 a.m.). Desert Corps : Damascus taken. Understand Lawrence's Arabs have entered. Desert Corps troops surrounded town all sides."

"1625 (4.25 p.m.). Desert Corps to General Head-quarters : Outskirts Damascus entered from northwards by Australian division last night. Colonel Lawrence and Arabs entered this morning. Our troops occupied clearing town collecting prisoners' material. Have left civilian administration in Vali's hands, with assistance Lawrence until arrival Clayton."

Abd el Kader[1] who had been thrown out of the Town Hall by Lawrence, went into the streets and preached that the Arab Army were only tools in Christian hands, and that it behoved sincere Moslems to strike a last blow for the faith against the Sherifians and the British. He was captured, but his fellow conspirator Mohammed Said hid and was not discovered.

It had been decided to shoot them both when captured, but before Said was found Feisal arrived and began his rule in proper oriental style by a general amnesty.

Abd el Kader did not profit long by his reprieve. He was too impatient to be a good conspirator. He took up his arms, and galloped down the street to Feisal's house, firing shot after shot at the door. He shouted to him to come out and meet him. The sentry took cover for a time, but eventually lost patience and put a bullet through his head.

London had wired to Allenby on October 1 :

---

[1] The man who betrayed Lawrence during his raid on the Yarmak valley, see pp. 109-10.

"At your arrival at Damascus you are authorised by His Majesty's Government to hoist the Arab flag there."

However, it was not until the 3rd that he saw Feisal. The Sherifian commander, attended by a resplendent bodyguard of kinsfolk and supporters, had entered Damascus at full gallop amid shouts and yells of victory. Allenby came up to the Town Hall at the head of a long line of high-powered motor cars, dignified enough, but an unimaginative and mechanical entry for a man whose brilliant use of cavalry had helped to sweep the Turks from Palestine and Syria.

Lawrence attended the meeting as a matter of course, and skilled as he was at reading Feisal's moods, even he was astounded at the dismay and puzzlement so evident on the Emir's face when the British Commander-in-Chief announced that he was prepared to recognise the inclusion of Damascus in the area to be controlled by the Arabs.

Was this not known in the beginning, he asked. Why tell it at the end?

During the last days of September the Turkish sanitary arrangements had utterly collapsed. The hospitals were full of dead and dying. In the streets, carts rumbled along from dawn to dark, piled high with dead. Occasionally a stiff bundle would fall off to the delight of the crowds of jeering children who were escorting them to the vast burial field just outside the city. They would rush forward, hold the head and feet, and with a " one, two and three " sling the body back again.

"WHEN THE LION WITHDRAWS THE HYENAS PLAY"

ALLENBY'S orders now reflected the inevitable conflictions of the absolutely opposed Arab and French agreements with Britain. His talk with Feisal on the 3rd included a request to the Arab Prince "not to issue any proclamations without consulting him," but one had already been issued to the people of Syria, informing them that Hussein's Government embraced all Syrian towns, the government being based upon the equality of all Arab-speaking peoples, irrespective of race and religion.

The Chief of the Lebanon Druse brought in to Allenby's headquarters a proclamation from the Damascus authorities calling upon the Lebanon authorities to uphold Feisal. Allenby told him to tear it up. "No orders are valid," he said, "except those issued through my Military Governor."

In Beirut the Arabs had cleared the enemy out long before the arrival of the British or the French, and had taken over the municipal government. Then Colonel Pieappe assumed some sort of control, and trouble developed at once because both the French and Arab flags were flying. The French ordered the Arabs to lower their flag, and the latter, naturally, ignored them. Allenby wired Feisal, asking him to use all his diplomacy in lessening the tension, with the result the Arabs there made a tacit acceptance of orders, not from the French, though, but from the British military authorities.

Beirut had merely imitated the people of Damascus, turning on the Turkish Garrison and making them prisoners, following this with the hoisting of the Arab flag and a declaration of independence. Inhabitants of Tripoli followed suit on the 3rd, and on the 5th Baalbek in the south and Latakia in the north raised the Arab standard. On the 7th Antioch flew the new flag.

On the 8th the Allied troops entered Beirut, after all news of the Arab rising had been suppressed in the newspapers. France had to have the honour of claiming its liberation from the Turks. Then Allenby organised a drive to Aleppo, and the Town Hall fell to a bombing party of the Arab army. From there they marched to Muslimiya, the junction of the Syrian, Baghdad and Anatolian railways, and there, with the capture of the station the day before the Turks asked for an armistice, the Arabs reached the climax of their military achievements.

Lawrence had disappeared completely, and Feisal floundered in bewilderment. There was no Arab independence. His rule in Damascus was under the surveillance of a misunderstanding military machine : they were talking of the recognition of Arab independence in this and that area, with the British and French alternatively predominant. The Syrian zone was already preserved for the judgment of a distant peace conference, Palestine was barred, and Feisal warned in person by Allenby that he must not attempt, for the present, any control of any of the districts.

The request to Feisal to withdraw his representative from Beirut resulted in a very spirited communication being sent to Allenby. After the usual complimentary preamble, Feisal plunged straight into the heart of matters :

" I am ready to obey your orders in everything, but at the same time the withdrawal from Beirut of . . . my Arab Military Governor there, who went because the people asked for him, is a matter not affecting my personal honour, but the cause of which I am guardian.

" It is still unfortunately beyond doubt that the Arab people of Syria view with a distrust which is traditional the intentions of the French Government toward their Syria. I would urge most strongly that if you wish to allay this feeling you will arrange for a joint formal declaration to be issued by the British and French Governments that there will be no annexation by a foreign power in Syria, including the Lebanon, and that at the end of the war its peoples will be allowed freely to determine their own future.

" As regards the situation in Beirut, I feel I must ask, in view of the clearly stated sentiments of the population that the Arab flag may continue to be flown, together with the flags of the Allies, when my governor is withdrawn, and that the existing machinery of the Arab Government remains in existence under your Military Governor. If your Excellency approves, please send the following to Shukri el Ayubi (the governor) confidentially, from me : ' Return at once to Damascus to discuss with me urgent matters. Arab troops should be placed at disposal of the military governor appointed by General Allenby.'

" I am visiting you at General Headquarters to obtain your advice on the whole question of policy."

While the letter gave a hint of conciliation, Allenby found the discussion with Feisal and his advisers a very different matter. There was no Lawrence to bridge the gulf, and after six hours of argument, in which there was no abatement of the definite anti-French attitude of the Arabs, Allenby found it politic to recommend that Feisal's suggestion of the issue of a diplomatic joint declaration be adopted. It would at least help to smooth away some of the Arab prejudice, and prevent, he said, any suspicion that the appointment of a French military governor would involve political consequences to the prejudice of Arab interests.

The appeal with regard to the flags might also be met, he said, as this was a matter of honour, and not of expediency. He emphasised that the difficulties had nothing whatever to do with " promises," but that they were the outcome of a very real prejudice on the part of the Arabs against any suggestion of a purely French administration.

Allenby did, however, find it necessary to warn Feisal that while he was recognising Arab independence in certain areas under the Sykes-Picot agreement, French interests must be accepted as predominant in Syria. If Feisal made any attempt to control the " blue " area, he said, his case would be prejudiced at once, and so far as the Lebanon was concerned, the situation there was far too delicate for him to turn his eyes in that direction.

" A CAMEL DOES NOT SELL HIS HUMP, AND WATER IN A JUG DOES NOT TURN TO SOUR MILK "

THE Arab agitation against " broken promises," and the hint of definite trouble with the French, provoked questions in the House of Commons, and in an attempt to reassure public opinion Lord Robert Cecil told the House on October 31, as an instance of Britain's attitude in the matter, that General Allenby was authorised on October 1 to allow the Arab flag to be hoisted at Damascus.

Lawrence, meanwhile, realising the Arabs would soon know of their " betrayal," had hurried to London, arriving there on October 24. His presence there, strangely enough coincided with an investiture, and the day before Turkey signed the armistice he was invited to Buckingham Palace.

For about an hour and a half before the actual ceremony King George and Queen Mary heard Lawrence's own story, and, at the end, his King and Queen listened with grave and troubled faces while he told them, quietly yet firmly, that he had pledged his word to Feisal, and the British Government were now about to let the Arabs down through the Sykes-Picot agreement. He, Lawrence, had been made an Emir among the Arabs, and intended to stick to them through thick and thin, and, if necessary, to oppose the French in order to recover Syria.

Lawrence went on to explain that he did not know that he had ever been gazetted, or what the etiquette was in such matters, but he hoped the King would forgive any want of courtesy on his part in not taking the decorations.

The interview was at an end, and as Lawrence, naturally, had to attend the investiture as a Royal Command, there was nothing but a whispered question from King George, an obvious refusal, and Lawrence passed out of the wondering company, leaving his decorations in the hands of a flustered courtier. Very few knew of Lawrence's private talk with his Sovereign, and when the news leaked out, the services were full of talk of " insult to the King," *ad nauseam.*

The capture of Aleppo and the subsequent armistice with Turkey forced the British cabinet into an immediate review of their position in relation to Syria, Palestine and Mesopotamia. The possibility of British troops invading Syria had been envisaged in the early days of the war, and this fact, together with the probable consequences of peace, had really led to the Sykes-Picot agreement.

Official quarters were quite frank in regard to their opinions about the obstacle to a satisfactory solution of the problems, particularly in connection with Syria. It was known before, and it was perfectly obvious now, that France would be intensely jealous of interference in Syria. The claim was regarded as a sentimental one, for it had no relation to any military conquest, and the 1916 agreement, now impracticable because of altered circumstances, threatened to become a source of danger to Britain's friendship with France.

The Arab revolt had been viewed by all those outside it as a strategic exercise. The Anglo-Arab conquest of Syria, and the major hand which the Arabs themselves had taken in its deliverance from Ottoman rule—for there had been very little military assistance from the French—had really discredited the 1916 arrangement. There was a feeling that efforts should be made to secure its cancellation. The Arabs' distrust of the French was intense. It was the former, largely, who had conquered Syria. Had the French ever done so, they asked.

It was not an easy time for British advisers. For imperial reasons it would be better to have an Arab state in Syria than a French administration, for despite France's alliance with Britain, her hold on Syria would be a rivalry to British interests not only in Syria but elsewhere in the Middle East.

Secret diplomacy had dragged Britain into a situation which had all the elements of a dangerous quarrel between the interested parties, and it was not unnatural that her cabinet viewed with eagerness the avenue of escape offered by President Wilson's democratic solution of popular determination. In this way the Sykes-Picot agreement could be circumvented, for it would secure that in any conference dealing with the partition of Turkey, and in particular the disposal of Syria, the Arabs would have equal representation with the British, French, American and Italians.

The danger was obviously recognized, and on November 9

a joint declaration was issued by the British and French governments :

" The French Government, in agreement with the British Government, has decided to issue the following joint declaration in order to give to the *non-Turkish population between the Taurus and the Persian Gulf* (my italics—E.R.) the assurance that the two countries, each in its own sphere, intend to secure for them the amplest autonomy, with the aim of guaranteeing their liberation and the development of their civilization.

" The aim which France and Britain have in view in prosecuting in the east the war let loose by German ambition is the complete and final liberation of the peoples so long oppressed by the Turks, and the establishment of national governments and administrations deriving their authority from the initiative and free choice of the native populations.

" In order to give effect to these intentions, France and Great Britain have agreed to encourage and assist the establishment of native governments and administrations in Syria and Mesopotamia already liberated by the allies, and in the territories which they are proceeding to liberate, and they have agreed to recognize such governments as soon as they are effectively established.

" So far from desiring to impose specific institutions upon the populations of these regions, their sole object is to ensure, by their support and effective assistance, that the governments and administrations adopted by these regions of their own free will shall be exercised in the normal way. The function which the allied governments claim for themselves in the liberated territories is to ensure impartial and equal justice for all ; to facilitate the economic development of the country by encouraging local initiative ; to promote the diffusion of education, and to put an end to the divisions too long exploited by Turkish policy."

The full text appeared in French and in France only. The English version omitted the whole of the first paragraph, an omission which could bear an unfortunate interpretation.

A week later, Lawrence submitted to the Government a comprehensive scheme for dealing with the question. In this he advocated three Arab states outside the Hejaz and its dependencies :

Lower Mesopotamia (under Abdullah) ;

Upper Mesopotamia (under Zeid) ;

Syria (under Feisal).

He suggested that Hussein should remain King of the Hejaz, the succession being carried on by his eldest son, Ali.

The boundaries he suggested between Upper and Lower Mesopotamia would run from the confluence of the Tigris and the Great Zab to Anah, on the Euphrates, and from there to Biridjik. The Euphrates itself would form the western boundary of Upper Mesopotamia. The northern boundary would lie through Urfa and Diarbekir to the Tigris.

Both states, it was suggested, should be in the sphere of British influence, and Lower Mesopotamia itself placed under effective British control.

Colonel A. T. Wilson, acting Civil Commissioner for Iraq, opposed the scheme. He considered it unworkable.

M. Clemenceau and Lloyd George, however, were already discussing the details of an arrangement which would satisfy their respective governments and at the same time, as they thought, clear up the confusion of the war-time agreements. The Arabs being impracticable folk, they argued, it followed that their desires were impracticable, and gradually the territorial problem raised by their demands dropped down the scale until they became a purely secondary consideration.

The area of battle shifted from straightforward hostilities to the quicksands of diplomacy. Lawrence left for Paris, and Feisal joined him there in an attempt to snatch a remnant from the " bargain-sale." They were armed with many documentary promises, but there were too many barriers to their fulfilment.

Feisal, believing in the value of propaganda, had ideas about getting all the principal organisations and municipalities throughout Arabia to send telegrams to the Peace Conference, demanding independence for their countries and naming himself as their representative, but Lawrence gently discouraged him.

The joint declaration of November 8 had been an Anglo-French attempt to amalgamate all their promises to the Arabs in a plausible whole. But it could not cancel the requirements of the Sykes-Picot agreement, and it would be impossible for Britain to avoid meeting the bill incurred by the Balfour declaration.

As Jemal Pasha had written to Feisal in 1917[1]: "You really think you can establish an Arab Government, but if . . . Palestine is to be international, Syria French, Iraq and Mesopotamia British, how can such an Arab government be ?"

That was the question to which Lawrence and Feisal sought an answer.

[1] See p. 118.

"WHEN THE DOGS ARE SATED THEY MAKE PRESENTS TO EACH OTHER OF WHAT REMAINS"

THERE was plenty of speculation, but little of truth, in the reports of Lawrence's activities during the Peace Conference, and no useful source of information on his work was available until David Hunter Miller published his monumental diary.

"One evening in January" (he wrote) "I dined with Lord Robert Cecil at the Majestic. There were seven of us, the others being Colonel Lawrence ; Lionel Curtis, a gentleman who had spent some years recently in Poland and its vicinity ; M. Westongard ; Mr. Bullitt and Lord Robert Cecil's secretary. Somewhat to my surprise the conversation did not turn to the League of Nations, except indirectly.

"The discussion was about Poland, and Colonel Lawrence's expeditions and excursions, and the future of the Turkish empire. There was a unanimous opinion among the British present that the United States should take Constantinople, and agreement, though reluctant, on the part of Colonel Lawrence, that the United States should administer Syria.[1]

"Colonel Lawrence's attitude is distinctly anti-French ; in fact, he said so to me as we walked home together. His story was most remarkable. Perhaps the two most interesting things were these : first in talking of the pilgrimages of the Mohammedans to Mecca, he said that the matter had now been arranged so that the pilgrims were not robbed ; second, that Prince Feisal, who is now in Paris, made a speech at Glasgow in Arabic which he (Colonel Lawrence) interpreted. After the speech various persons told Colonel Lawrence that the gestures and facial expressions of the Prince were such that they could practically understand what he said before the interpretation.

[1] One of the first proposals was the formation of a great federation of all the Arab states from the Red Sea to the Persian Gulf, free from any Turkish domination and under the protection of the United States. "The Arabs of this most ancient race," Feisal said to the press on January 19—Lawrence acting as his interpreter— "desire to become the youngest independent State in Asia, and they appeal to America as the most powerful protector of the freedom of man."

" As a matter of fact, he said, before the Prince got up to speak, he leaned over to Colonel Lawrence and said to him in Arabic, ' Instead of making a speech I am going to get up and recite a page from the Koran, and as your interpretation you can say anything you damn well please.' "

On January 29 Feisal submitted a memorandum to the conference, translated by Lawrence :

" The country from the line Alexandretta—Persia south-ward " (it began) " to the Indian Ocean is inhabited by ' Arabs '—by which we mean people of a Semitic stock, closely related and speaking the same language—Arabic. The non-Arabic speaking elements in this area do not, I believe, exceed one per cent. of the whole.

" The aim of the Arab nationalist movement (of which my father became the leader in war after combined appeals from the Syrian and Mesopotamian branches) is to unite the Arabs eventually into one nation. As an old member of the Syrian Committee I commanded the Syrian revolt, and had under me Syrians, Mesopotamians and Arabs.

" We believe that our ideal of Arab unity in Asia is justified beyond need of argument by the general principles laid down by the Allies, when the United States joined them. If argument is required we would point to our splendid past, the tenacity with which our race had for six hundred years resisted Turkish attempts to absorb us, and in a lesser degree, to what we tried our best to do, in this war, as one of the allies.

" My father has a privileged place among the Arabs as their successful leader in this war, and as the head of their greatest family. He is convinced of the ultimate triumph of the ideal of unity, if no attempt is now made to force it by imposing an artificial political unity on the whole, or to hinder it by dividing the areas as spoils of war among the great powers.

" The idea of unity of the Arabs in Asia has been made more easy of late years since the development of railways, telegraphs and air routes. In old days the area was too huge and in places necessarily too thinly peopled to com-municate common ideals readily.

" The various provinces of Arab Asia, Syria, Iraq, Jezireh, Hejaz, Nejd, and Yemen are very different economically and socially, and it is impossible to constrain them into one frame of government.

" We believe that Syria, an agricultural and industrial area, thickly peopled with sedentary classes, is sufficiently advanced politically to manage her own internal affairs. We feel also that foreign technical advice and help will contribute much to our national growth. We are willing to pay for this help in cash ; we cannot sacrifice for it any part of the freedom we have just won for ourselves by force of arms.

" In Jezireh and Iraq are two huge provinces made up of three civilian towns divided up by wastes thinly peopled by semi-nomadic tribes. The world wishes to exploit Mesopotamia rapidly and we therefore believe that the system of government there will have to be buttressed by men and material resources of a great foreign power. We ask, however, that the government be Arab in principle and spirit, a selective rather than an elective government being necessarily followed in the neglected districts until time makes a broader basis possible. The immediate duty of the Arab Government there would be to furnish the educational processes which are to advance the tribes to the material level of the towns.

" The Hejaz is mainly a tribal area and the government will remain, as in the past, subject to these patriarchial conditions. We understand this better than Europe, and propose therefore that the Hejaz should retain complete autonomy.

" The Yemen and the Nejd are not likely to submit their cases to the Peace Conference. They will look after themselves and adjust their relations with the Hejaz and elsewhere.

" In Palestine a very large majority of the people are Arabs. The Jews are the nearest to Arabs in blood ; there is no conflict of character between the two races, and in their principles they are absolutely at one. But I think the Arabs must not assume the responsibility of holding the scales between the different faiths and races of this one province in view of the old historic past frictions and religious differences. They would wish for the effective interposition of a great trustee so long as the local administration commends itself by its activity in the development of local conditions.

" In discussing these provinces in detail I do not pretend to superior competence. The powers will, I hope, find better

means to give fuller effect to the aims of our national movement.

" Why I came to Europe on behalf of my father and the
Arabs of Asia was to say that they are expecting the great
powers at the Conference not to attach undue importance
to apparent superficial diversities and not to consider them
only from the lower ground of existing European material
interests. They expect the Powers to think of them as one
people, jealous of their own language and liberty, and
asking that no step should be taken inconsistent with the
prospect of an eventual union of these races under one
sovereign government.

" In emphasising the differences in the social conditions
of our provinces, I do not wish to give the impression that
there exists any real conflict of ideals, material interests,
creeds or character, rendering our union impossible. The
greatest obstacle we have to overcome is local ignorance,
for which the Turkish government is largely responsible.

" In our opinion, if our independence be constituted and
our local competence established, the natural influence of
race, language and interest will soon draw us together into
one people, but for this the great powers will have to ensure
us open internal frontiers, common railways and telegraphs,
and uniform systems of education. To achieve this they must
lay aside the thought of individual profits and all their old
jealousies.

" In a word, we ask you not to force your civilisation as a
whole upon us, but to allow us to select what serves us from
your previous experience.

" In return we can offer you little but gratitude."

A week later, on February 6, the Emir addressed the dele-
gates at the Quai d'Orsay. First he recapitulated the main
points in the memorandum, and in a desperate attempt to
sway the conference into granting the Arabs the independence
which European diplomats were blockading, he spoke of
" some 20,000 killed " in the Arab army's fights to win its
freedom.

David Hunter Miller[1] gave a full account of this meeting.
" Feisal " (he wrote) " said that in Damascus, Beirut, Tripoli,
Aleppo, Latakia and the other districts of Syria the civilian

[1] Diary of the Conference of Paris.

population declared their independence and hoisted the Arab flag before the Allied troops arrived. The Allied Commander-in-Chief insisted afterwards that the flags should be removed, and installed a temporary military governor. This, he (Allenby) explained to the Arabs, was only until the Peace Conference had settled the future of the country. Had the Arabs known that it was in compliance with a secret treaty, they would never have permitted it.

"Lloyd George asked how many Arab troops the Hejaz had put into the field. Feisal replied that it was impossible to give the exact figure, but including the Hejaz army the Arabs had put into the field about 100,000 men.

"Lloyd George asked whether the Hejaz troops had taken part on the Mesopotamian front. He answered in the negative. Lloyd George then said he would like the Emir to give a short account of the services rendered by the Arab forces in the defeat of the Turks army.

"Feisal said that when his father revolted against the Turks he was hereditary Governor of Mecca—a position held by the family for eight hundred years. He had no arms, mountain guns, ammunition or supplies and only took Mecca with difficulty. He was unable to take Medina.

"The Turks then sent 35,000 men to retake Medina. God helped the Arabs, and the English also sent them material assistance. Officers and volunteers from the old Turks army joined them and formed the nucleus of a regular force. In fourteen months the Arabs advanced eight hundred miles to the north and cut the Hejaz railway south of Ma'an. This was an important military achievement, as the Turks at Medina threatened the rear of the Arab forces.

"He then attacked Ma'an by a frontal attack without any hope of success in order to help General Allenby's preparations and to prevent a Turkish concentration. He had placed his army voluntarily under Allenby's command and had thus co-operated with them. General Allenby then asked the Arab forces to attack the three railways at Deraa. The Arab army did its duty and cut these lines two days before General Allenby's attack, which eventually led him to Damascus.

"The Arab army entered Damascus together with General Allenby's forces. From that point the Arab revolt spread like flame and in one bound reached Latakia, which was entered by the Arabs the day before the French entered Beirut.

Throughout these operations the Arab plans had been subordinate to Allenby's.

" Pichon asked whether the French had taken any part in the operations. Feisal said that he had had with him a French detachment of four 6.5 mountain guns and 2.85 mm. guns. This contingent had done wonderful work.

" ' With regard to Palestine, for its universal character, I leave it to one side,' he said, ' for the mutual consideration of all parties interested. With this exception I ask for the independence of the Arab areas I have enumerated in my memorandum. When the principle is admitted, I ask that the various provinces on the principle of self-determination be allowed to indicate to the League of Nations the nature of the assistance they require. If the indications before you in any one case are not conclusive as to their wishes for their complete independence or for their mandatory powers, I suggest then an international enquiry, made in the area concerned, might be a quick, easy, sure and just way of determining their wishes. I am delighted to defend my national interests,' he concluded, ' and I am sorry that I had to speak in Arabic.' "

Lawrence again acted as translator, and then submitted a written translation for the records of the conference. There were three mis-statements, and as Lawrence neither corrected nor minimised them it must be presumed that they were part of his propagandist efforts. The " 100,000 men," " 20,000 killed " and " the Turks sent 35,000 men to take Medina "— these were exaggerations, but they passed into history.

With regard to Palestine, Lawrence, Weizmann and Feisal had been in close and quite friendly touch on this question, and their conversations had ended in the following Treaty of Friendship, signed in London on January 3, 1919.

" H.R.H. Emir Feisal, representing and acting on behalf of the Arab Kingdom of the Hejaz, and Dr. Chaim Weizmann, representing and acting on behalf of the Zionist organisation, mindful of the racial kinship and ancient bonds existing between the Arab and the Jewish people, and that the surest means of working out the consummation of their national aspirations is through the closest possible collaboration in the development of the Arab state and Palestine, and being desirous further of confirming the good understanding which exists between them, have agreed upon the following articles :

(1) The Arab State and Palestine in all their relations and undertakings shall be controlled by the most cordial goodwill and understanding and to this end duly accredited agents of the Arabs and Jews shall be established and maintained in the respective territories.

(2) Following the completion of the deliberations of the Peace Conference, the definite boundaries between the Arab State and Palestine shall be determined by a commission to be agreed upon by the parties hereto.

(3) In the establishment of the constitution and administration of Palestine, all such measures shall be adopted as will afford the fullest guarantees for carrying into effect the British Government's declaration of November 2nd, 1917.

(4) All the necessary measures shall be taken to encourage and stimulate immigration of Jews into Palestine on a large scale, and as quickly as possible to settle Jewish immigrants upon the land through closer settlement and intensive cultivation of the soil. In taking such measures the Arab peasant and tenant farmers shall be protected in their rights and shall be assisted in forwarding their economic development.

(5) No regulation nor law shall be made prohibiting or interfering in any way with the free exercise of religion ; and further the free exercise and enjoyment of religious profession and worship without discrimination or preference shall forever be allowed. No religious test shall ever be required for the exercise of civil or political rights.

(6) Mohammedan holy places shall be under Mohammedan control.

(7) The Zionist organisation proposed to send to Palestine a commission of experts to make a survey of the economic possibilities of the country and to report upon the best means for its development. The organisation will place the commission at the disposal of the Arab state for the purpose of a survey of the economic possibilities of the Arab state and to report upon the best means for its development. The organisation will use the best efforts to assist the Arab state in providing means for developing the natural resources and economic possibilities thereof.

(8) The parties hereto agree to act in complete accord and harmony on all matters embraced herein before the Peace Conference.

(9) Any matters in dispute which may arise between the contracting parties shall be referred to the British Government for arbitration.

(Sgd.) CHAIM WEIZMANN.
FEISAL BIN HUSSEIN.

January 3rd, 1919.

The document ended with a reservation, translated from the Arabic by Lawrence, which read :

" If the Arabs are established as I have asked in my manifesto of 4-1-1919, addressed to the British Secretary of State for Foreign Affairs, I will carry out what is written in this agreement.

" If changes are made, I cannot be answerable for failing to carry out this agreement."

A few days after the Emir's address at the Quai d'Orsay the Zionist case was presented to the Council of Ten by Doctor Weizmann and M. Sokolow, on behalf of the Zionist Organisation and the Jews of Palestine respectively.[1]

On February 15 President Wilson read his proclamation to the League of Nations. " At the end of the session," commented the *Corriere della Sera* that day, " the representatives of the Hejaz intervened ; motionless as two statues the Emir Feisal and Lawrence, the second delegate of the Hejaz, had remained imposing under the silk turbans, and only towards the end, unexpectedly, Lawrence raised his hand to be allowed to speak. He was brief, clear, and empirical.

" ' Since the League of Nations protects the little countries which are not yet ripe for an independent life and provides for the application of the principle of the mandate to them, the Hejaz demands the definition of what this mandate, on which the future of so many peoples will depend, is. They must have the right to choose the power which is to aid them,

---

[1] " The Emir Feisal, in concluding this agreement in his father's name, was not, it is true, directly representing the Arabs of Palestine, but the Arabs . . . regarded Syria as one country, and in Syria the Emir's leadership had been accepted. If his hopes, indeed, had been fulfilled, the development of the situation in Palestine might have been far more peaceful than it has been. As it was, the Agreement marks the one brief moment in the whole story at which a genuine harmony was established between Arab and Jewish statesmanship."—Palestine Royal Commission Report, July 1937.

but they must enjoy the possibility of knowing their fate within the limits admitted by the League of Nations. Now there are secret treaties between the great powers, treaties arranging for the division of the Asiatic territories which were oppressed by the tyrannies of the Turks. It was just that these should be suppressed.'

" Lawrence was listened to in a surprised silence, but he went forward unmoved, speaking in the most perfect French with a sacerdotal gravity, and the Emir, face ecstatic and stroking his beard with the gold tassels which hung down from his Arab headdress, gave the speaker brief but insistent hints."

Lawrence did his best in these peace talks. He did not trouble to hide his anti-French attitude, but he knew that the history of the Arab revolt was an admixture of specious diplomacy and politic deceit. There were signatures to treaties with the Arabs, and signatures to treaties with France, and it was obvious which would have to be honoured.

The French and British delegations were not so much concerned with the Arabs' fight for independence. They had to get the Sykes-Picot agreement out of the tangle. Britain wanted Mosul, and France wanted all Syria.

On the same day that Wilson's proclamation was read, the French handed a scheme of agreement to the British Government in an attempt to bridge the differences between the two. (Lloyd George had first broached the subject of the exchange of Syria for Mosul to M. Clemenceau towards the end of 1918.)

An accompanying letter asked for a recognition of " the historic and traditional case " for including Syria in the French zone. It also asked that Syria should be treated as one unit, and that France should be allowed to take the mandate for the whole region.

At a subsequent meeting in Lloyd George's flat in the Rue Nitot, at which President Wilson was present, the subject of the 1916 treaties was mentioned. (According to a speech by M. Briand, made during a debate in the French Chamber on June 25, 1920, Lloyd George's report was " They— the treaties—have now been altered. I have been promised the cession of Mosul and Palestine," and M. Briand stated, the remark passed unchallenged.)

On March 20, at a meeting of the Supreme Council at Lloyd George's Paris flat, M. Clemenceau, turning to Lloyd

George himself, said, " When I went to London last autumn I said to you ' Let me know what you want in Asia, so that we may do away with any cause of misunderstanding between us.' You said to me ' We want Mosul, which the Sykes-Picot agreement puts in the French zone.' I promised to settle the matter, and have done so in spite of the opposition of the Quai d'Orsay.'[1]

The history of this diplomatic wrangling is not easy to follow in its tortuous progress, but once more Miller's diary supplied the essential particulars :

" 26.3.19

" An informal meeting of the British and French experts on the Syrian question took place here on Tuesday night. It was attended by Colonel Lawrence, Miss Gertrude Bell, and Sir Valentine Chirol on behalf of the British. . . .

" Upon being urged to express his views on the Syrian question, Colonel Lawrence admitted that the proposal of sending a commission to Syria had been promoted by the failure of the French authorities to approach the Emir Feisal in a conciliatory way, and that it would undoubtedly be far better if the commission could stay on in Paris and come to an agreement upon general principles before going to Syria in order to clear up on the spot any details of procedure and local organisation.

" After considerable discussions, all present agreed that if some responsible representative of the French Government would approach Feisal, a settlement might quickly be attained on the following lines :

" France to receive a mandate for Syria ; the Syrians to elect their Prince in a national assembly to be convened by suitable methods at Damascus (the only serious candidate for the rulership of Syria would be Feisal, who already enjoys the support of a large majority of the population) ; the position of France in regard to Syria to be analagous to that of the British in regard to the Sultans of Egypt or the British Minister resident towards the semi-independent rulers of native states in India; the Lebanon and possibly the Druse country to enjoy an autonomy under Feisal and the mandatory authority of France.

[1] " Woodrow Wilson and World Settlement " (R. Stannard Baker).

" It was understood that the Frenchmen present would bring the possibility and the expediency of taking steps towards such a settlement to the notice of the French Government.

" Colonel Lawrence made it clear that the movement for Arab unity possessed no serious value for the present or indeed for the near future. He added that there should be no political connection between Feisal and his father, the King of the Hejaz. The frontiers of Syria he contended should not be drawn in accordance with the Sykes-Picot agreement, which was geographically and politically absurd, inasmuch as it divided Syria from east to west instead of dividing it naturally from north to south. He added that a proper territorial division would take account of the economic independence of Arab tribes upon certain states, and added that this principle would extend the centre of economic dependence upon Damascus and therefore the boundaries of Syria from the south-east of the Jordan. . . ."

" THE DREAM OF THE CAT IS ALL ABOUT THE MICE "

For a month or so little or no progress was made in Arabian affairs, and in May 1920, Lawrence suddenly decided to fly to Egypt. At the same time a British Handley-Page squadron was at the Bue aerodrome in Paris, on its way to Egypt. Henderson, the commander of the Squadron, who had acted as Lawrence's pilot on many occasions in the early days of the Hejaz fighting, found to his delight that he was to have " T.E." as a passenger.

Most of the machines were in trouble all the way to Marseilles, so at Lyons Lawrence was transferred to one piloted by Lieutenants Spratt and Prince. They reached Pisa, the next official stop, but for some unexplained reason they tried to reach Rome before dark. The aerodrome at Centocelle was not prepared for them, and in the absence of guiding flares the machine over-shot the landing ground and crashed into a quarry. Both the R.A.F. men were killed instantaneously, but " T.E." and two mechanics had a miraculous escape, Lawrence getting away with a broken collar-bone and severe bruises.

Lawrence did not stop. As soon as the squadron re-formed, he flew on with Henderson to Taranto, where he refused the Commanding Officer's hospitality, quite nicely, had his food from the men's mess, and slept under one of the 'planes.

Athens was reached via Valona, then Suda Bay, Crete. Here an attack of sand-fly fever incapacitated all the pilots, and during the convalescent period a relief machine to replace the one smashed in Rome arrived with one passenger— H. St. John Philby !

Such was fate's queer trick. Lawrence and Ibn Saud's adviser had been in opposition in Paris, and the former had decided to fly to Cairo to gain an advantage in the bargaining. St. John Philby had followed, and who knows what influence this chance meeting had on the future of the Arab tribes ?

However, Lawrence was back in Paris in the autumn,

prepared with further " ammunition " for the Arab cause. The Miller diary again filled up the picture :

" September 12 : Mr. Polk dined with Lloyd George. There were present Allenby and other members of the cabinet. He discussed in detail the situation in Palestine, Syria and Mesopotamia. The British thought that Clemenceau was not willing to go into a serious discussion of the Syrian matter until after the elections. Lloyd George said he had the agreement with Feisal in 1915 with which they were familiar, and the Sykes-Picot agreement in '16 with France. He intended to live up to both agreements, but he thought the French were insisting on certain towns—Aleppo, Homs and Damascus—being given to them.

" Allenby had stated that Feisal did not trust the French and since the British garrisons which are now in Syria had been withdrawn to be replaced by France, Feisal would attempt to attack the French.

" Lloyd George said he had invited Feisal to London and would explain the situation, but somehow he had resolved to withdraw the British garrison in Syria. Allenby argued that the withdrawal was a mistake. Lloyd George apparently made two points, one that he must withdraw for the purpose of economy, two that he intends to carry out his obligations to Feisal."

Three days later, there was another meeting, this time in Clemenceau's room. " Lloyd George " (the diary continued) " had taken on himself the responsibility of sending for Emir Feisal because the British Government had entered into certain engagements with Hussein in return for his support. There was the suggestion in the French press that the British Government had not told the French Government of these engagements. He then handed to Clemenceau a document prepared in the British Foreign Office on the question of whether the French Government had been notified of the engagements made by the British Government and King Hussein. Lloyd George said that the Sykes-Picot agreement also had been based on the engagements of the British Government and the Arabs. Emir Feisal claimed that the British Government had given away something promised to him : the British Government could not accept that view.

" In communications with Hussein they had always made it clear that in their view the country west of Damascus, Homs,

Hama and Aleppo was not Arab in character. He hoped to make this clear to Feisal on his arrival."

The immediate result of the agreement between Lloyd George and Clemenceau in September was that the British troops should be withdrawn and replaced by French forces, but that the four towns of Damascus, Homs, Hama and Aleppo for the time being should be left out of the zone of direct military occupation and that the French troops should not proceed thither.

In October Feisal received a letter from the Foreign Office which dealt with the correspondence and notes concerning the agreements. "From this correspondence," wrote Curzon, " two things are clear. First that the British Government are bound by their undertaking to King Hussein to recognise the establishment of an independent Arab state comprising within its borders the four towns of Damascus, Homs, Hama, and Aleppo ; and second that his British Majesty's Government made it absolutely clear to your illustrious father before the entry of the Arabs into the war that they regarded France as having special rights in the area west of the four towns."

For the time being, Feisal had to be content with that definition of the Arabs' standing in the matter.

In December, the dispatches prepared by Wingate on " the military operations in the Hejaz from the 9th June, 1916 to 31st January, 1919," so long kept from the public, appeared in their final form.

No. 1 and No. 2 had been held up during the War because it was feared that their publication would give the Germans and the Turks a very valuable field for propaganda in commenting on the use of Christian officers, etc., in the Holy places of Islam.

When the third and last dispatch was compiled the armistice had been signed, and at that time there seemed no reason for further postponement of their publication. All three were therefore incorporated in one, but relations with the French, particularly in regard to Arabian and Syrian matters, were becoming quite strained in the peace discussion—and the dispatches were held up once more.

Another hindrance to their appearance had been the delicate state of Moslem opinion. Allenby was consulted in the matter, and he thought it would not be wise to announce publicly, at any rate at that time, Britain's prominent share in operations conducted in sacred territories.

A little later Hussein and Ibn Saud were in actual conflict in the neighbourhood of the Holy Places, and the British Government were placed in a very awkward predicament. They had to give Hussein some support at the risk of wounding the susceptibilities of the larger section of Indian Moslems, who still regarded him as a rebel against the Caliphate.

Added to this was confidential information regarding the very strong anti-British and anti-foreign feeling among the Moslem populations of Syria and Mesopotamia. Consequently the publication of the dominant share Britain had taken in the Arab revolt would not help matters.

The situation eased a little, but it was as well that the dispatches had not yet appeared. Paradoxically enough, India asked for some prominence to be given to the services rendered by the Indian section during the Hejaz campaign, and in an endeavour to placate French opinion emphasis was laid on the value of the work done by the French detachment.

Finally, having been watered down to a solution considered as harmless to Moslem feelings, supplemented with an honourable mention for the Indians, and with a pat on the back for the French, the *London Gazette* published the three dispatches as one on December 15, 1919.

The first phase, covered in his report dated June 25, 1917—apart from the actual recommendations—made one reference to Lawrence. After writing of " the necessity of providing additional officers to assist Lieut.-Colonel Wilson (on whom to date had fallen the whole of the difficult task of guiding and advising Arab leaders both in military and political matters)," Wingate commented that " a considerable number of Arabs were trained in demolition work and are now operating against the railway under the personal direction of Lieut.-Colonel S. F. Newcombe, D.S.O., R.E., Captain T. E. Lawrence, and Lieut. H. Garland."

The second dispatch, dated June 15, 1918, mentioned Lawrence twice—referring to the " Howeitat under Auda abu Tayi, accompanied by Captain (now Lieut-.Colonel) Lawrence," and then " early in July, as the result of an operation, brilliantly planned and executed by Captain Lawrence, Akaba . . . was captured."

The third dispatch, of December 17, 1918, mainly concerned

with operations in Southern Arabia, referred to "the great victory achieved by the Army under General Allenby in Syria, and its corollary, the entry of the Arab forces under Emir Feisal, after a series of cleverly-planned and daring flanking operations, into Damascus . . . in which Lieut.-Colonel T. E. Lawrence played so distinguished a role."

Wingate had been generous in his recommendations, so much so that permanent officialdom, viewing them in the only light under which they ever examined them—added a reproving " minute " to the file :

> " Please note in connection with awards, the allowance is one per cent ' mentions ' and half per cent ' rewards.' This is the percentage laid down by the army in connection with all theatres of war."

P*

" IF BEGGING SHOULD UNFORTUNATELY BE THY LOT, KNOCK AT THE LARGE GATES ONLY "

WHILE the peace discussions had been going on, Lawrence had spent some time in Feisal's temporary Paris home in the Avenue Bois du Boulogne, drafting his version of the Arab revolt. The tale was told before Lawrence left Paris, and in the autumn it had been revised. Travelling through to London, Lawrence left his case containing the manuscript, together with many photographs then destined to illustrate it, on the railway station at Reading, and it disappeared. It was a bitter blow to him, and it was only after persistent pleas from Hogarth and others that he settled down to the colossal task of re-writing the story.

Feisal also was busy. He knew he was reaching for a crown in Syria which would make his head more than uneasy. Added to this, the Baghdadis around him were preparing for the establishment of their Iraqi kingdom.

Colonel Wilson was troubled in Iraq by what he termed Syrian-financed propaganda, which was being used to encourage anti-British action. The clamour for Arab self-government was growing louder. When Baghdad was captured in March, 1917, Basrah, it had been declared, would remain British, and Baghdad would belong to the Arabs. Surely, then, this was one of the promises that could be kept ?[1] All such discussions affecting minorities were lost in the welter of the major Anglo-French problems, but while Feisal was in Europe trying to strengthen his position, disturbances broke out on the Iraqi-Syrian frontier. Feisal denied all knowledge

[1] " In the Hejaz the Arabs have expelled the Turks and Germans who oppressed them and have proclaimed Sherif Hussein as their King, and His Lordship rules in independence and freedom and is the ally of the nations who are fighting against the power of Turkey and Germany. So indeed are the noble Arabs, the Lords of Nejd, Kuwait, and Asir. Many noble Arabs have perished in the cause of freedom at the hands of those alien rulers, the Turks, who oppressed them.

" It is the determination of the Government of Great Britain and the Great Powers allied to Great Britain that these noble Arabs shall not have suffered in vain. It is the desire and hope of the British people and the nations in alliance with them that the Arab race may rise once more to greatness and renown amongst

of the affair. The British heard him doubtfully, but the French were definitely suspicious. Britain wanted to reprove this Iraqi gesture, and yet maintain friendly relations with Feisal and his Baghdadis. Not only were the oil wells an important consideration, but the country itself was a flank to the sea-route to India. Britain did not want enemies there.

In March, 1920, there was a Syrian National Congress in Damascus, at which the independence of Syria was declared, with Feisal as King. " After all we have suffered, the Arabs will not be content to be enslaved," Feisal told them. " All we ask from Europe is recognition of our right as a living nation to a free life and complete independence."

Then followed the San Remo conference, held from April 18 to 27. Lloyd George himself described the result. " The San Remo conference was a triumph of goodwill," he said. " Everyone went away, I am sure, happier than after any other conference, and we shall be going together side by side with a great unity of purpose, which will promote good understanding. . . . The mandate for Syria has been accorded to France ; the mandate for Mesopotamia, including Mosul, has been given to Britain."

The conference put an end to Feisal's first post-war triumph. It sealed the doom of Arab Independence. In July a French army, with tanks, aeroplanes, and Senegalese, marched on Damascus. The Arab Government, which had rejected the French mandate, was overthrown, and Feisal exiled.

There was some heart-burning in England over the matter. Mr. Bonar Law was asked in the House of Commons whether the British Government intended to remonstrate with the French because of their proceedings in Syria. His reply was brutally frank. France would be just as entitled, he said, to reproach Britain for certain of her proceedings in Mesopotamia.

The resentful nationalist supporters of Feisal, forseeing defeat of their Syrian aspirations, had transferred their activities to Iraq. They fomented trouble among the Euphrates tribes.

---

the peoples of the earth and that it shall bind itself, to this end, in unity and accord.
" O, people of Baghdad ! remember that for twenty-six generations you have suffered under strange tyrants who have ever endeavoured to set one Arab house against another in order that they might profit by your dissensions. Therefore I am commanded to invite you . . . to participate in the management of your civil affairs, in collaboration with the political representatives of Great Britain who accompany the British Army, so that you may unite with your kinsmen in the north, east, south and west in realising the aspirations."—Proclamation broadcast, under instructions, by General Maude.

The mosques and holy cities were full of agitators, and just at the time that the French were preparing to eject Feisal from Damascus, rebellion broke out in the Lower and Middle Euphrates against weakened British forces.

The rebellion spread rapidly. Individual British officers were murdered, supply steamers attacked, garrisons besieged, and the railways cut. During four anxious months nearly 70,000 British troops were brought into action, and millions of pounds poured out before the trouble was quelled.

Having gone to this centre of agitation from his exile, Feisal came to the front again, both pushed and willing to be pushed. Lawrence saw no reason why he should not be advanced to the head of the Arab administration there. After all, he argued, the loss of Syria was more the result of French machinations rather than default on the part of Feisal.

It is probable that it was Lawrence's ceaseless propaganda which led to a change of policy on the part of the British Government at this time. He had written several articles for the more important of the British national dailies, which became the focal points of heated controversies, and after Syrian and Mesopotamian affairs had faded away in a momentary eclipse, the British Government decided to tackle the Middle East problems at once.

In 1921 Churchill, then Colonial Secretary, formed what was termed the Near East department. He appointed Lawrence to act as Adviser on Arab affairs, with Major Young as head of the Administrative section.

For some months these two, with other experts, attended meetings and had innumerable talks in Egypt, Palestine and Trans-Jordan, attempting to straighten out the many problems which had arisen, particularly since Feisal's expulsion from Damascus.

There was one significant meeting at Ma'an, where Abdullah, using his own words " intended to stay to keep my Brother's (Feisal's) seat warm." The latter was on his way to Jeddah to have a talk with his father. Churchill himself was in Jerusalem, busy in an attempt to secure a re-orientation of British policy towards the various Arab potentates, and Trans-Jordan, in its proximity to the disaffected Syrian area, presented many difficulties.

Churchill told Abdullah that the British Government's only concern was to see that the French were not annoyed by their neighbours, particularly while Feisal's candidature for Iraq was in the balance. Abdullah guaranteed that he would keep Trans-Jordan quiet, but he wanted Churchill to understand that the French peace moves with the Turks, their concentrations of troops in the south, and the tightening of their hold on the Hauran and the Druse countries was no happy augury for future peace.

Lawrence's committee, or rather the Committee on which he served, had the particular problem of the political subsidies in the Arabian peninsula. In the end they arrived at the conclusion that Ibn Saud and Hussein should each be paid £100,000 per annum.

Ibn Saud they considered to be the greatest factor in Arabian politics, not so much because of the help he could be to Britain, but rather because of the harm he could do. While he himself was a moderating influence, Ibn Saud commanded forces which could—and would at the slightest encouragement —invade the more important areas of Arabia at will. Therefore the committee attempted to placate him by giving him equal status with Hussein, but in return he had to promise to refrain from armed action (1) against Iraq, (2) against Koweit, (3) against the Hejaz. He was told, very firmly, that his subsidy had been increased from £60,000 to £100,000 per annum so that he would be able to dictate policy to his followers and thus be in a position to comply more exactly with British wishes. Friendly relations between Ibn Saud and his rival, Hussein, were urged by the commissioners ; moreover they countenanced the assumption of the title of Sultan of Nejd by the Wahabi chief.

Hussein's subsidy was conditional upon the ratification of the Treaty of Versailles ; recognition and respect of British treaties with Ibn Saud and the Idrisi ; improved pilgrimage conditions ; prevention of anti-British and pan-Islamic intrigue ; prevention of anti-French action by the Sherifians.

From the military point of view, Britain ignored Hussein, but as guardian of the Holy places his friendship or enmity meant, at this time, the difference between peace and dangerous unrest in the Moslem world.

Meanwhile, Feisal had returned from Mecca, and Ja'afer Pasha, as loyal to him as ever, had gone to Baghdad, and on August 23, 1921, Feisal, swearing support of British policy,

The Moslem Sphere of Interest.

became King of Iraq. Lawrence had accomplished some part of his purpose.[1]

He undertook one more important diplomatic journey, down to Jeddah, to persuade the ageing Hussein to agree to the various clauses of the Anglo-Arab Treaty, which was intended to clear the air of the many political sandstorms. Lawrence did not succeed. Hussein was wilful and obstinate, he was angry over Ibn Saud's equality in subsidy, his new title—and after a very futile month Lawrence returned, with the treaty still unsigned.[2]

It was a curious journey—twelve days in Egypt, four to Jeddah ; a stay there from July 29 to August 14 ; then a trip to Aden ; back again to Jeddah on August 29, which port he finally left on September 21. He went from Egypt to Jerusalem, arriving there on October 3, and staying until the 12th. From the beginning of October until this time he was in and out of Jerusalem, and travelling all over Trans-Jordan. He returned to England just before Christmas, 1921.

Then Lawrence thought his usefulness to the Arabs and to the British Government was ended, and forthwith resigned his post.

He fled to the Royal Air Force, taking the name of Ross, but between times managed to supervise the setting up of a 200,000 word draft of the *Revolt*, in Oxford. He had eight copies made and bound.

[1] " When years afterwards I asked King Feisal for his impressions of Lawrence . . . he evaded the question. ' Lawrence,' he said. ' He said many things about me which are not a bit true, and I should probably say things about him which would not be true either. He was a genius, of course, but not for this age.'

" ' For a past age ? ' I suggested. . . .

" ' On the contrary, for the future. A hundred years hence, perhaps two hundred years, he might be understood, but not to-day.' " (Mrs. Stuart Erskine, in her book " Feisal of Irak.")

[2] " Did he (Colonel Lawrence) not know the Arabs ? Had he not to his credit the greatest achievement in the Anglo-Arab annals of the century ? The Foreign Office therefore entrusted him with the Treaty, and sent with him as aid in council a noted Syrian pan-Arabist, who was then the Agent of Feisal in London.

" But these gentlemen, both capable in their respective sphere, had to deal with a veteran of the Yildiz diplomacy. The descendant of the Prophet would not be forced, and Colonel Lawrence, all his triumphs to the contrary, spent a whole month in Jeddah to no purpose. He had apparently lost his cunning. Alas ! He also lost his temper, which is very rare in a British diplomatic agent. In justice to Lawrence, however, I must say that the Syrian's dictatorial manner was, to say the least, unwarranted ; and it mattered not what his preference was, whether his sentiment was pro-British or pro-Arab. He had already failed, though serving King Feisal faithfully in the past, to uphold the cause ; he could not save King Feisal in the Syrian debacle ; and he had come to advise the father of Feisal to sign a treaty in which the ceding of Syria to the French was practically guaranteed."—" Around the Coasts of Arabia," by Ameen Rihani.

By Christmas he had been hunted out into the open again by the Press. He consigned his manuscript to the Bodleian, and masked his feelings in an obstinate silence, while Press, Parliament and the Air authorities fought over him.

In February 1923 he was " discharged " from the Air Force, and the next month he enlisted in the Tank Corps, this time in the formally adopted name of Shaw, having been assured that if he served two years " without incident," he could rejoin the Air Force.

His Tank Corps service was notable for the fact that he never appeared on parade, and was rarely, if ever seen in the Mess-room. More often than not he would patronise one of the little civilian canteens in the depot at Bovington. The one fact the men of the depot—quite naturally—did note was that " Shaw " never appeared on pay parade.

However, the Tank Corps men, despite their curiosity regarding the mystery recruit, gave him better shelter than Uxbridge did, and in August 1925 Lawrence got his transfer back to the R.A.F. He was stationed at Cranwell, and after a spell there was transferred, in December 1926, to India.

The earlier part of Lawrence's Indian service found him slightly rebellious against rather severe camp restrictions, but he had some compensation, however, for he was engaged in a translation of Homer's " Odyssey," which matched his moods and saved him from stagnation.

Fate butted in with the Afghan rebellion in February 1928, against King Amanullah, for the news had also leaked out that Lawrence was on the North-West frontier. Rumour did the rest, with the able aid of the British press. (Actually, he was at Karachi during the first half of the year, and at Miranshah until the end of the year.)

The British Minister at Kabul had been so embarrassed with representations from the Afghan Government that in the end he found it advisable to recommend that " Aircraftsman Shaw be sent back to England at once." He left India before the rebellion actually broke out, but the home authorities bungled his landing at Plymouth. An Admiralty launch went out to his boat in the ordinary course of its duties, and for " convenience," Shaw was brought to port in the launch. The press fastened on the incident, magnified it, and forced the matter into Parliament.

For months there had been rumours about Lawrence's

" missions." Wherever disorders occurred in the Indian states, there he was reported to be, acting as the head of an extensive, all-seeing intelligence service on the Afghan border. Wherever agitation was reported in southern and western Asia, fantastic stories abounded about his activities there. One—typical of many—said that a fakir who had been arrested while sitting in the dust at an Indian funeral, was actually " the famous Lawrence of Arabia," working his magic in all the mystical draperies of the East.

" If he is doing special duties," an influential London journal demanded, " Colonel Lawrence should be transferred to another sphere and given the appropriate status. If he is not, the air authorities should consider seriously the effect of his ambiguous position on officers and men, as well as on public opinion here and abroad."

On January 28, a few days before he landed, a Labour member asked in the House of Commons how long Lawrence had been on the North-West frontier ; had he carried out the ordinary duties of his rank, and had he been granted leave at any time during his period of service in India ?

It was obvious the British authorities intended to leave no room for further rumours. " Aircraftsman Shaw was posted to No. 20 Squadron, Peshawar, from Karachi, on 26th May, 1928." He had carried out his ordinary duties, the reply continued, and " he was not granted any leave while with the squadron."

Supplementing this, the questioner wanted to know whether Lawrence's real name was known when he enlisted, but Sir Samuel Hoare did not answer this until January 30, when he replied that " Colonel Lawrence's identity was known when he transferred from the Army to the Air Force under the name of Shaw. He preferred to be known by that name, and no objection was raised to his being accepted for service under it."

When, therefore, Lawrence disembarked so " mysteriously " —he had his meals in private throughout the journey, came a report from the boat—the authorities had to face further questions.

Why, the House asked, was the launch used ? Was Lawrence mixed up in any way with the troubles on the North-West Frontier ? Had the Government recalled him because of representations made from India ? In view of the mysterious way in which he had returned, was it true that he was still in India, and that someone else had been brought home?

The " noise " died down, and for a year Lawrence was busy at Calshot working on motor-boat design and equipment. He also had something to do with the arrangement for the Schneider Trophy race of 1929, ostensibly a very humble connection but described in very well-informed circles as " important."

Then the Soviet Government brought members of the Industrial Party to trial for treason, and the proceedings in Moscow from November 25 to December 12, 1930, had their repercussions throughout the European chancelleries.

For some time Soviet agencies had been held responsible for the circulation of reports regarding Lawrence's activities, in which he was generally charged as being the chief of a propaganda service directed against the Russian government and influence, but those who thought they knew all Lawrence had done, rubbed their eyes in wonderment as they read the evidence given by the accused in the Moscow trial.

According to sworn statements, Lawrence had undertaken negotiations with the Industrial Party in London. The object of these meetings was to prepare a revolution against the Soviet Government in Russia, to be accompanied by armed intervention, in conjunction with the rebels, on the part of Great Britain, France and the border states. Imperialistic French circles would then receive payment of the Tsarist debts, while England would receive the Caucasian oilfields.

Two extracts from the official shorthand notes of the trial read as follows :

" L. K. Ramzin (one of the accused) second day, 26.11.30 : During this same trip abroad in 1928 we held three meetings in London. . . . Finally a third meeting was organised in London with Colonel Lawrence. Engineer Simon Larikhey and I were present.

" The meeting was held in one of the British automobile clubs. The meeting was quite short, lasting about forty minutes, and was more in the nature of making one another's acquaintance. At this meeting I was told that British military circles were in favour of intervention, and were beginning preparations for it. At the same time contacts were established through British firms in Moscow, since diplomatic relations with England had not yet been renewed. On the basis of these meetings and information received from various sources it is clear that the leading role in the organisation of intervention from abroad undoubtedly belongs to France."

" V. A. Laritchev (second day) : Perhaps it would be worth while mentioning our meetings with Colonel Lawrence and the other chiefs of the British general staff, who I had met on Strizhov's instructions (Strizhov had been abroad but could not get to England and pass on the necessary information regarding the preparation of bases in the Black Sea). I promised to hand on this information, and did so. . . . In these conversations we had in England and especially in the talk we had with Colonel Lawrence we were naturally interested in getting to know the attitude British circles had displayed in the question of intervention. . . ."

Publicity and Parliament combined once more, but Mr. L'Estrange Malone (who himself had served in the Red Sea during the early part of the Sherifian revolt, and had some knowledge of Lawrence's work) asked for a definite reply in the House of Commons that would at least satisfy the British public. It seemed impossible to convince foreign opinion that Lawrence was not the greatest British Secret Service Agent the world had ever known.

Mr. L'Estrange Malone asked the Under Secretary of State for Air : " Whether, in view of the statements made in the Russian State Trial to the effect that Colonel T. E. Lawrence, alias Aircraftsman Shaw, was in London in 1927 engaged in a conspiracy against the Soviet Government, he would state the dates of Aircraftsman Shaw's departure to and return from India, and what leave if any he had during that period of service ? "

Mr. Montague replied : " Aircraftsman Shaw sailed for India on December 7, 1926, arrived on January 7, 1927, and served in that country till January 12, 1929, when he embarked for home, arriving on February 2, 1929. He was not granted any leave while serving in India."

Viscountess Astor : " Is it not true that Aircraftsman Shaw is leading a perfectly quiet, respectable, and useful life ? "

As with so many supplementary questions, there was no

reply to this latter remark, but while British opinion felt that whoever was manufacturing mystery, it was not Lawrence, the secret service legend could not die.

Hong Kong reported in the latter part of 1929 that Lawrence was in the district " on important investigations," and repeated the story early in 1930. Later in the year he was supposedly busy in China making secret investigations for the guidance of British representatives who were dealing with extra-territoriality negotiations.

On July 17, 1931, Soviet agents in Bukhara ascribed tribal revolts there to the " machinations of Colonel Lawrence." They also said that " his influence is spreading through Turkestan and it will be impossible to quell the revolts in any way permanently unless a powerful Soviet garrison is established in that region." (The puzzling fact here is that the Soviet Foreign Commissiarat in Moscow already had information to the effect that Lawrence had been " killed in an aeroplane disaster in England " earlier in the year. What had actually happened was that Lawrence had been conspicuous in rescue work when a giant seaplane crashed near Calshot in February 1931, nine of the crew being killed.)

Later he was reported to be behind some religious riots in Asia Minor, and then Hong Kong sheltered him again, " for reasons unknown."

For a few months there were no more sensational reports, until on July 7, 1932, a German wireless station broadcast was received in Baghdad announcing that " Lawrence was engineering a pact between Tibet and Great Britain."

From enquiries made abroad, it was still evident that the Russians believed that it was a " double " who had been enrolled in the Royal Air Force as a " blind " to the real Lawrence's activities, and this version was the one generally accepted on the Continent.

When it was announced that Aircraftsman Shaw had applied for his discharge from the Royal Air Force, Berlin actually stated on the same day that he was " on his way to Turkey or Abyssinia."

This was in March 1933, but as he was not yet out of his period of service the authorities ignored his appeal for release " for private reasons." He had plenty to do, for while he still insisted on retaining the lowest rank, he gave invaluable aid in the development of the high-speed motor-boats which were being built for work with the Air Force. He was continually testing their engines, and taking the boats out for trials along the coast.

Special boats were constructed for bombing practice for the seaplane, and Lawrence was among the volunteers who, manning these strange craft, twisted and turned and sped along the sea while seaplanes used them as " marks " and attempted to hit them with bombs.

Following his return to England early in 1929, he had filled in his spare time finishing the translation of the " Odyssey," begun in India in 1928. He completed it in August 1931, and it was published a year later. When, with this out of the way, the boats passed from the experimental stage to actual use, Lawrence began to ease the pressure he put on his life. He had driven himself mercilessly, both in his own service and in that of his country.

Waiting for his discharge, he began to devote more of his spare time to his cottage in Clouds Hill, Moreton, the Dorsetshire haven of rest which he had purchased years before. He journeyed between camp and home on his Brough motorcycle, always at high speed, flashing from the turmoil of the depot to the peace of his retreat.

He kept in touch with a small circle of friends, immersed himself in the creation of another book, and began to revel in the fact that at long last he was being left alone. He began to plan his retirement, and when in March 1935 the authorities finally released him, he went straight to Clouds Hill, to freedom.

He settled down in his small cottage, making occasional journeys into Dorchester for shopping, or disappearing for a solitary tour on his motor-cycle when and where his fancy led him.

Sometimes he paid visits to the Tank Corps Depot at Bovington, scene of his service with that arm of the Forces. His new-won freedom had, imperceptibly, broken through his reserve, although he was always a subject for comment as he went about the countryside.

On May 13 a " flash " message over the newspaper tapes galvanised the world :

" Lawrence of Arabia injured in cycle collision Moreton Dorset."

Circumstances conspired to surround the accident with the inevitable mystery the public like to associate with his name. The news on the first day was a mass of conflicting rumours, not only as to how the accident happened, but regarding the extent of his injuries.

The military flung a cordon of guards round the hospital; two boys concerned in the collision were warned " not to talk "; the hospital authorities, anxious to maintain secrecy, denied all reports of serious injury; and yet the first rumour which leaked through this " screen "—that Lawrence had a fractured skull and was in a critical condition—was no more than truth.

The following day the hospital announced that " Lawrence is in a serious condition with head injuries," and when it was learned that three specialists had been rushed to the hospital, including Sir Farquhar Buzzard, the King's Honorary Physician, most people felt that this was no accident; this was tragedy.

Hope flared up a little, when two bulletins mentioned " a chance," but this quickly faded, and the watching world could only marvel that life should hang so tenaciously to what was now known to be a terribly shattered mind and body.

Six days the specialists strove to keep death away, hovering round Lawrence's unconscious form, feeding him artificially, administering oxygen and drugs towards the end.

At three o'clock on Sunday morning, May 19, his gallant heart began to fail, and for another five hours all that was possible was an agonising watching, waiting for the almost imperceptible flutter of life to cease.

At 8.40 that Sunday morning, a single message went flashing round the world:

" Lawrence dead."

Lawrence's restless soul had found peace, but the Press was not content. Running parallel with world-wide tributes were the most fantastic rumours, wilder than many of the legends linked with his Arabian adventures.

" Britain was in peril because Lawrence had died with his brain still holding the secrets of the country's war 'planes "; that was one.

" The man in hospital was not Lawrence, who is on a secret mission in the Far East " began another story, and yet another fastened on some slight heath fires which had been started near Clouds Hill and said they were the work of foreign agents, who were trying to obtain or destroy invaluable documents.

Even the inquest was an unsatisfactory affair, and despite the verdict of " accidental death " everyone present was left with a funny little doubt. One military witness testified that just before the collision a black car, travelling very swiftly in the opposite direction, passed Lawrence, and he saw the latter swerve. The collision with the boys followed immediately after, so violent an impact that he was thrown 130 feet from his machine.

There was no corroboration of the story, and the police reported that they had been unable to trace such a car. The witness was recalled, but, as he said, as he did not know it was Lawrence on the motor-cycle until after the accident he had no incentive to suggest a mystery. " I saw the car," he repeated, " a black one."

* * * * *

They buried Lawrence in the quiet of the English countryside. There was a simple, plain coffin, a four-wheel hand trestle to carry it, an evergreen lined grave without monument or wreaths, a few quiet words, the shortest of prayers —and he was gone.

In that small circle round the grave were his relatives, great soldiers and statesmen, a few of the officers and men who had been with him in Arabia, and some of the very few he had welcomed into his friendship ; and in their hearts must have echoed this tribute from the ruler of the empire for which Lawrence had sacrificed the best a man has—his honour :

" The King gratefully recognises his distinguished services to his country, and feels that it is tragic that the end should have come in this manner to a life so full of promise."

END

ACKNOWLEDGEMENT is offered for the help given by reference to the following publications, from which quotations have been taken in some instances :

Military Operations, Egypt and Palestine. Compiled by CAPTAIN CYRIL FALLS. Maps by MAJOR A. F. BECKE.

My Diary at the Conference of Paris. DAVID HUNTER MILLER.

The Independent Arab. SIR HUBERT YOUNG.

Dead Towns and Living Men. C. L. WOOLLEY.

Mons, Anzac and Kut. By an M.P. (HON. AUBREY HERBERT).

La Révolté Arabe. EUGENE JUNG.

La Procès des Industriels de Moscou-Stenographie Intégrale. (Printed in Paris, 1931.)

C. M. Doughty. D. G. HOGARTH.

Documenti per la Storia della Pace Orientale (1915-32). A. GIANNINI.

Around the Coasts of Arabia. AMEEN RIHANI.

Une Campagne du Hedjas. (Published in Paris, 1919.)

Russian State Documents. (Published in Moscow in 1919, 1920 and 1924.)

Palestine Royal Commission Report, 1937, and other Government papers.

Thanks are also due to War Office, British Museum, and Chatham House officials for help in consulting official records.

INDEX

This is merely selective, to indicate particular events, and some of the participants in them.